Look Who   )!

"A fabulous downtown reference."
— Michael Musto, *The Village Voice*

"*CityTripping* is informative, colorful, and exciting, with real insights into what it's like to be young in New York. I've recommended it to all my friends!"
— David Lauren, *Swing* magazine

"A quick-witted, anecdotal paperback guide to experiencing and appreciating New York in all its diversity, from the tried-and-true to the weird and wacky."
— *New York Times*

"The hippest, smartest, funniest guide to the city we've ever seen."
— *Where New York*

"A must-have for anyone in their teens and 20s who wants to be 'on top' of a city known to crush its fair share of people."
— *XY Magazine*

"A cool new reference for free-spirited twentysomethings."
— *New York Daily News*

"Young [and] hip ... CityTripping.com has arrived."
— *Time Out New York*

"CityTripping.com is the scrappier and hipper counterpart to corporate behemoth Citysearch."
— *Rolling Stone*

Also from CityTripping Productions:
CityTripping New York: A Guide for Nighthawks, Foodies, Culture Vultures, Fashion Fetishists, Downtown Addicts, and the Generally Style-Obsessed,
by Tom Dolby (City & Company Publishers).
To order, contact your local bookseller or go to **www.citytripping.com**.

CITYTRIPPING™

los angeles
www.citytripping.com

your guide to

« restaurants

« nightlife

« shopping

« culture

« fitness

« hotels

illustrations | celia calle

foreword | ben stein

introduction | dennis hensley

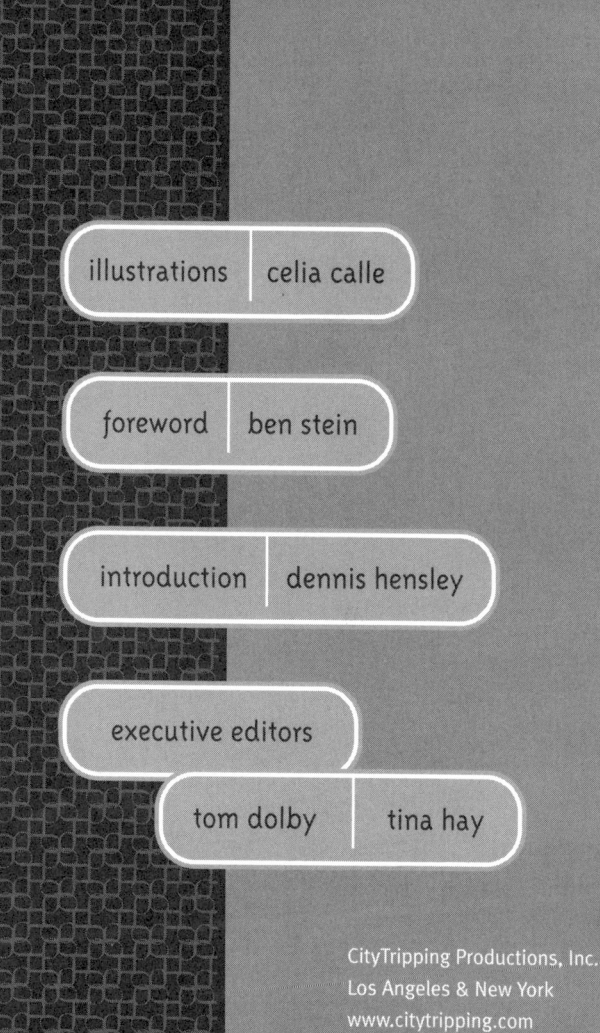

executive editors

tom dolby | tina hay

CityTripping Productions, Inc.
Los Angeles & New York
www.citytripping.com

Copyright © 2000 by CityTripping Productions, Inc.
Foreword copyright © 2000 by Ben Stein.
Introduction copyright © 2000 by Dennis Hensley.
Illustrations copyright © 2000 by Celia Calle.
All rights reserved. No part of this book may be reproduced without written permission from the publisher.

Library of Congress Cataloging-in-Publication Data available on request.
ISBN 1-885492-97-9

First Edition
Printed in the United States of America

CityTripping Productions, Inc.
Los Angeles Office
9454 Wilshire Boulevard, Suite 600
Beverly Hills CA 90212
310-205-3997
310-271-3540 fax
www.citytripping-la.com
laeditor@citytripping.com

New York Office
151 West 25th Street, 4th Floor
New York NY 10001
212-924-5683
212-924-5845 fax
www.citytripping-ny.com
editor@citytripping.com

Distributed by City & Company
22 West 23rd Street, 5th floor
New York NY 10010
212-366-1988
212-242-0415 fax
www.cityandcompany.com
cityco@mindspring.com

Publisher's Note: Neither CityTripping Productions nor City & Company has any interest, financial or personal, in the locations listed in this book. No fees were paid or services rendered in exchange for inclusion in these pages. While every effort was made to ensure accuracy at the time of publication, it is always advisable to call ahead for up-to-date fees and hours.

Executive Editors: Tom Dolby and Tina Hay
Managing Editors: Kevin Arnovitz and Tom Williams

CityTripping Productions, Inc.
CEO/Director of NY Operation: Tom Dolby
President/Director of LA Operation: Tina Hay
CFO/Director of Business Development: Kenneth Henderson

Foreword: Ben Stein
Introduction: Dennis Hensley
Major Los Angeles Neighborhoods: Kevin Arnovitz
Eating Out: Jane Tunks
Nightlife: Sara Scribner
Shopping: Jane Tunks and Kevin Arnovitz
Coffee: Kevin Arnovitz and Tommy Nguyen
Culture and the Arts: Jane Tunks
Work that Body: Kevin Arnovitz and Tommy Nguyen
Sleeping Around: Noa Jones and Kevin Arnovitz
Getting Around: Jane Tunks

Special thanks: Eliot, Ellen and Staci Arnovitz, Wendi Bohl, Peter Brown, Celia Calle, Melisa Coburn, Ray, Dagmar, and David Dolby, Tracy Guth, John, Mehrzad, and David Hay, Lutfallah and Maliheh Hay, Dennis Hensley, Tonya Hudson, Mahin and Yahya Kamran, Joey Kotfica, Load Media, Atoosa and Alex Nehorai, Charles Ogilvie, Tina Paul, Katharine Sands, Helene Silver, Michael Stabile, Ben Stein, Jason Stevens.

what's in here

12 foreword

14 introduction

16 letter from the editors

19 how this book works

20 map

21 major los angeles neighborhoods
Santa Monica • Venice • Brentwood • Westwood and the Westside • Beverly Hills • West Hollywood and Robertson Boulevard • Beverly Center and Melrose and Fairfax Avenues • Hancock Park and Larchmont • Hollywood • Los Feliz Silver Lake • Downtown • South Bay Beach Towns

30 eating out

31 Introduction and Tips

33 **Main Listings** Café Stella • Canal Club • Dominick's • El Coyote • Fred 62 Gladstone's 4 Fish Malibu • Hal's Bar & Grill • James' Beach • Les Deux Café Lucques • Millie's Diner • Phillipe's The Original • Red • Swingers • Taylor's Prime Steaks • Zen Grill

45 **Specialty Listings** Breakfast • California Pizza • Celebrity-Owned • Drive-Thru Global Cuisine • Hamburgers • Happy Hour • Late Night • Mexican • Old School Power Eating • Supper Clubs • Sushi • Truly Tacky • Vegetarian

64 Index by Neighborhood

71 Index by Type

74 Index by Price

citytripping los angeles

78 nightlife

79 Introduction and Tips

81 Getting Good Press

82 Coping with the Velvet Rope

83 **Main Listings: Bars and Lounges** Bar Marmont • Bigfoot Lodge • Cat Club Daddy's • The Dresden Room • Encounter • Formosa Café • North • Sky Bar

89 **Specialty Listings: Bars and Lounges** Dive Bars • Glitzy Joints • Go Retro Martini Nation • Pub Crawling

94 **Main Listings: Clubs** The Derby • The Playroom • Spaceland • Viper Room

97 **Specialty Listings: Clubs** Dance Clubs • Drag Revues • Gay and Lesbian Glamorama • Gothic Fetish • Latin Flavor • Live Music • Rave On • Strip Clubs

106 Index by Neighborhood

110 Index by Type

114 shopping

115 Introduction and Tips

116 **Main Listings: Clothing** American Rag • Curve • Decades, Inc. • Fred Segal Janice McCarty • Lisa Kline • Lura Starr • Maxfield • NYSE • Oliver Peoples Planet Funk • Polka Dots and Moonbeams • Product • Re-Mix • Slow • Tracey Ross • Urban Outfitters • Vin Baker • Wasteland • X-Large/X-Girl

130 **Specialty Listings: Clothing** Celebrity-Worn • Club Clothes • Designer Duds Lingerie and Beyond • Malls • Melrose Streetwear • Rodeo Drive • Screw Retail Streetwear on La Brea • Vintage Threads

145 **Main Listings: Glamour and Grunge** Black Wave Tattoo • House of Freaks Valerie

147 **Specialty Listings: Glamour and Grunge** Beauty School Dropout • Brows and Nails • Hair Today • Spa Day

150 **Main Listings: Outfitting Your Pad** Blueprint • Ilan Dei Studios • In House Postobello • Rose Bowl Flea Market • Shabby Chic • Shelter • Sonrisa

154 **Specialty Listings: Outfitting Your Pad** Chain Stores • Mid-Century Modern Oriental • Poster Heaven

157 **Main Listings: Housewares and Gifts** Daisy Arts • Illume • Ozzie & Moosy Soolip • Uncle Jer's • Zipper

159 **Specialty Listings: Housewares and Gifts** Kitsch

160 **Main Listings: Foodstuffs** Trader Joe's

161 **Specialty Listings: Foodstuffs** Farmers Markets • Gourmet Food • Markets Wine and Roses

164 **Main Listings: Books** Book Soup • Midnight Special • Vroman's

166 **Specialty Listings: Books** Neighborhood Independents • Specialty Bookstores Superstores • Used Books

169 **Main Listings: Music and Video** Virgin Megastore • Tower Records

170 **Specialty Listings: Music and Video** Music Afficionados • Video and Munchies

172 Index by Neighborhood

183 Index by Type

188 culture and the arts

189 Introduction

190 **Main Listings: Film** American Cinematique

192 **Specialty Listings: Film** Drive-ins • Film Festivals • Film Societies and Smaller Film Venues • Movie Houses

200 **Main Listings: Live Performance** Center Theater Group • Geffen Playhouse Hollywood Bowl

202 **Specialty Listings: Live Performance** Cabaret • Comedy • Improv Theaters • NoHo Theater Scene • Spoken Word • Theater Row • Theater and Performance Art

209 **Main Listings: Museums** Armand Hammer Museum of Art • Getty Center Griffith Observatory • Los Angeles Country Museum of Art • Museum of Contemporary Art • Museum of Tolerance • Santa Monica Museum of Art

215 **Specialty Listings: Museums** Hollywood Museums • Miracle Mile • Modern Chic • Offbeat Museums

219 **Specialty Listings: Galleries and Arts Festivals** Bergamot Station • Eastside Art Crawl • 6150 Wilshire • Arts Festivals

224 Index by Neighborhood
230 Index by Type

234 work that body

235 Introduction

236 **Main Listings** Barry's Boot Camp • Billy Blanks' World Training Center • Crunch
Gold's Gym Hollywood • Sportsclub LA • Rockreation • Silver Lake Dog Park

240 **Specialty Listings** A Day at the Beach • Bowling • Catch Some Waves • Gear Up
Golf for Hipsters • In-line Skating • Jogging • Pilates • Skateboard City
Spinning • Take a Hike • Yoga

248 Index by Neighborhood
250 Index by Type

252 coffee

253 Introduction

254 **Main Listings** The Abbey • Anastasia's Asylum • Back Door Bakery & Café
Bourgeois Pig • Cacao • Café Tropical • The Coffee Table • Home • Urth Café
Wednesday's House

258 **Specialty Listings** Chain Gang • Late Night • Screenwriter's Blues • To a Tea

261 Index by Neighborhood

264 sleeping around: hotels

265 Introduction and Tips

266 **Main Listings: Expensive** Argyle • Chateau Marmont • Mondrian
The Standard • W Hotel

270 **Specialty Listings: Expensive** Downtown, Upmarket • Living it Up
Staying by the Sea

272 **Main Listings: Moderately Priced** Avalon • Beverly Plaza Hotel • Hollywood
Roosevelt Hotel • Le Parc

274 **Specialty Listings: Moderately Priced** Farther Afield

275 **Main Listings: Cheap** Banana Bungalow • Best Western Hollywood Hills Hotel

276 **Specialty Listings: Cheap** Budget Bonanza

277 Index by Neighborhood

278 Index by Price

280 get out of town: las vegas

281 Introduction and Tips

283 **Main Listings: To Sleep and Wager** Bellagio • Desert Inn • Hard Rock Hotel & Casino • Mandalay Bay • Mirage

287 **Main Listings: Eating Out in Vegas** Aureole • Binion's Ranch Steakhouse China Grill • Mr. Lucky's • Nobu • Pink Taco • RumJungle

290 **Specialty Listings: Eating Out in Vegas** Gorging Yourself • LA Annexes

292 **Main Listings: Nightlife in Vegas** Baby's • Gipsy • Hard Rock Casino Bar House of Blues • Red Dragon Lounge • Red Square

294 **Quickies** Best Place to Score a Lapdance • Best Place to Play Eighteen • Best Place to Learn Craps • Best Place to Blow Your Winnings • Best Place to Outfit Yourself Vegas-style

296 Index by Type

298 getting around

302 full alphebetical index

312 who we are

foreword

glorious los angeles!

Mighty imperial capital of the empire of mass culture, of popular taste, of how to dress, wear your hair, walk your walk, love your lover for the whole world, and maybe for outer space as far as we know. The British Empire is gone, and so is the Soviet Union. But the global sway of Hollywood — which by now is all of Los Angeles — is broader and more uncontested than ever. No mud hut in Rwanda, no rattling tour bus in Bangladesh, no swanky townhouse in Belgravia, no, not even the streets of Baghdad or Beijing, is free of the influence of Hollywood and the music, movies, and TV — and now Internet content — that it makes.

Imperial City in the Palms, new Rome with freeways that sends out its conquerors by radio wave and electron and celluloid and digital embroidery! Hail Los Angeles, queen of cities, bow down, ye mighty politicians and come here and beg for our money. Humble yourselves, you grand soldiers and sailors and plead to have us memorialize your lives so you can have the only immortality you can be sure of.

We are the epicenter. Of earthquakes and fires, but also of manmade earthshaking and fire.

But what kind of city are we? The most opaque of places, so spread out that our best spots are invisible, a woman so big, a giant, a super Anita-Ekberg-from-outer-space type woman, that her beauty cannot be found unless you know exactly where to look. It's 60 miles from the western edge of Malibu to downtown Los Angeles and Little Tokyo. It's a hard day's drive on the freeway from Beverly Hills to Disney World. It takes stamina to drive (even without rush hour) from Warner Brothers in Burbank to Sony-Columbia in Culver City.

How can the local, the traveler, the tourist, the businesswoman making a deal, the newcomer looking for action know where to go? There is no one cute neighborhood like Greenwich Village in New York or Georgetown in Washington, D.C. There is no center for anything, but instead an unending multi-centered metroplex, an organism that travelers from the East or West have no idea how to navigate.

That's where the *CityTripping Los Angeles* guide helps the lover find the centers of pleasure, the shopper find the dream widget, the diner find the sushi that's better than sex, the dancer find the club where the people are hipper than hip.

In astonishingly well-written prose that zings to the point of shopping for the young, dining for the middle-aged, and power voyeurism for the lusty, *CityTripping Los Angeles* takes you to what counts in food, sex, buying, sleeping, and looking in every part of the grand imperium that is LA.

I have lived here for almost a quarter of a century and I did not know where to find retro bars, Irish pubs, or where to get a fresh steak 24 hours a day. Even for me, who has crawled down these roads of power for two decades, *CityTripping Los Angeles* has organized how I'll eat and shop and schmooze far better than I would have thought possible.

If Caesar's Rome had a guidebook like this, the Vandals would have come in a lot sooner. Now you've got it. Come in, have a good time and be awed. And don't be scared. You can check out any time you like, but as to leaving...

Ben Stein

introduction

a friend of mine once observed that when it comes to living, loving, and laboring in Los Angeles, one can get away with anything. "I mean, when I was at Yale," I remember her saying over lunch on Ventura Boulevard in the Valley, "there were certain things that just weren't done. Here, you can pull whatever kind of shit you want. There is no such thing as bad form." I remember being titillated by her remark, but also overwhelmed. Okay, so anything goes here in the land of La-La, but where do I go? It's a question I continue to ask myself as the years whiz by.

I still remember fondly my first night as an official Los Angeleno. It was the fall of 1986 and after driving my overstuffed Pontiac Grand Prix all the way to Pico and Robertson from Phoenix, AZ, I was too pooped to party but not too pooped to eat. It was late at night, I knew no one, and I was scared of driving where there might be other cars. Still, my stomach was growling like a Foley artist on *Jurassic Park*, so I hopped back in the car and left it up to the universe. Well, the universe must have just gotten laid, for it led me straight to the safe, juicy, high-fat haven of Johnnie's, a pastrami joint in West LA. With jukeboxes on every table, waitresses with names like Mavis, and the most mouth-wateringly sinful pastrami sandwich a body could hope for, Johnnie's was "all that" long before Rachael Leigh Cook and Freddie Prinze Jr. were even born. The nadir of my Johnnie's fanaticism came the night I took a visiting friend there and who should we see knocking back a basket of fries in a corner booth but Weird Al Yankovic, presumably taking a break from all that lampooning? Though my friend and I resisted the urge to disturb Al's meal, a geeky guy sitting at the counter was less controlled and shouted, "Hey, Weird!" across the diner. I found his greeting, well, weird, but Al didn't seem to mind. He was tossing his lip over a massive French dip and couldn't have been happier. That's the magic of Johnnie's. Though it would be years before I could correctly pronounce the street it's on,

Sepulveda — Craig Clybourn, the hero of my novel *Misadventures in the (213)* is plagued with similar pronunciation problems — I was happy to have found my first official LA hang.

Through the years I've happened on several funky funspots — Heavy Rotation records on Ventura Boulevard, the All-Star Coffeehouse in the bottom of Hollywood's historic Hotel Knickerbocker, the Will Geer Theater in Topanga Canyon, Arby's — but I've never been as on top of the scene as I could have been had I shown up in town with *CityTripping* tucked into my *Thomas Guide*. Case in point, why has it taken me 12 years to discover Dragstrip 66, the low-on-attitude, heavy-on-hotties Saturday night dance club at Rudolpho's in Silver Lake? Why, until recently, did I think Runyon Canyon was the guy that wrote *Guys and Dolls* and not a great place for a hike? And why, oh why do I continue to pay $16.99 for the latest 'N Sync CD when there are scads of slightly-soiled, used copies available around town for a song? Screw Calgon. CityTripping, take me away! There is so much on these sun-drenched streets to see, buy, imbibe, and gawk at — a pal of mine once saw Marilyn Manson buying towels at Bed, Bath, and Beyond, though I can't promise you'll be so lucky — that staying home and watching *E! News Daily* is just not a viable option.

So what are you waiting for, Angelyne to screech up in her pink Corvette to take you on a shopping spree at Fred Segal? It's never going to happen and trust me, she's much more fun from a distance. You have to be your own Angelyne, we all do, but luckily, we've got *CityTripping* to turn to. Trip on, little campers.

Dennis Hensley

letter from the editors

there's something cinematic about

arriving in Los Angeles as a newcomer, or even rediscovering it as a native. You know the shot: You're driving along a wide, palm-dotted boulevard in your convertible, stereo blasting something so very now while working a deal on your cell phone. The fact that it's January and the temperature is hovering at 68 degrees only adds to your satisfaction.

When you live in Los Angeles, you're forever pinching yourself in a state of disbelief. "I can't believe I actually live here!" is a common refrain. Soon you find yourself bumping into Heather Graham while rifling through the sale rack at Fred Segal or sitting next to Sean Hayes at Mandarette, and life really starts to imitate art — or at least the movies. That's the initial appeal of Los Angeles: It's a life composed of interconnected fantasies that begin to resemble scenes on an audition reel.

The fact that so many of us came out to Los Angeles with the singular purpose of "making it" adds to the aura of fantasy in the city. People don't merely exist; they feed on the success and failure of their personal story. In fact, life in Los Angeles becomes an art form — as does everything that goes with living: having drinks, doing lunch, working a party, flirting, creating the perfect day at the beach.

After you get over the thrill of sidewalk dining in February and random celebrity sightings, your informational needs will become more specific: At which sushi bar can I rub elbows with the writing staff of *Buffy*? Where can I kickbox alongside the flavor of the month? Where do the development brats hang out on Thursday nights? Where does punk rock still reign in LA? And, of course, the ever-important, Where should I get my hair done? The answers aren't obvious. Unearthing them can take months, even years of mastering Los Angeles. At CityTripping we feel that you have an unalienable right to make your real life conform to your dream life. That's why we've compiled *CityTripping Los Angeles*. We offer this book as a menu of suggestions, but our most profound advice is this: Discover your own places. Become a regular. Create your own aesthetic. Most venues in this book weren't ordained as cool. They managed to tap a sensibility with which others identified and, hence, coolness was born.

The sum of Los Angeles is less about geography and more about exploration. Sure, it's difficult to stumble across a cozy cafe or a stellar bar spontaneously; that sort of discovery often requires that you get out of your car. But that doesn't mean that cultivating a lifestyle needs to be a painstaking process. Actually, we like the fact that striking gold is a little bit harder in Los Angeles than in other cities. This means, after all, that the true urban adventurer wins. Although it's not immediately apparent to visitors or newcomers, Los Angeles does have a soul — a sense of self that defies swift classification. When you discover that soul, you'll know you've arrived. We hope *CityTripping* will help speed you along your journey.

The Editors

how this book works

this book is divided into two types of listings: long and short. The long listings are our top picks, the most interesting and multifaceted selections in each category; they are organized alphabetically. The short listings are grouped together according to theme, such as supper clubs, dive bars, or vintage clothing. You'll find these short listings on the pages with a gray background. At the end of each chapter, there are indexes by neighborhood, type of venue, and — for restaurants and hotels — by price. And at the end of the book, you'll find a full alphebetical index of all entries.

We hope you enjoy this book as much as we enjoyed putting it together. If there's something you'd like to see in the next edition or its online companion, drop us a note at laeditor@citytripping.com. Have fun!

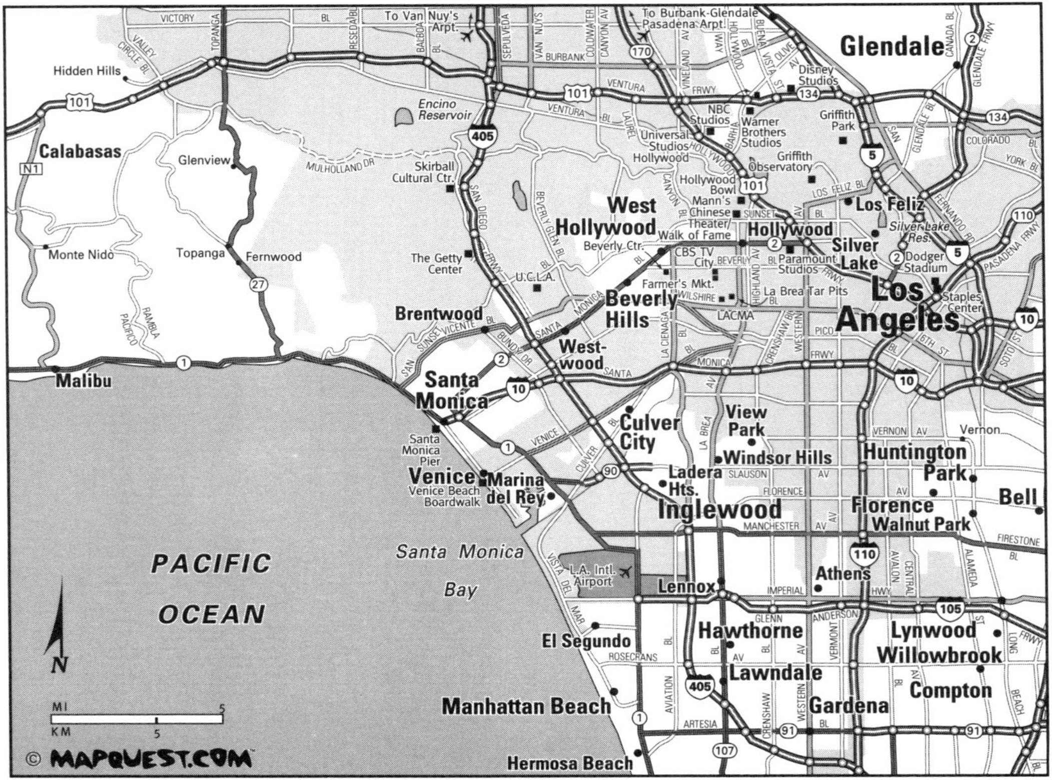
Glendale
Los Angeles
Hidden Hills
Calabasas
Glenview
Monte Nido
Topanga
Fernwood
Malibu
Encino Reservoir
Skirball Cultural Ctr.
The Getty Center
Brentwood
U.C.L.A.
West Hollywood
Beverly Hills
Westwood
Santa Monica
Santa Monica Pier
Venice
Venice Beach Boardwalk
Marina del Rey
Culver City
View Park
Windsor Hills
Ladera Hts.
Inglewood
Hollywood
Los Feliz
Silver Lake
Silver Lake Res.
Dodger Stadium
Staples Center
Griffith Park
Griffith Observatory
Disney Studios
Warner Brothers Studios
NBC Studios
Universal Studios Hollywood
Hollywood Bowl
Mann's Chinese Theater/ Walk of Fame
Beverly Ctr.
CBS TV City
Farmer's Mkt.
Paramount Studios
La Brea Tar Pits
LACMA
Huntington Park
Vernon
Bell
Florence
Walnut Park
Athens
Lennox
L.A. Intl. Airport
El Segundo
Hawthorne
Lawndale
Gardena
Lynwood
Willowbrook
Compton
Manhattan Beach
Hermosa Beach
Santa Monica Bay
PACIFIC OCEAN
To Van Nuy's Arpt.
To Burbank-Glendale Pasadena Arpt.
N
MI 5
KM 5
© MAPQUEST.COM

neighborhoods

while the description may seem odd for a place whose soul and character have long been ridiculed, Los Angeles is very much a city of neighborhoods. Because the landscape is so vast, residents establish a center of gravity for themselves and then draw boundaries around that focal point — not necessarily because they're provincial or snobbish, but because trying to conquer the entire grid would be unmanageable. As a result, you have a city of people who govern their daily lives by certain geographical precepts: "I don't go east of La Cienega;" "Silver Lake is in the middle of nowhere;" "Why are we schlepping to Santa Monica?"

In Los Angeles, there is no middle of nowhere, and what constitutes a schlepp is defined less by conventional wisdom than by what you consider your personal ground zero.

Santa Monica

Perched on the Pacific with clean air, cool breezes, and cute-as-can-be shops and restaurants, Santa Monica can legitimately claim to be Los Angeles's most liveable corner. Quintessentially LA stores such as **Shabby Chic** dot Montana Avenue, a perfect place to brunch and stroll on a Sunday afternoon. The **Third Street Promenade** is a pleasant take on an outdoor mall and includes all the essential retail fare, from **Urban Outfitters** to **Restoration Hardware.** If you crave a corn dog and a ride on a rickety Ferris wheel, take a stroll on the **Santa Monica Pier.** In any case, you'll feel a whole lot better after some smooth cocktails overlooking the sea at **Shutters on the Beach**. After dark, Santa Monica evolves from sunny suburb to nighttime playground. The crowd at the **Buffalo Club** and **Sugar** will be noticeably blonder and more pressed than those on the Eastside. But the vodka at **Voda** flows freely — and in a lush, inviting setting.

Venice

Just down Ocean Avenue from Santa Monica, Venice is a neighborhood that's been labeled "transitional" for more than 20 years. This misnomer obscures the fact that Venice is what it is — an eccentric beach town with more flip-flops than Fluevogs. Hippies, ageless surf bums, and musicians have lent the neighborhood a Bohemian character that is considerably less pristine than that of Santa Monica. Look hard enough, though, and you'll uncover plenty for the urbane in Venice. Take Abbot Kinney Way, where the most interesting recent developments have occurred. Here, the design boom has invaded, bringing along with it some of the better kitsch shops in Southern California. And you won't find a better weekend brunch for the money than that served at airy **Joe's**. Architects have also feasted on Venice's old spaces: Brian Murphy designed Dennis Hopper's fortress, and Frank Gehry dreamt up the **Norton House** and **Chiat-Day Building**, where you'll find the huge pair of Oldenburg binoculars. But the main attraction continues to be the freak show that is the Ocean Front Walk, better known as the **Boardwalk** at Venice Beach. Street performers, psychedelic merchants, and fortune-tellers dominate this stretch of sidewalk that embodies California in all of its bizarro behavior.

Brentwood

Traveling east on San Vicente Boulevard from Santa Monica, you'll cross into Brentwood at 26th Street. O.J. and Monica have lent Brentwood some unwarranted notoriety, but that doesn't change the fact that residents of this neighborhood wouldn't live anyplace else. Brentwood folks feel that they have everything they need at their doorstep: neighborhood cafés on San Vicente and Montana within walking distance, boutiques that residents have grown up with, and a stylish charm that continues to seduce those looking for a true neighborhood in an often impersonal city. For a good sampling of Brentwood chic and likely star sightings, hit the shops at **Brentwood Gardens** on San Vicente. If the script on the **Ron Herman** store facade looks familiar, it is; trendy Melrose emporium **Fred Segal** is Herman's baby.

Westwood and the Westside

East of the 405 and north of bustling Wilshire Boulevard lies the quasi-college town of Westwood Village, home to UCLA. The demographic here errs on the young and cute side, but head south and you'll find the Westside teeming with a young Hollywood element that prefers not to pay the steep rents in Beverly Hills. One of the better jazz venues in town, **Lunaria**,

neighborhoods | 23

sits on a nondescript stretch of Santa Monica Boulevard. And there isn't a better concentration of great cinemas than those in Westwood; it's no coincidence that Westwood Village hosts more than its fair share of Hollywood premieres. Check the papers and set a date to catch a flick at the **Nuart**, a terrific art cinema in the Asian enclave of Sawtelle.

Beverly Hills

Traveling east on Wilshire or Sunset Boulevard from Westwood, you'll hit the most recognizable neighborhood in the nation, and certainly among the most expensive. The storefronts of the Golden Triangle, Beverly Hills' retail district, read like a *Who's Who* of international fashion. Travel south to Wilshire Boulevard and you'll find the "big three" department stores of **Barneys**, **Saks**, and **Neiman Marcus**, where agents from the "big four" talent agencies of CAA, ICM, WMA, and UTA (not to mention upstart powerhouse Endeavor) hurry through lunchtime buying binges from their neighboring offices. CAA's IM Pei-designed home base (still owned by Michael Ovitz) sits unassumingly at the corner of Wilshire and Santa Monica and is worth checking out, if only for the gargantuan Lichtenstein painting in the lobby. North of Sunset, the homes may lack architectural consistency (and, many aesthetes would argue, good taste), but their addresses place them on some of the most desirable residential real estate in the world.

West Hollywood and Robertson Boulevard

Divided from Beverly Hills by Doheny Drive, West Hollywood has something for everyone, despite its largely gay reputation. Santa Monica Boulevard has long served as the unofficial Main Street for the gay boys of Los Angeles. **Revolver** and **Rage** are standard cruise-and-model video bars; a lot of guys also like to start their evenings at **Merrick's** or **Cobalt Cantina** to load up on margaritas. **The Abbey**, just south of the Boulevard on Robertson, features a pleasant outdoor courtyard and serves as a multi-purpose venue, a place to meet up with friends, get pissed on Cosmos or spiked on caffeine, or grab a salad or dessert. Girls, travel farther south on Robertson toward Beverly and Third and you can shop 'til the debt comes home. Women's fashion boutiques have crowded this stretch of Robertson south of the antique district that runs the gamut from **Agnes b.** to **Cynthia Rowley** to designer boutique **Madison**. If you have ten grand to drop on a bed, pop into **Diva**, at the northwest corner of Beverly and Robertson, or **Look**, across the street. Fatigued? Take lunch with the beautiful ones at the health-conscious **Newsroom**. And when it gets dark on a red-letter date like Halloween or New Year's Eve, it's common for West Hollywood's finest to close Santa Monica Boulevard to all but foot traffic and let the Angelenos have a car-free good time.

Beverly Center and Melrose and Fairfax Avenues

This pocket of the city sits south of West Hollywood, east of Beverly Hills, and west of Hancock Park. The neighborhood's main drags are Melrose Avenue, Beverly Boulevard, and Third Street between La Cienega and La Brea. Although the area lacks a proper name, you'd be hard-pressed to find a list of LA's hottest spots for bar-hopping, shopping, and noshing that doesn't include dozens of entries in this three-square-mile zone. Don't miss **Fred Segal**, Los Angeles's fabulous boutique-style department store, on Melrose Avenue at Crescent Heights. Progressive design shops are opening up in droves along Beverly Boulevard, as well as brand-name boutiques such as **Todd Oldham's** storefront. Third Street has quickly become home to the largest concentration of offbeat boutiques, cafés, and fashion designers in Los Angeles. And, lest we forget, this area is youth culture central. Whether you're looking for clubwear, vintage wax, or a navel piercing, you should start on Melrose between Fairfax and La Brea, where you'll find a combination of thrift stores, club gear, record shops, shoe stores, and other general (yet delightful) foolishness. On Fairfax, old Los Angeles and the hipster scene meld at the 24-hour **Canter's Deli** and its sidekick the **Kibbitz Room**, where punk bands rock while you gobble your blintzes and matzo-ball soup. While you may be initially suspicious of the **Farmer's Market** at Third and Fairfax, rest assured that it's not touristy, but rather an amalgam of young and old Angelenos, where bluehairs fondle the produce and screenwriters pick up a copy of *Variety* before sitting down for French toast at **Kokomo's**.

Hancock Park and Larchmont

Keep going east on Third Street or Beverly Boulevard and you'll enter the enclaves of Hancock Park and Larchmont. Back when Beverly Hills was still considered the country, LA's economic elite were concentrated in Hancock Park. Once one of the most segregated neighborhoods, the doors have opened recently, although the revivalist mansions remain. Today these residences are as likely to be inhabited by young gay couples from the entertainment industry as older downtown-establishment WASP families. Just to the east of the multimillion-dollar homes is the more modest Larchmont Village, a neighborhood that's emerging as a "Brentwood East" and whose quaint main drag, Larchmont Boulevard, resembles the shopping district of every moneyed suburb across the country. Under the shadow of the monolithic Paramount Studios just to the north, Larchmont denizens stroll along their quiet boulevard to quaint cafés and local shops. With gritty and increasingly funky Koreatown just blocks to the east and hipster hangouts like **The Martini Lounge** and **Kane** within walking distance (yes, you heard right — residents of Larchmont actually like to walk) on Melrose, Larchmont is as popular a relocation site as there is in Los Angeles.

Hollywood

North of Hancock Park and south of the hills sits Hollywood, which, despite popular assumptions, is not its own city, but rather a part of the City of Los Angeles. It often comes as a shock to non-Angelenos that Hollywood, despite the cache of its name, is one of the city's more depressed neighborhoods north of the 10. That said, there's plenty more to Hollywood than stars on the sidewalk. To wit, nightlife has flourished in this area: weekly dance parties, which once thrived in neighboring West Hollywood, have picked up stakes and moved to new digs at Hollywood's **Playroom**. For industry boys, Tuesday nights have become synonymous with Beige at **360**. A narrow stretch of Cahuenga north of Sunset boasts the **Catalina Bar & Grill**, the city's best jazz venue, and **The Burgundy Room**, which is not a manufactured dive but a real drinker's paradise. For live music, both **Hell's Gate** and **Dragonfly** continue to pull in great acts. Amid the blight of the Hollywood flats, a formerly bleak stretch of Santa Monica Boulevard just west of Cahuenga has sprouted a number of independent stages for performance art and neighborhood theater. From the look of things, a new spate of cafés and bars is not far away.

Los Feliz

Drive along Hollywood Boulevard or Franklin Avenue east from Hollywood and you'll enter the pleasant confines of Los Feliz. It wasn't long ago that Los Feliz (pronounced "Los FEE-liz") was regarded by Westsiders as the far eastern frontier of Los Angeles. But as some locals will tell you, "Madonna changed everything." Whether or not the pop diva's arrival in the neighborhood actually affected the area's growth,

Los Feliz has emerged as a great place to eat, play, shop, and live. Thank restaurateur Fred Eric for the tony, eclectic **Vida**, which has established itself as the anchor for a burgeoning collection of restaurants along Hillhurst and Vermont Avenues and an active bar scene among music industry types. Both Hillhurst and Vermont have sprung boutiques ranging from glitter-rayon to ska-punk in their style and selection. In addition, Los Feliz has always had its share of venerable watering holes: **The Dresden Room** and the newer **Good Luck Bar** are as hot as ever with the Eastside contingent.

Silver Lake

East on Sunset or (for a more inviting tour) just over the Franklin Hills, Silver Lake used to be Los Angeles's best-kept secret, with its beautiful hills and unpretentious charm. At least once a week, you're destined to hear a self-proclaimed urban theorist declare, "Silver Lake is what Los Feliz was three years ago." Silver Lake loyalists, however, will argue that their quaint neighborhood has always been there, merely unnoticed by everyone else. You can't ignore the fact that with nightspots like **Spaceland** and restaurants with the panache of **Café Stella**, Silver Lake has earned itself a permanent place on the map. Gritty Sunset Boulevard in Silver Lake may not be picturesque (for that, take a drive along the reservoir on West Silver Lake Boulevard), but institutions like **Millie's** and emporiums of the sublime such as **Ka Boom** will get your attention. Don't look now, but **Delirium-Tremens Gallery**, along with a couple of other studios, has opened on Echo Park Avenue, stretching Silver Lake's sphere of influence even farther east.

Downtown

Keep driving on Sunset Boulevard toward the skyscrapers and you'll finally arrive downtown. You've probably heard the rip on Los Angeles a thousand times: "There's nothing downtown," or "There's no city." You may even know people who have lived in Los Angeles for years who have ventured downtown only once or twice for a play at the **Mark Taper Forum** or the **Ahmanson Theater**. If you choose to subscribe to this refrain, then you're likely to miss a dynamic scene, and one that's increasingly important in the city's growing artistic identity. Take the **Brewery Arts Complex**, a renovated industrial space that houses several hundred artists in live/work loft spaces (it can take over a year to get off the waiting list). A restaurant and a café exist on site, and the biannual ArtWalk in October and April, when resident artists open up their lofts and exhibit their work, shouldn't be missed. Up in Chinatown, have a drink at **Quon Brothers**, where Mommy will serve you graciously as you listen to live jazz. Down in Japantown, the **Koma Cocktail Lounge** serves up smooth sake. Restaurateurs are taking the lead downtown as well. Susan Feinger and Mary Sue Milliken have created a clean, tantalizing space with **Ciudad**, not to mention some tasty Pan-American fare. And if you can find it, **R-23**, tightly nestled between loading docks, serves up some of the best sushi this side of the Pacific.

South Bay Beach Towns

The string of beach towns south of Palos Verdes has more in common in mood and feel with San Diego than with Los Angeles. Although some urbane Angelenos don't give this area a second thought, Manhattan Beach, Redondo Beach, and Hermosa Beach can stake their claim as the birthplace of the surf-grunge movement. If you're looking for a shirt-and-shoes-optional sort of Saturday, or a getaway from the noir-shrouded world of Los Angeles, head down the bay to the **Manhattan Beach Strand** for some rays and the best beach volleyball in the world, followed by an evening with the blonde glitterati at **The Lighthouse Café** in Hermosa Beach.

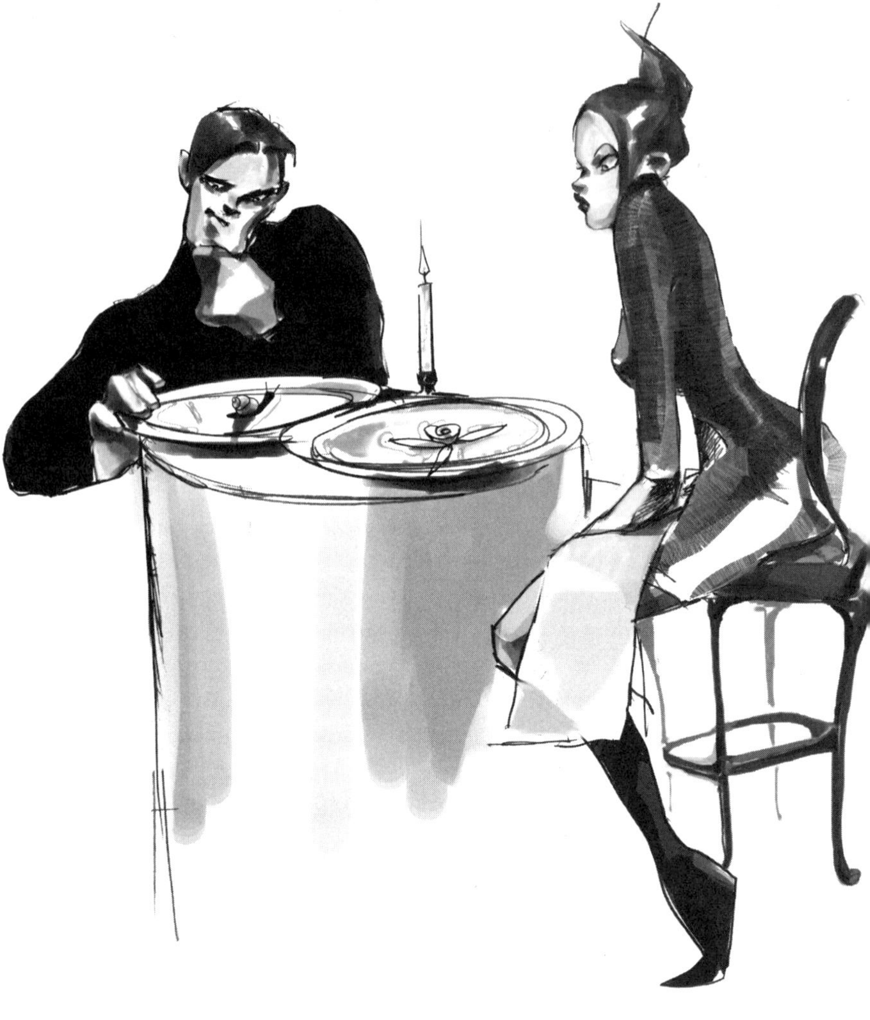

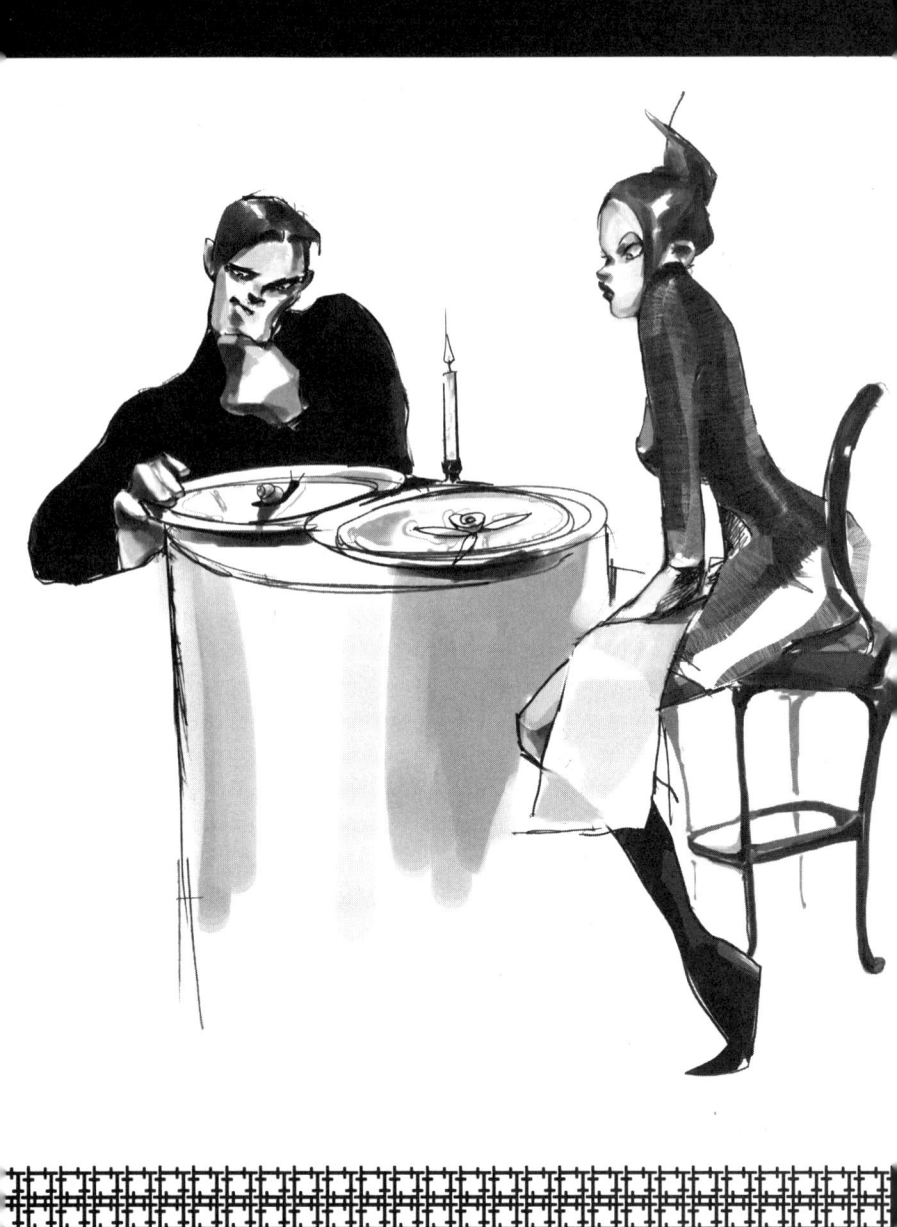

eating out

california cuisine has evolved as a genre unto itself over the past twenty years, though ask someone what it means and you're likely to get a blank stare. Like pornography, you know California cooking when you see it, though a good set of guidelines would be fresh, light food with an emphasis on presentation and the fusion of disparate tastes. And in Los Angeles, where you eat that food and under whose tutelage it's prepared make all the difference. Restaurants, like virtually everything else in Los Angeles, succeed on the value of celebrity and panache. Who frequents the place and how they gleam against the stylized décor may be more important than what's on the menu.

That's not always the case, though. For every movie-set restaurant owned and operated by a superchef where a reservation may seem like an impossibility, there's an authentic neighborhood joint — maybe a Korean barbecue, a burger stand, or a tacqueria — that's cultivated a fiercely loyal following. Given Los Angeles's diversity, it'll come as no surprise that ethnic food is a culinary mainstay and source of adventure. Saying you're going out for Mexican food is insufficient unless you specify its specific variety; likewise, Chinese food comes in a multitude of regional styles. And no city has mastered the art of the dive quite like Los Angeles, whose drive-up or drive-in burger stands came of age during the automobile revolution that gave the city its notoriety. Los Angeles's restaurant scene — a lively blend of high and low cuisine — mirrors its civic culture.

dining tips to start you off

» For restaurants that cater to the scenester element, call ahead for a reservation, even if your plans haven't gelled yet. You can always cancel or change it later.

» Smoking is not permitted in restaurants. A small number of places have patios that allow you to spark up, but they're far and few between.

» More so than most cities, you can get away with casual attire at most restaurants in Los Angeles, even at some of the trendier spots. Be advised, though, that some restaurants will turn a nose up at sloppiness and others simply won't allow it. If you're concerned, call ahead to ask if there's a dress code; even if there's no official one, they may be able to give you some tips on feeling comfortable.

» Be prepared to pay cash, as some restaurants don't accept credit cards. If this is a concern, be sure to call ahead.

key

Prices are for dinner for one, including drink, tax, and tip. Lunch is usually 25 percent less.

$ — $15 and under
$$ — $16-$25
$$$ — $26 and over

CAFÉ STELLA *3932 Sunset Blvd. at Santa Monica Blvd., Silver Lake, 323-666-0265; Hours: Tue-Sat 6pm-11pm $$*

This cozy bistro is tucked away in a courtyard off of Silver Lake's main drag, making it easy for the tattooed denizens who refuse to go west of Vermont to dig into classic, old-school French cooking. Straight out of a Godard film, the small storefront dining room barely fits a half dozen tables for two. A dozen more spill out into the courtyard, a romantic space strung with pretty lights overhead. The no-nonsense, one-page menu favors textbook bistro fare: poulet a l'estragon, steak au poivre, steak Provençal, pork tenderloin in a mushroom cream sauce, and tuna in a curry cream sauce. Zone dieters beware: heavy starters like French onion soup, escargots, and goat cheese and tapenade on baguette set the stage for the classically executed meal to come. End it all with desserts like pot au chocolate and crème brûlée, or an ennui-infused shot of espresso and a cigarette. This snug hideaway is the perfect venue for a romantic dinner, and it's not too expensive, either. Two can eat a three-course meal for $50, but it'll cost a little more if you indulge in the other great French contribution to the world, wine. Keep in mind, too, that it's cash only.

CANAL CLUB *2025 Pacific Ave. bet. Brooks Ave. and Venice Blvd., Venice, 310-823-3878; Hours: daily 5pm-10pm $$$*

In a landmark Frank Gehry-designed space, the Canal Club makes a specialty of high-end beach eats from around the world. The centerpiece of this restaurant is the bar, which

eating out

opens an hour before dinner and is almost immediately elbow-to-elbow with good-looking barflies seeking truth through the demon god of alcohol. Polynesian cocktails are the house specialty and are made from freshly squeezed fruit juices and premium rum. Drawing his inspiration from Cuba, Mexico, Spain, Italy, Greece, China, Thailand, and France, the chef has created a delightfully eclectic appetizer-driven menu: the "raw and roe bar" doles out oysters on the half shell and sushi, and exotic Cuban pressed sandwiches — pork and Manchego cheese or chicken and brie — are sided with darkly fried shoestring potatoes.

DOMINICK'S *8715 Beverly Blvd. bet. Robertson and San Vicente Blvds., West Hollywood, 310-652-7272; Hours: Mon-Thu 6:30pm-12:30am; Fri-Sat 6:30pm-2am $$$*

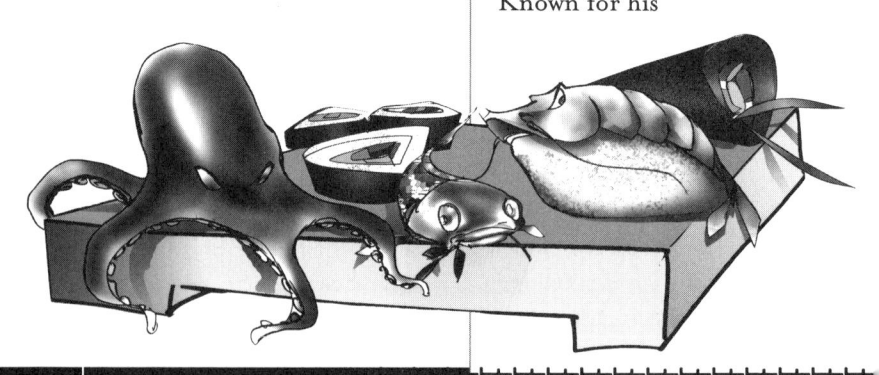

The latest offering from serial restaurateur Fred "62" Eric, this venerable steak house has been retooled and redesigned for the martini crowd, who come to this late-night haunt to see and be seen. The post-nuclear, nautical-themed room has a shiny green ceiling, wood-paneled walls, and snug green leatherette booths. If you can't hear your dining companion over the constant din, there's also a swanky but quiet outdoor patio with a fireplace where you can dine more peacefully. Known for his eccentric dishes and wacky presentation, Eric doesn't disappoint with Dominick's menu. The Captain's Calamari, a brown paper bag overflowing with crisply fried calamari, is a good place to start. The whimsically named Mac Daddy and Cheese is a rich concoction of macaroni baked with cheese, cream, and a strong dose of pasilla chile. For dessert, don't miss the S.S. Wonka, a dark chocolate-dipped waffle and banana topped with caramel and marshmallows wrapped around a flagpole-disguised skewer.

EL COYOTE *7312 Beverly Blvd. bet. Fairfax and La Brea Aves., Los Angeles, 323-939-2255; Hours: Sun-Thu 11am-10pm; Fri-Sat 11am-11pm $*
No one can fully experience the joy of life in Los Angeles without eating at El Coyote at least once. After a few of its margaritas, even the most hardened New Yorker will concede with a fixed grin and glazed eyes that he loves LA. Open for over 70 years, this revered institution serves the strongest and cheapest margaritas in town, making alcoholics of four generations of Angelenos, who will wait up to an hour to dine in the kitschy atmosphere — think tawdry oil paintings, Tijuana tchotchkes, and garishly painted walls — at super-cheap prices. The industrial-strength libations are only $3.25 a pop — but be careful, as just two El Coyote margaritas will knock you on the floor. The average-quality Mexican food is secondary to the restaurant's cultural significance: This is not so much a restaurant as a place where underage Angelenos test out their fake IDs as teenagers, drown their sorrows as clock-punching adults, and celebrate their birthdays all their lives. Fun morbid fact: It's also where Sharon Tate ate her last meal before her run-in with the Mansons.

FRED 62 *1850 N. Vermont Ave. bet. Franklin Ave. and Hollywood Blvd., Los Feliz, 323-667-0062; Hours: open 24 hours $*

When it's 3am and you can't decide between a steaming bowl of udon, a tofu scramble, or a good old-fashioned hamburger, Fred 62 is there — 24 hours a day, seven days a week. "Eat Now, Dine Later" is the motto of this quirky diner with a high kitsch factor and a charmingly eclectic menu. Booths are '60s-era wraparound bucket seats complete with headrests, and there's a jukebox stocked with favorites from James Brown to Sonic Youth. Chef Fred Eric pulls out all the childhood breakfast treats, like Pop-Tarts that you can toast at your table, Eggs in the Hole (a slice of toast with a cutout hole that holds a fried egg), two kinds of French toast (try the cornflake-encrusted version), and sour-cream-and-buttermilk pancakes (and don't forget the real maple syrup). Lunch and dinner options include burgers, meat loaf, chicken-fried steak, and five types of Asian noodles, including the classic Japanese udon and Seoul-Full Noodles, a Korean-inspired dish. If it's classic diner fare you want, go for the Juicy Lucy Burger, a stack of beef, cheese, and any toppings you desire on a massive bun.

GLADSTONE'S 4 FISH MALIBU
17300 Pacific Coast Hwy. at Sunset Blvd., Topanga Beach, 310-454-3474; Hours: Mon-Fri 11am-11pm; Sat-Sun 7am-11pm $$

Expect a long wait at Gladstone's, especially during the summer, when this Malibu landmark is packed to the gills with locals and out-of-towners looking for an awesome coastline view. The surf and turf menu goes on for days, leaving no glassy-eyed creature uncooked, with portions so huge that even your grandmother would have to throw some out. Only the freshest fish is served at Gladstone's, which gets shipments of seafood from the Atlantic, Pacific, and the Gulf of Mexico daily. It's hard to choose from the long list of appetizers, with dishes like fresh shucked oysters, an iced seafood combo (shrimp, crab, oysters, calamari, ceviche, and mussels), Boston and Manhattan chowders, steamed Eastern Littleneck clams, and coconut shrimp. And each main course offering — halibut, sea bass, swordfish, mahimahi, ahi, red snapper, and catfish — is cooked at least three different ways. Hungry for dessert? Gladstone's signature mile-high chocolate cake is a mammoth, triple-layer chocoholic's wet dream. On Saturdays and Sundays, the Malibu Beach Brunch serves all the usual egg dishes until 12:30pm — and the bar is open for your favorite hangover cure bright and early.

HAL'S BAR & GRILL *1349 Abbot Kinney Way bet. Brooks and California Aves., Venice, 310-396-3105; Hours: Mon-Thu 11:30am-10:30pm; Fri 11:30am-11pm; Sat-Sun 10am-10:30pm $$$*

Perched among the antiques and collectibles stores on Abbot Kinney Way, Hal's caters to the artsy Venice crowd, who treat it as their local watering hole. Compositions by well-known neighborhood artists like Chuck Arnoldi and Laddie Dill crowd the walls, hearkening back to the joint's origins as a hangout for Venice-area artists. Despite the fact that the neighborhood is leaning more toward wanna-be actors and actresses these days, homesick New Yorkers still love this place for its SoHo vibe. The New American menu changes weekly, with inventive dishes like duck-breast risotto with wild mushrooms, thyme, and asparagus, and a delicious stew of veal sweetbreads with wild mushrooms served in a bowl of spinach. Hal's signature thick, juicy hamburger and extra-crispy fries are always on offer, as well as a good hunk of steak and a beautifully cooked salmon. The Caesar salad is also said by many to be the best in town. The food here rocks, the atmosphere crackles, and there's a decent list of inexpensive wines to boot.

JAMES' BEACH *60 N. Venice Blvd. bet. Speedway and Pacific Aves., Venice, 310-823-5396; Hours: Wed-Sun 11:30am-3pm, 6pm-10:30pm; Mon-Tue 6pm-10:30pm $$$*

Less than a block away from the modern-day circus that is the Venice Beach Boardwalk, this casual restaurant turns out some damn good beach food seven days a week. Although only four years old, this hip neighborhood hang has become an institution, attracting locals from across the spectrum: stalwart hippies, European expatriates, refugees from the animation lab on a dinner break, you name it. Weight watchers should go for the rotating selection of low-calorie Swimsuit Specials, while big eaters can't miss with the golden fried chicken, East Coast-style beach lobster, and tuna tartare. Thursdays through Saturdays, James' Beach serves its late-night menu until 1am, featuring such goodies as sevruga caviar, steak frites, and freshly baked chocolate chip cookies. Keep in mind, too, that the Sunday brunch is one of the tastiest in town.

LES DEUX CAFÉ *1638 N. Las Palmas Ave. bet. Hollywood and Sunset Blvds., Hollywood, 323-465-0509; Hours: Mon-Fri 11:30am-2:30pm, 6:30pm-1am; Sat-Sun 6:30pm-1am $$$*

The coolness quotient is high at this unmarked French boîte in the back streets of downtown Hollywood. Whoever has the most attitude wins at this terminally hip hang, but regulars swear that Les Deux isn't pretentious: Just walk in like you own the place and you'll have a good time. Owner and hostess Michelle Lamy treats the restaurant as her home, making every night feel like a house party for all of her closest friends — East Coast refugees, wanna-be superstars, and the local intelligentsia — who nibble on the rustic French food before moving on to the cabaret room, where they mingle till the wee hours. Head-turning celebrities are usually on hand: Madonna had her after-Grammy party here and Sting his birthday celebration. The main room is a refurbished Arts and Crafts-style bungalow with dark, dimly lit wood walls. There is also an elegant garden out back, with a bubbling fountain and a handful of olive trees. Some of Les Deux's critics call the food boring and overpriced, but people come here for the scene, not the food, silly. Nevertheless, Lamy insists that Les Deux's food is perfectly seasoned, and to prove her point, there are no salt or pepper shakers on the table. The restaurant's supporters say it serves up the best cheese plate in the city, and they recommend dishes like raclette, warm oysters, and skate in brown butter.

LUCQUES *8474 Melrose Ave. at La Cienega Blvd., West Hollywood, 323-655-6277; Hours: Tue-Sat 6pm-12am; Sun 6pm-10pm $$$*
Everyone from Westside foodies to Eastside culture vultures has been flocking to Lucques since it opened in 1998. This red-hot California-Mediterranean restaurant is booked weeks in advance, so reservations are a must. For the financially challenged, there's a $30 three-course prix fixe dinner on Sundays — a deal for a place that costs up to $50 a head otherwise. Young up-and-coming chef Suzanne Goin put in time at Campanile and Berkeley's

famous Chez Panisse before transforming silent-screen star Harold Lloyd's carriage house into a model of clubby hipness. Still, Lucques maintains an understated elegance, with leather sofas at the fireplace, olive walls, and a romantic, high-walled patio. Unlike most restaurants of the moment, Lucques isn't pretentious or fussy; you will always feel welcome here. The one-page menu is seasonal, inspired by the produce Goin culls from local farmer's markets. Recommended dishes from past menus include roasted beet salad, cured pork chops, and grilled quail with couscous stuffing. Desserts are also spectacular here, with a pillowy vanilla pot de crème, blood orange sorbet, and fall fruits mulled in red wine. Lucques has the extra added attraction of a bar with its own late-night menu, with steak frites bernaise, a tomato tart, and a sinful cheese plate, all served till midnight.

MILLIE'S DINER *3524 Sunset Blvd. bet. Hyperion Ave. and Silver Lake Blvd., Silver Lake, 323-664-0404; Hours: Mon-Fri 7am-3pm; Sat-Sun 7am-4pm $*

Millie's is the place to go for that ceremonial first breakfast out when you and your new lover are ready to admit that you are now, officially, an item. It's arguably the most important social center in Silver Lake. Unemployed musicians, local celebrities, and slumming Westsiders make up the denizens at this local institution, where gleaming Formica tabletops and vintage jukeboxes evoke a retro mood. Millie's is open only for breakfast and lunch, and there's plenty of comfort food on the menu, including pork chops, chicken fried steak, and three kinds of grilled cheese sandwiches, as well as the Usual (two pancakes, two strips of bacon, and two eggs with a side of rosemary potatoes). But to truly take advantage of the menu, indulge in the house specialty, the Devil's Mess-scrambled eggs, bubbling over with melted cheddar cheese and spicy Cajun sausage, topped with salsa, guacamole, and sour cream. Vegetarians can opt for the Eleanor R. Special — two eggs over easy, oozing cheese over a layer of sizzling-hot rosemary potatoes and garnished with salsa and sour cream. On each table, there are at least seven bottles of hot sauce — one of which is sure to set even the most jaded taste buds on fire.

PHILLIPE THE ORIGINAL

1001 N. Alameda St. at Main St., Chinatown, 213-628-3781; Hours: daily 6am-10pm $

There are always long lines at Philippe's ten carving stations, where you can grab a slice of Los Angeles history at bargain prices — a first-class meal runs under $5 here. Since 1908, this funky downtown establishment has been making succulent, French-dipped prime beef sandwiches to order, dishing 'em out to city hall employees, jurists on duty, and out-of-work loafers. The big dippers can also be stuffed with pork, turkey, or lamb. Whatever sandwich you choose, try a dab of Philippe's hotter-than-hot house mustard. And don't forget the awesome side dishes — vinegary homemade cole slaw, award-winning potato salad, pickled eggs, and, to top it off, freshly baked doughnuts. Home of the 9 cent cup of coffee (decaf is outrageously priced at 20 cents), Philippe's also has a wide selection of premium California wines, most priced at $3 a glass. The communal tables and sawdust-covered floor have welcomed weirdos and malcontents for decades. A retired circus group used to meet here weekly throughout the '50s and '60s, and today Philippe's is the site of the monthly meeting of local anarchists and art terrorists, the Los Angeles Cacophony Society.

RED *7450 Beverly Blvd. bet. Fairfax and La Brea Aves., Los Angeles, 323-937-0331; Hours: daily 8am-11pm $$*

So cool that the letters of its name are all lowercase, this California-style café has been comfortable with its place on the hipness scale (medium-high) for a while now. Inspired by the all-red interior, the svelte and almost-famous come here for the health-conscious menu. Although it's open for dinner, lunch is the stock-in-trade at this casually cool neighborhood spot. Tables spill out onto the sidewalk, and dogs are welcome at the outdoor tables (be forewarned that if the dining room is packed, it'll be a noisy, clanging mess). The kitchen turns out simple fare like soups, sandwiches, and grilled fish and chicken. Vegetarians also rave about Red's homemade veggie burger; unlike the usual cardboard-colored mush, this burger's red and infused with (gasp!) flavor. At dinnertime, go for the more substantial seared Chilean sea bass, grilled salmon in cabernet sauce, or shiitake and tomato penne pasta.

42 | eating out

SWINGERS *8020 Beverly Blvd. bet. Crescent Heights Blvd. and Fairfax Ave., Los Angeles, 323-653-5858; Hours: daily 6:30am-4am $*

This painfully hip coffee shop pioneered the "slovenly motel diner-turned-retro hip diner" formula. Open since 1993, it's been luring the tattooed and pierced twentysomething crowd with its supercharged smart drinks (remember when that was the new thing?) and drop-dead-gorgeous waitstaff ever since. Touring bands like Stereolab stay at the Beverly Laurel Motor Hotel and then roll in to Swingers midday for their breakfast, which, fortunately for this clientele, is served all day. The decor is an homage to the days when blue-collar was cool — think bright orange walls, red plaid booths, and a prominent jukebox. The menu is classic atomic age with an MTV spin: veggie burgers, smoothies, and vegetarian chili complement the beef burgers, skin-on French fries, club sandwiches, and Cobb salad. But breakfast is the meal of the day here, whether it's 3am or 3pm, with overflowing three-egg omelettes, cream cheese-and-bacon-stuffed French toast, and a wacky take on eggs Benedict.

TAYLOR'S PRIME STEAKS

3361 W. 8th St. bet. Western and Normandie Aves., Koreatown, 213-382-8449; Hours: Mon-Fri 11:30am-11pm; Sat-Sun 4pm-11pm $$

The ultimate in decadence is a rare slab of meat and a stiff drink. Skip the new steak houses that are all the rage in LA and experience the real deal in Koreatown. There's no cooler place to indulge in the sins of the flesh than this old-time steak house tucked away on a rather average-looking block. Creaky waitresses call you "sugar" while you snuggle into the dark embrace of a red Naugahyde booth with your sweetheart. The menu is standard steak house fare, but turned out with a flourish as only a veteran kitchen can. And with the old-time prices, too: Taylor's dishes out the lowest-priced prime aged steak in the area. A nicely charred yet blood-rare steak with all the trimmings (soup or salad, veggies, and a potato of your choice) is less than $20 — and that's the most expensive steak. The porterhouse T-bone is the most tasty, and the house steak, the culotte, is also very good. Classic starters like Caesar salad and jumbo shrimp cocktail are up to par; as for the side dishes, pass on the too-crispy cottage fries and opt for the mashed or baked potato instead.

ZEN GRILL *8432 W. 3rd St. bet. La Cienega and Crescent Heights Blvds., Los Angeles, 323-655-9991; Hours: Mon-Sat 11:30am-11pm; Sun 3pm-10pm $$* If your pockets don't run deep but you still want to eat elbow-to-elbow with the in crowd in a coolly elegant space, hightail it over to Zen Grill, popular for its moderate prices and fresh, tasty food. This eclectic Pan-Asian restaurant packs in young, ambitious upstarts with its fusion cuisine, taking its cues from the kitchens of Japan, India, Malaysia, Korea, Vietnam, and India. The casual atmosphere seduces with its red walls, Chinese lanterns, and exposed beams, if not with the clattering noise of this small restaurant. Adventurous diners can expand their horizons with Malaysian laksa soup and Korean-style barbecued ribs. Fusion classics like teriyaki Chilean sea bass, pan-fried tofu steak, crispy calamari salad, and a sashimi tuna rice tower round out the menu.

BREAKFAST

Ah, the most important meal of the day. Where else to eat it but **Home** *(1760 Hillhurst Ave., Los Feliz, 323-669-0211)*, where you can choose between Wonder Bread toast, Pop-Tarts, Cap'n Crunch, and chocolate milk? Those with bigger appetites should head to **Eat Well** *(3916 Sunset Blvd., Silver Lake, 323-664-1624)* for its Big Mess, an everything-but-the-kitchen-sink molten mass of eggs, spicy sausage, veggies, and cheese. The **Hollywood Hills Coffee Shop** *(6145 Franklin Ave., Hollywood, 323-467-7678)* doles out wacky renditions of archetypal diner fare, like cinnamon French toast made from croissants. Young celebs like Brad Pitt, Drew Barrymore, and Gwyneth Paltrow have all been spotted in the red vinyl booths. *Swingers* was filmed here, and it was the real-life hangout of out-of-work actors Vince Vaughn and company before they hit the big time; fledgling screenwriters and actors still pack the joint, hoping to follow in their footsteps. The locals-only **Village Coffee Shop** *(2695 Beachwood Dr., Hollywood, 323-467-5398)* is nestled in the peaceful Beachwood Canyon neighborhood at the foot of the hill that boasts the Hollywood sign. Get off the beaten path and chow down on greasy omelettes and fluffy pancakes, sans tourists. **Kokomo Café** *(Farmer's Market, 6333 3rd St., Los Angeles, 323-933-0773)* is a midtown favorite, with retro breakfasts like eggs sardou (poached eggs set on artichokes, topped with spinach and hollandaise) and pain perdu (French toast with apples, nuts, and homemade maple syrup) served in the open-air Farmer's Market. **Who's on Third?** *(8369 3rd St., Los Angeles, 323-651-2928)*, in the shadow of the Beverly Center, is always packed in the morning hours. Think comfort food with a healthy twist, like egg-white omelettes and low-fat hollandaise. At **Hugo's** *(8401 Santa Monica Blvd., West Hollywood, 323-654-3993)* specialty is Pasta Mama, a mix of fresh pasta, eggs, and Parmesan cheese. Other dishes include the tofu scramble and five kinds of griddle cakes. At **Quality Food & Beverage** *(8030 3rd St., Los Angeles, 323-658-5959)*, the stark '40s-style decor sets the tone for the old-fashioned home cooking it serves its dyed-in-the-wool hipster clientele. **King's Road Café** *(8361 Beverly Blvd., Los Angeles, 323-655-9044)* attracts the Hollywood actor and screenwriter crowd, who love the fontina omelettes and eggs prosciutto, and the de rigeur espresso drinks. Farther West is **John O'Groats** *(10516 Pico Blvd., West LA, 310-204-0692)*, which pulls people in droves for its morning repast; there's always a wait at this restaurant, but the homey biscuits, home fries, and overstuffed omelettes make it worth the wait. **Blueberry** *(510 Santa Monica Blvd., Santa Monica, 310-394-7766)* serves its signature blueberry pancakes along with eggs and waffles to the beautiful downtown Santa Monica crowd. Eggs come every which way at the **Omelette Parlor** *(2732 Main St., Santa Monica, 310-399-7892)*. There's always a wait for these masterpieces, priced at only $5.99. To please the muscle-bound bodybuilding geeks in Venice Beach are the **Rose Café** *(220 Rose Ave., Santa Monica, 310-399-0711)*, with omelettes, frittatas, and pancakes galore and, across the street, the **Firehouse** *(213 Rose Ave., Santa Monica, 310-392-4275)*, where all the dishes can be cooked with a fitness buff's low-fat, high-protein needs in mind.

CALIFORNIA PIZZA

Celebrity chef Wolfgang Puck's flagship restaurant, **Spago** *(1114 Horn Ave., West Hollywood, 310-652-4025)* invented California's famous gourmet pizza. His signature pie — the crème fraîche topped with smoked salmon — isn't on the menu, but it's still available if you ask nicely. Puck's designer pies can also be found at one of the **Wolfgang Puck Cafés** scattered around town *(8000 Sunset Blvd., West Hollywood, 323-650-7300; call for other locations)*. Over the hill, within the confines of the San Fernando Valley, Spago's first pizza chef, Ed LaDou, now has his very own **Caioti Pizza Café** *(4346 Tujunga Ave., Studio City, 818-761-3588)*. Legend has it that Caioti's walnut Gorgonzola salad slathered with balsamic vinaigrette induces labor in extremely pregnant women. In between stints at Spago and his own cafés, LaDou helped create the new-wave pizzas that fill the menu at **California Pizza Kitchen** chain, dotted all around town *(11677 San Vicente Blvd., Brentwood, 310-826-3573; call for other locations)*. Ensconced in Caioti's former Laurel Canyon location, **Pace** *(2100 Laurel Canyon Blvd., West Hollywood, 323-654-8583)* is continuing the oddball pizza tradition with crackly-crusted pizzas named after mythological figures like Aphrodite and Zeus. It's not all newfangled, though: **Antica Pizzeria** *(8022 3rd St., Los Angeles, 323-658-7607)* has the only authentic version of the thick-crust Neapolitan pizza in the entire United States. The blistery pies are slathered with crushed-tomato sauce and molten mozzarella cheese, plus the fresh toppings of your choice. **Casa Bianca** *(1650 Colorado Blvd., Eagle Rock, 323-256-9617)* serves crispy, thin-crusted pies schmeared with a tangy tomato sauce and chewy mozzarella cheese. Many Big Apple émigrés say **Joe Peep's** *(12460 Magnolia Blvd., North Hollywood, 818-506-4133)* has the best New York-style pizza in town. Fold a thick slice yourself from the "5,969 calorie" menu and see what you think. The celebrity-owned **Mulberry Street Pizza** *(347 N. Canon Dr., Beverly Hills, 310-278-9911)* is also a cheap place to grab a to-die-for New York-style slice. **Vito's** *(814 N. Vermont Ave., Los Angeles, 323-667-2723)* packs in Eastsiders and expat New Yorkers to its hole in the wall, where they toss authentic thin-crusted pies that scream outer borough.

CELEBRITY-OWNED

No, you haven't entered an outtake from *The Player*. Celebrities are notorious for throwing their weight behind newly opened restaurants to gain a little street cred. Elbow past the throngs at **Ago** *(8478 Melrose Ave., West Hollywood,*

323-655-6333), a regional Italian restaurant co-owned by Robert DeNiro and Miramax's Bob and Harvey Weinstein. Rumor has it that Quentin Tarantino coldcocked a colleague there at a business dinner. Speaking of Miramax, the studio's favorite sons, Matt Damon and Ben Affleck, have invested in **Continental** *(8400 Wilshire Blvd., Beverly Hills, 323-782-9717)*, another in a series of ecclectic eateries with an inspiring menu. The most famous Jewish mother in town, Leah Adler, a.k.a. Steven Spielberg's mom, was running the **Milky Way** *(9108 Pico Blvd., West LA, 310-859-0004)* long before kid-loving extraterrestrials and killer sharks dominated the big screen. The strictly kosher restaurant (which serves dairy products, but no meat) is a favorite of Kirk Douglas and Jason Alexander, who brings his own parents here for dinner. The menu is more creative than you would think, with dishes like chimichangas, seafood paella, and Cajun blackened snapper. Of course, it's closed on Saturdays, a gentle reminder to get your ass to temple. **Reign** *(180 N. Robertson Blvd., Beverly Hills, 310-273-4463)* — owned by wide receiver Keyshawn Johnson — doles out an upscale take on soul food in a hip Hollywood environment. Crab cakes, fried chicken, collard greens, peach cobbler: all the down-home Southern favorites are here. And Marla Gibbs — Florence the maid on *The Jeffersons* — is investing in the hood with **Marla's Jazz Supper Club** *(2323 W. Martin Luther King, Jr. Blvd., Leimert Park, 323-294-8430)*. This New Orleans-style restaurant is sporadically closed, so call before you make the trip to South Central.

DRIVE-THRU

Dining while driving is essential to life in any auto-centric city. Just make sure to take lots of napkins to keep your steering wheel grease-free. If you call ten minutes beforehand, the curbside service at **Langer's Deli** *(704 S. Alvarado St., Downtown, 213-483-8050)* will deliver the city's best pastrami sandwich to your window as soon as you pull up. The tender, thick-cut sugar-cured beef is a one-handed eating masterpiece. Right next to the 405, **Rubin's Red Hot** *(15322 Ventura Blvd., Sherman Oaks, 818-905-6515)* will hand you a frankfurter in a seeded bun topped with pickles, tomatoes, chopped onion, and bright-green relish. Re-live the '50s at **Bob's Big Boy** *(4211 Riverside Dr., Burbank, 818-843-9334)* every Saturday and Sunday night, when carhops deliver burgers, fries, and shakes to your car. On Fridays, restored hot rods and classic cars fill up the parking lot (though unfortunately, for insurance reasons, the staff can't wear roller skates anymore).

Fans of **Krispy Kreme** *(1801 W. Imperial Highway, La Habra, 562-690-2650; 7249 Van Nuys Blvd., Van Nuys, 818-908-9113)* drive for miles to get the hot glazed doughnuts fresh off the conveyor belts. But the original drive-thru doughnut is the **Donut Hole** *(15300 Amar Rd., La Puente, 626-968-2912)*, with its two drive-in 26-foot-high fiberglass chocolate doughnuts.

GLOBAL CUISINE

For those who live to eat, Los Angeles is a chowhound's paradise. The cross-cultural pollination of the city creates unlimited territory for expanding one's taste buds. And at under $10 a person, you can eat your way around the world without draining your wallet — or even leaving the city. To wit: Located next to a freeway interchange, **King Taco No. 2** *(4504 E. 3rd St., East LA, 323-264-4067)* is so popular that the mammoth parking lot turns into a hopping tailgate party on the weekends. This East LA gem serves tacos and burritos made from sweetbreads, marrow guts, and brains, as well as the more pedestrian carne asada, chicken, and pork with your choice of sauces-mild green or roaring-hot red. The best burritos can be found at **Manuel's El Tepeyac** *(812 N. Evergreen, East LA, 323-267-8668)*. Try the Hollenbeck burrito; its namesake is the local police division. A little more fancy is Mexican steak house **Gallo's Grill** *(4533 Cesar E. Chavez Ave., East LA, 323- 980-8669)* where you can get steaks and brochettes brought sizzling to your table with fresh tortillas and four homemade salsas. In Koreatown, **Guelaguetza** *(3337 8th St., Koreatown, 213-427-0601)* dishes out authentic Oaxacan dishes like mole, banana leaf-wrapped tamales, *clayudas* (a Oaxacan-style pizza), and regional drinks like *tejate* and *horchata*. If you love Greek favorites like crisply charred lamb chops, flaky spanakopita, and grape leaves, head downtown to **Papa Cristos** *(2771 Pico Blvd., Koreatown, 323-737-2880)*, a lunch counter inside a Greek market that's well worth the trek. Buy some fresh baklava at the market to end a perfect Greek meal. At **Zankou Chicken** *(5065 Sunset Blvd., Hollywood, 323-665-7842)*, the Middle Eastern rotisserie chicken is so good that it garnered a mention on Beck's album *Midnight Vultures*. The ethnic enclave of Thai Town, on Hollywood Boulevard between Western and Vermont, hosts scores of fierce Thai restaurants; you'll do well at any of the restaurants on this strip. For the best Thai noodles, **Sanamluang** *(5176 Hollywood Blvd., Hollywood,*

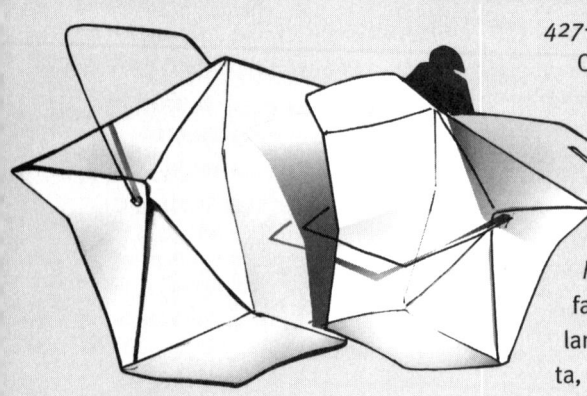

323-660-8006) is the place to go, and **Kruang Tedd** *(5151 Hollywood Blvd., Hollywood, 323-663-9988)* is ground zero for exotic Thai bar snacks like chile-fried peanuts. A mini-strip of Ethiopian restaurants can be found on Fairfax Avenue just south of Olympic, with the most popular among them, **Nyala** *(1076 S. Fairfax Ave., Los Angeles, 323-936-5918)*, upholding a tradition of Northern African home-style cooking. The roasted chicken dinner at Cuban restaurant **Versailles** *(1415 S. La Cienega Blvd., Los Angeles, 310-289-0392; 10319 Venice Blvd., Palms, 310-558-3168)* is a veritable feast, with heavily garlicked chicken with onions, black beans, rice and fried plantains. Culinary pilgrims will be richly rewarded at **Itacho** *(7311 Beverly Blvd., Los Angeles, 323-938-9009)* which serves traditional Japanese tapas-like dishes that are hard to find on this side of the Pacific. For perfect Japanese udon and soba noodles, hit one of **Mishima**'s two locations *(11301 Olympic Blvd., West LA, 310-473-5297; 8474 3rd St., Los Angeles, 323-782-0181)*. Juliette Lewis slums with the Silver Lake crowd at Lebanese restaurant **Marouch** *(4905 Santa Monica Blvd., Silver Lake, 323-662-9325)*, scarfing on chicken schwerma and baba ghanoush. You'll be slaving over the hot grill cooking your own at **Soot Bull Jeep** *(3136 8th St., Koreatown, 213-387-3865)*, one of several outstanding spots for Korean barbecue in town. For Chinese food, dim sum aficionados favor **Empress Pavilion** *(988 N. Hill St., Chinatown, 213-617-9898)*. And finally, where else can you get steamed lobster on a paper plate but at **Neptune's Net** *(42505 Pacific Coast Hwy., Malibu, 310-457-3095)*, in the most northern part of Malibu, just across the county line.

HAMBURGERS

So the first McDonald's was opened outside of Los Angeles? Big deal. The slavishly burger-bound will find much better patties to fry in the city of angels. Culinary pilgrims from across the country throng to **Cassell's** *(3266 6th St., Koreatown, 213-387-5502)* for the perfect hamburger — at under $6 a pop. Depending on your level of devotion, 6 or 12 ounces of freshly ground USDA prime beef are broiled to order and served up naked on a monstrous bun. Cassell's closes at 4pm and is cash only, so don't miss this chance at ground beef nirvana. **Pie 'n' Burger** *(913 E. California Blvd., Pasadena, 626-795-1123)* chars its burger to a crisp without sacrificing juiciness, serving it up on a toasted bun with crisp lettuce and barely melted American cheese. The Westside's best-loved burger can be had at the **Apple Pan** *(10801 Pico Blvd., West LA, 310-475-3585)*, with its medium-thick patty, fresh lettuce, slices of dill pickle, and sharp Tillamook Cheddar cheese on a lightly toasted bun. Prepare to be baffled at the 150 permutations of hamburger at **Hampton's Hollywood Café** *(1342 N. Highland Ave., Hollywood, 323-469-1090)*. These gourmet concoctions range from the traditional cheeseburger to veggie, turkey, alligator, venison, and buffalo burgers. If you've ever yearned for a peanut butter-covered alligator burger, this is

eating out

the place to go. Oh, and SAG members get a 10 percent discount, while agents get 10 percent added to their bills. Who ever said Hollywood was fair? Inspiring its own cult following is the **In-N-Out Burger** *(7009 Sunset Blvd., Hollywood, 1-800-786-1000; call for other locations)* Double Double-double cheese, double meat cooked to order and handed to you at the drive-thru window. When Los Angeles's own Kosovo POW was released, his mom flew to Germany with a sack of these grease bombs to remind him of home. But the greasiest local heartburner is the double chili cheeseburger at **Tommy's** *(2575 Beverly Blvd., Los Angeles, 213-389-9060, locations throughout LA)*. These places are always hopping, no matter what the hour. Herbivores looking for ersatz meat fixes should hightail it over to **Astro Burger** *(5601 Melrose Ave., Hollywood, 323-469-1924)*, where there are over ten takes on the garden burger.

HAPPY HOUR

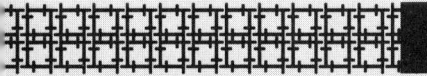

Even the most devoted boozers have to eat sometime. So get thee to the city's best happy hours to fill up your stomach before a long night of pub-crawling. **McCormick & Schmick's** *(Library Tower, 633 W. 5th St., Downtown, 213-629-1929; 2 Rodeo Dr., Beverly Hills, 310-859-0434)* is hands down the best happy hour (3pm-7pm) in Los Angeles. This seafood restaurant packs 'em in for the $1.95 munchies — crispy calamari, mozzarella bruschetta topped with juicy bay shrimp, and toasted focaccia smeared with chevre. Another hot downtown happy hour, **Ciudad** *(445 S. Figueroa St., Downtown, 213-486-5171)*, is the latest venture of the Food Network's *Too Hot Tamales*, Mary Sue Milliken and Susan Feniger. Featuring Pan-Latin American cuisine, the *cuchifritos* (bar snacks) are served from 3pm to 7pm daily. Close to the ocean are several more worthwhile happy hour hangouts. The Tamales' other restaurant is the famous **Border Grill** *(1445 4th St., Santa Monica, 310-451-1655)*, with free chips, quesadillas, and three kinds of salsa as well as discount drinks. In the middle of town is **Cava** *(8384 3rd St., Los Angeles, 323-658-8898)*, a Spanish and Latin American-influenced restaurant that serves $2 glasses of killer sangria between 4:30pm and 7pm weekdays. Pasta and tortilla chips are free for the masses, and tapas are available at a discounted price. **The World Café** *(2820 Main St., Santa Monica, 310-392-1661)* doles out free mini pizzas and homemade potato chips to the inebriated during its happy hour every day. There are also Internet stations available for e-mail addicts.

LATE NIGHT

Los Angeles offers starving night owls grub ranging from Thai and Japanese to soul food and Indian. Silver Lake and Los Feliz, epicenter of the local music scene, feed flocks of post-rock clubgoers after 2am. A favorite of the Beastie Boys and Keanu Reeves, **Electric Lotus** *(4656 Franklin Ave., Los Feliz, 323-953-0040)* offers North Indian cuisine cooked in olive oil instead of ghee to placate the local vegans. The place is open until 3am nightly, and there is usually a DJ spinning live. For a greasy spoon, head to the **Astro Family Restaurant** *(2300 Fletcher Dr., Silver Lake, 323-663-9241)*, the closest late-night food source to megaclub Spaceland, for its heart attack-inducing diner classics. Downtown also has a handful of joints open well into the wee hours. When only the most expensive meal will do, **Pacific Dining Car** *(1310 W. 6th St., Downtown, 213-483-6000)* doles out mesquite-grilled, prime-aged beef 24 hours a day, and breakfast is served after 11pm. Around the corner from the Museum of Contemporary Art's Temporary Contemporary, Little Tokyo's Japanese coffee shop **Suehiro** *(337 E. 1st St., Little Tokyo, 213-*

626-9132) dishes out tempura, teriyaki, rice bowls, and steaming noodles to an insomniac art school crowd. If hot dogs are your thing, head to **Pink's** (709 N. La Brea Ave., Hollywood, 323-931-4223), where Angelenos have been standing in line for these famous grease bombs for over 60 years. **Roscoe's House of Chicken 'n' Waffles** (1514 N. Gower St., Hollywood, 323-466-7453) specializes in down-home Southern specialties like fried chicken and waffles, chicken livers, giblets, and grits. **Caffé Luna** (7463 Melrose Ave., Hollywood, 323-655-8647) dishes out pasta, thin-crust pizza, and panini sandwiches till 5am to a hip young Hollywood crowd. **Mel's Drive-In** (8585 Sunset Blvd., West Hollywood, 310-854-7201) has reinvented the space once occupied by Sunset Strip's legendary 1960s night owl hangout Ben Frank's. Burgers, shakes, and fries anchor the menu, but Mel's also does a sideline in vegetarian and fat-free dishes. For old-guard Jewish comfort food, **Canter's** (419 N. Fairfax Ave., Los Angeles, 323-651-2030) has always been a stronghold of the late-night dining scene; cold cuts and matzo-ball soup are served around the clock. For a late-night dose of sushi, **Shibucho** (3114 Beverly Blvd., Koreatown, 213-387-8498) is an elegant sushi bar open until 3am.

MEXICAN

Influenced by its roots as a little pueblo in Mexico, Los Angeles has a wide variety of Mexican restaurants, from the cheese-covered masses of Tex-Mex combination dinners to the refined dishes of regional Mexico. The granddaddy of all LA-area Mexican restaurants is **El Cholo** (1121 S. Western Ave., Koreatown, 323-734-2773; 1025 Wilshire Blvd., Santa Monica, 310-899-1106). Open since 1927, this venerable establishment is famous for its strong margaritas and summer-only green corn tamales. Homestyle California-Mexican cooking is the strong suit here, with chicken enchiladas and shrimp fajitas among the best-loved dishes. Nestled next to

eating out

Paramount Studios, **Lucy's El Adobe Café** *(5536 Melrose Ave., Hollywood, 323-462-9421)* serves up classic Mexican cuisine to industry honchos and lackeys alike. At the **Gardens of Taxco** *(1113 N. Harper Ave., West Hollywood, 323-654-1746)*, the chicken and shrimp dishes taste as if they were born in the sauce at this family-run restaurant. There is no written menu, but your server will singsong his way through the dishes (most under $15 for four courses) for you. **Mexico City** *(2121 Hillhurst Ave., Los Feliz, 323-661-7227)* is a Los Feliz neighborhood dive, doling out authentic Mexican dishes to a super-cool Eastside crowd. The green mole and garlic shrimp are to die for. **La Serenata de Garibaldi** *(1842 E. 1st St., Boyle Heights, 323-265-2887; 1416 4th St., Santa Monica, 310-656-7017)*, hailed as the home of the finest Mexican seafood in town, is a bit overrated, but it offers a good chance to sample fresh mahimahi, shrimp, and sea bass in a dozen possible sauces.

OLD SCHOOL

These restaurants are the last bastion of high-cholesterol, artery-clogging slabs of meat, where the ghosts of movie stars go to inhale the scent of horseradish. Open since 1919, **Musso & Frank Grill** *(6667 Hollywood Blvd., Hollywood, 323-467-7788)* is the oldest restaurant in Hollywood. The venerable institution is most famous for its ice-cold martini, indisputably Hollywood's best, which inspired faultless prose from the likes of Fitzgerald, Faulkner, and Chandler. Surly old waiters bring heart-stopping platters of beef Stroganoff, chicken pot pie, and funnel cakes, as well as prime aged slabs of New York steak and prime rib. Longtime favorite the **Original Pantry Café** *(877 S. Figueroa St., Downtown, 213-972-9279)* is now owned by Mayor Riordan, but it's still open 24 hours with steaks and chops on a chalkboard menu. For the real old school, **Cole's P.E. Buffet** *(118 E. 6th St., Downtown,*

213-622-4090) has been around since 1908. Still dishing up succulent beef sandwiches, the bar also serves imported German brews on tap for cheap. Scenes from the *X-Files*, *LA Confidential*, and *Forrest Gump* were all filmed here; occasionally, local cabaret band the Centimeters hosts live shows at Cole's. **Miceli's** *(1646 N. Las Palmas Ave., Hollywood, 323-466-3438)* has been serving traditional Italian-American fare since 1949 from its nook just south of Hollywood Boulevard. The decor is unabashedly tacky, with dozens of straw Chianti bottles hanging from the walls; the owner claims that this is the first pizzeria opened west of the Mississippi.

POWER EATING

With connections — and by being seen at the right restaurants — you can meet all the major players in Hollywood in less than a week. Wanna-be members of Tinseltown's elite, take note: Practice your air kiss and study this list. From industry moguls to the hottest superstars, from breakfast to lunch to dinner, here's where the game is played. Taking over for old-guard breakfast favorite the Beverly Hills Hotel's **Polo Lounge** *(9641 Sunset Blvd., Beverly Hills, 310-276-2251)*, the Four Seasons' **Gardens** *(300 S. Doheny Dr., Beverly Hills, 310-273-2222)* is favored by studio chiefs like Sherry Lansing for their morning repast. All the major studios have press junkets at the Four Seasons, so it's guaranteed to be full of industry swine fueling up before a big day of schmoozing. But loyalists still prefer the Polo Lounge and its calories-be-damned eggs Benedict and apple pancakes. Bloodthirsty agents go to the Peninsula Hotel's **Belvedere** *(9882 Little Santa Monica Blvd., Beverly Hills, 310-788-2306)*, which is next door to CAA and near rival powerhouse William Morris. The venerable Jewish deli **Nate 'n' Al's** *(414 N. Beverly Dr., Beverly Hills, 310-274-0101)* also feeds CEOs and their minions, who are comforted from the stress of deal-making by the matzo-ball soup, deli sandwiches,

eating out 57

and grandmotherly service. As far as lunch goes, **The Grill** *(9560 Dayton Way, Beverly Hills, 310-276-0615)* is the only place where deals are cut between the hours of 1 and 2pm. Runners-up include rival steak house **The Palm** *(9001 Santa Monica Blvd., West Hollywood, 310-550-8811)*, the power spot of choice for music industry moguls. **Maple Drive** *(345 N. Maple Dr., Beverly Hills, 310-274-9800)* is the veritable commissary for upstairs moviemaking company Castle Rock. And due to their proximity to Twentieth Century Fox, **Primi** *(10543 Pico Blvd., West LA, 310-475-9235)* and **Osteria Romana Orsini** *(9575 Pico Blvd., West LA, 310-277-6050)* are packed with bigwigs at lunch hour daily. For the valley studios (Universal, Disney, anything pornographic), there is **Ca' del Sole** *(4100 Cahuenga Blvd., North Hollywood, 818-985-4669)*, one of the few choices for execs working in the area. For dinner, Monday night at **Morton's** *(8764 Melrose Ave., West Hollywood, 310-276-5205)* has long been considered the only game in town; career-making and -breaking deals are brokered here weekly over plates of hearty American food. Elsewhere, celebrities also sup at **Spago Beverly Hills** *(176 N. Canon Dr., Beverly Hills, 310-385-0880)*, the latest must-see restaurant from celebrity chef Wolfgang Puck, famous for his inventive California cuisine.

SUPPER CLUBS

The Cocktail Nation is flocking to a slew of new Los Angeles supper clubs that are no longer just for the retired set. The newest addition to the fold is the **Sunset Room** *(1430 Cahuenga Blvd., Hollywood, 323-463-0004)*, a deliberate throwback to the days when dining was an all-evening affair. The deep, inviting booths, the rich mahogany bar, and the outdoor patio create the perfect combination of Hollywood glamour and spacious comfort. Steak and martinis just won't go out of style at the **Coconut Club** *(Beverly Hilton Hotel, 9876 Wilshire Blvd., Beverly Hills, 310-285-1358)*, reminiscent of '40s-era Las Vegas, with snow-white vinyl booths, glittery palm trees, and neon monkeys. The cover is steep ($20) but worth it if you want to step into the swanky shoes of yesteryear. Tucked away in a West LA minimall, **Stevie Joe's Lounge and Supper Club** *(10433 National Blvd., West LA, 310-837-5245)* features a darkly lit interior that melds '30s-, '40s-, and '50s-style decor with palm fronds, velvet curtains, and pinup-girl oil paintings. The updated regional American classics on the menu include blackened turkey meat loaf and Maryland crab cakes, and there are a zillion martini choices on the drink list. Located in the burnished-maple space of a onetime speakeasy, **Flint's** *(3321 Pico Blvd., Santa Monica, 310-453-1331)* serves the food of a bygone era with a modern twist, like challah French toast and yellowfin tuna tartare, as well as more hearty old-time faves like osso buco. Sultry chanteuses and jazz combos often hold court, as well as more offbeat acts like the A/V Geeks, who show vintage educational reels like "Are You Popular?" and "Psychological Differences Between the Sexes." It's always a good night at the **La Boca del Conga Room** *(5364 Wilshire Blvd., Los Angeles, 323-938-1696)*, the hottest supper club around. Legends like Poncho Sanchez and the Buena Vista Social Club often heat up the dance floor at this club, which is co-owned by Latin superstars Jennifer Lopez and Jimmy Smits, among others. The brief menu is red-hot Nuevo Latino, with colorful drinks and such dishes as grilled chile-rubbed prawns and Ecuadorian-style tamales. **The Catalina Bar & Grill** *(1640 Cahuenga Blvd., Hollywood, 323-466-2210)* attracts international old guard beboppers, who make this elegant space their sole LA stop on cross-country jaunts. The menu is New American, with entrees like Cajun catfish, shrimp fettuccine, and roasted rack of lamb. **Atlas Bar & Grill** *(3760 Wilshire Blvd., Koreatown, 213-380-8400)* features local swing, lounge, Latin, and jazz bands, and a simple menu of global pastas, seafood, and chops. For over 35 years, **El Cid** *(4212 Sunset Blvd., Silver Lake, 323-668-0318)*

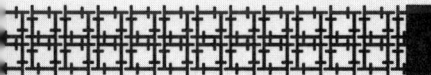

eating out

has been putting on lively flamenco floor shows in fantastically kitschy surroundings to accompany its traditional Spanish cuisine and potent sangria.

SUSHI

Los Angeles's proximity to the Pacific Ocean has blessed it with the freshest fish in the States. Be warned, though, that some of it is also the most expensive.

Supported by its claim to be the priciest sushi joint in North America, the chefs at Ginza Sushiko *(218 N. Rodeo Dr., Beverly Hills, 310-487-2251)* decide what you will eat. The fish here is said to have no equal and is flown in daily from Tokyo. Big spenders don't mind paying $250-$350 a person for these sublime concoctions. Slightly more economical and much more prestigious, **Matsuhisa** *(129 N. La Cienega Blvd., Beverly Hills, 310-659-9639)* is where celebrity chef Nobu Matsuhisa invented his signature Japanese-Peruvian cuisine. The *omakase* menu translates roughly to "do me what you will," a wise choice when dealing with a master — just don't faint when you get the check.

The hippest sushi bar in town is **R-23** *(923 E. 3rd St., Downtown, 213-687-7178)*, just a short drunken walk from the seminal punk rock club Al's Bar. Slurp down some of the best sushi around in stark, minimalist surroundings, favored by both artist types and city hall suits. The least pretentious of the city's offerings is definitely **Sushi Nozawa** *(11288 Ventura Blvd., Studio City, 818-508-7017)*, nestled in a bland minimall near Universal Studios. Chef Kazunori Nozawa rules with an iron fist — you will eat what he fixes you. The tap-dancing chefs at **Sushi on Tap** *(11056 Ventura Blvd., Studio City, 818-985-2254)* take breaks from slaving behind the sushi bar to execute a letter-perfect homage to Tin Pan Alley musicals. And finally, for the scene, the overpriced **Sushi Roku** *(8445 3rd St., Los Angeles, 323-655-6767)* caters to painfully hip Gen-Xers who love the exotic sakes as much as the fish.

TRULY TACKY

For those who feel the need to dine in a surreal wonderland, a handful of kitsch-filled paradises await. An aquarium, blowfish lights, nautical curios, and a 30-pound 22-year-old fish named Rufus are resplendent at **Bahooka's Ribs and Grog** *(4501 N. Rosemead Blvd., Rosemead, 626-285-1241)*. The food is nothing to write home about, but that's not why people come here. The deep fryer gets a lot of use, and the house special, Bahooka's Special Exotic Ribs, are glazed in molten rivers of sweet teriyaki sauce. **Damon's** *(317 N. Brand Blvd., Glendale, 818-507-1510)* does justice to the tacky tiki tradition with a tropical fish tank and murals of monkeys and native Hawaiians painted on the walls. **Clearman's North Woods Inn** *(7247 N. Rosemead Blvd., San Gabriel, 626-286-4022)* is an enormous log cabin-themed steak house (just up the street from Bahooka's) whose roof and eaves are covered with fake snow year-round. Animal heads and tastefully rendered naked ladies look on while you eat cheese bread and red-cabbage slaw. Silver Lake-adjacent, the **Lowenbrau Keller** *(3211 Beverly Blvd., Koreatown, 213-381-5723)* serves cholesterol-heavy German food in an overdone Teutonic setting. The dark and cavernous dining room is full of armored knights, gargoyles, wrought-iron chandeliers, and taxidermy. Schlocky German show tunes set the tone for the artery-clogging feast to come. The most stately cafeteria in the world may just be **Clifton's** *(648 S. Broadway, Downtown, 213-627-1673)*. Nothing compares to the faded grandeur of its ersatz redwood forest, full moon, deer, and meandering indoor stream and waterfall. The food is of the usual cafeteria steam table variety, but there's also carved-to-order ham and roast beef that makes a visit worthwhile.

VEGETARIAN

The land of paper-thin actresses and the men who love them supports a panoply of healthy vegetarian dining establishments. Fuel up on breakfast at **A Votre Santé** *(345 N. La Brea Ave., Hollywood, 323-857-0412)*, where you can get your tofu scrambled until 3pm daily, along with pancakes and egg white omelettes. Lunch and dinner options include salads, stir-fries, and healthy renditions of Mexican classics and Italian pastas. **Real Food Daily** *(514 Santa Monica Blvd., Santa Monica, 310-451-7544; 414 N. La Cienega Blvd., West Hollywood, 310-289-9910)* serves virtuous, organic vegetarian cuisine, with nary a trace of meat, dairy, unnecessary fats, wheat, or refined sugars. **Jack Sprat's Grille** *(10668 Pico Blvd., West LA, 310-837-6662)* serves low-fat American food so yummy that you can't tell it's good for you. **Newsroom Café** *(120 N. Robertson Blvd., West Hollywood, 310-652-4444)* draws the health-conscious industry crowd. Unlike many other veggie restaurants, the Newsroom also has a full liquor and coffee bar. Over in Santa Monica, **Pradeeps** *(1405 Montana Ave., Santa Monica, 310-393-1467)* serves authentic low-fat Indian food, as does **Chameli** *(8752 Valley Blvd., Rosemead, 626-280-1947)*, a little farther away. After a long day of strolling the Venice Beach boardwalk, nothing beats **Figtree's Café** *(429 Ocean Front Walk, Venice, 310-392-4937)* for healthy food and an ocean view. One of the vestiges of the '60s, when hippies ran Topanga Canyon, **Inn of the Seventh Ray** *(128 Old Topanga Rd., Topanga Canyon, 310-455-1311)* serves macrobiotic fare to New Agers and health freaks alike, who enjoy the woodsy paradise overlooking a creek.

index by neighborhood

santa monica/venice/malibu

Blueberry 510 Santa Monica Blvd. bet. 5th and 6th Sts., Santa Monica, 310-394-7766

Border Grill 1445 4th St. bet. Santa Monica Blvd. and Broadway, Santa Monica, 310-451-1655

Canal Club 2025 Pacific Ave. bet. Brooks Ave. and Venice Blvd., Venice, 310-823-3878

El Cholo 1025 Wilshire Blvd. at 11th St., Santa Monica, 310-899-1106

Figtree's Café 429 Ocean Front Walk bet. Rose and Brooks Aves., Venice, 310-392-4937

Firehouse 213 Rose Ave. at Main St., Santa Monica, 310-392-4275

Flint's 3321 Pico Blvd. bet. Cloverfield Blvd. and Bundy Dr., Santa Monica, 310-453-1331

Gladstone's 4 Fish Malibu 17300 Pacific Coast Hwy. at Sunset Blvd., Topanga Beach, 310-454-3474

Hal's Bar & Grill 1349 Abbot Kinney Way bet. Brooks and California Aves., Venice, 310-396-3105

Inn of the Seventh Ray 128 Old Topanga Rd. nr. Topanga Canyon Blvd., Topanga Canyon, 310-455-1311

James' Beach 60 N. Venice Blvd. bet. Speedway and Pacific Aves., Venice, 310-823-5396

La Serenata de Garibaldi 1416 4th St. bet. Santa Monica Blvd. and Broadway, Santa Monica, 310-656-7017

Neptune's Net 42505 Pacific Coast Hwy. nr. Deer Creek Rd., Malibu, 310-457-3095

Omelette Parlor 2732 Main St. bet. Ocean Park Blvd. and Rose Ave., Santa Monica, 310-399-7892

Pradeeps 1405 Montana Ave. at 14th St., Santa Monica, 310-393-1467

Real Food Daily 514 Santa Monica Blvd. bet. 5th and 6th Sts., Santa Monica, 310-451-7544

Rose Café 220 Rose Ave. at Main St., Santa Monica, 310-399-0711

World Café 2820 Main St. bet. Ocean Park Blvd. and Rose Ave., Santa Monica, 310-392-1661

brentwood/westwood/west la

Apple Pan 10801 Pico Blvd. bet. Westwood and Overland Aves., West LA, 310-475-3585

California Pizza Kitchen *11677 San Vicente Blvd. at Barrington Ave., Brentwood, 310-826-3573*

Jack Sprat's Grille *10668 Pico Blvd. bet. Overland Ave. and Beverly Glen Blvd., West LA, 310-837-6662*

Johnnie's Pastrami *4017 S. Sepulveda Blvd. bet. Washington Blvd. and Washington Pl., Culver City, 310-397-6654*

John O'Groats *10516 Pico Blvd. at Beverly Glen Blvd., West LA, 310-204-0692*

Milky *9108 Pico Blvd. bet. Beverly and Doheny Drs., West LA, 310-859-0004*

Mishima *11301 Olympic Blvd. at Sawtelle Blvd., West LA, 310-473-5297*

Osteria Romana Orsini *9575 Pico Blvd. bet. Beverwil and Beverly Drs., West LA, 310-277-6050*

Primi *10543 Pico Blvd. bet. Overland Ave. and Beverly Glen Blvd., West LA, 310-475-9235*

Stevie Joe's Lounge and Supper Club *10433 National Blvd. bet. Overland and Motor Aves., West LA, 310-837-5245*

Versailles *10319 Venice Blvd. at Motor Ave., Palms, 310-558-3168*

beverly hills

Belvedere *Peninsula Hotel, 9882 Little Santa Monica Blvd. bet. Century Park East and Wilshire Blvd., Beverly Hills, 310-788-2306*

Coconut Club *Beverly Hilton Hotel, 9876 Wilshire Blvd. at Santa Monica Blvd., Beverly Hills, 310-274-7777*

Continental *8400 Wilshire Blvd. bet. La Cienega and San Vicente Blvds., Beverly Hills, 323-782-9717*

Gardens *Four Seasons Hotel, 300 S. Doheny Dr. at Burton Way, Beverly Hills, 310-273-2222*

Ginza Sushiko *218 N. Rodeo Dr. at Wilshire Blvd., Beverly Hills, 310-487-2251*

The Grill *9560 Dayton Way at Wilshire Blvd., Beverly Hills, 310-276-0615*

Maple Drive *345 N. Maple Dr. bet. Beverly Blvd. and Burton Way, Beverly Hills, 310-274-9800*

Matsuhisa *129 N. La Cienega Blvd. bet. 3rd St. and Wilshire Blvd., Beverly Hills, 310-659-9639*

McCormick & Schmick's *2 Rodeo Dr. at Wilshire Blvd., Beverly Hills, 310-859-0434*

Mulberry Street Pizza *240 S. Beverly Dr. bet. Wilshire and Olympic Blvds., Beverly Hills, 310-247-8100*

Nate 'n' Al's 414 N. Beverly Dr. bet. Santa Monica and Wilshire Blvds., Beverly Hills, 310-274-0101

Polo Lounge Beverly Hills Hotel, 9641 Sunset Blvd. at Beverly Dr., Beverly Hills, 310-276-2251

Reign 180 N. Robertson Blvd. bet. Wilshire Blvd. and Clifton Way, Beverly Hills, 310-273-4463

Spago Beverly Hills 176 N. Canon Dr. nr. Wilshire Blvd., Beverly Hills, 310-385-0880

west hollywood

Ago 8478 Melrose Ave. at La Cienega Blvd., West Hollywood, 323-655-6333

Dominick's 8715 Beverly Blvd. bet. Robertson and San Vicente Blvds., West Hollywood, 310-652-7272

Gardens of Taxco 1113 N. Harper Ave. at Santa Monica Blvd., West Hollywood, 323-654-1746

Hugo's 8401 Santa Monica Blvd. bet. La Cienega and Crescent Heights Blvds., West Hollywood, 323-654-3993

Lucques 8474 Melrose Ave. at La Cienega Blvd., West Hollywood, 323-655-6277

Mel's Drive-In 8585 Sunset Blvd. bet. San Vicente and La Cienega Blvds., West Hollywood, 310-854-7201

Morton's 8764 Melrose Ave. at Robertson Blvd., West Hollywood, 310-276-5205

Newsroom Café 120 N. Robertson Blvd. bet. Beverly Blvd. and 3rd St., West Hollywood, 310-652-4444

Pacé 2100 Laurel Canyon Blvd. bet. Mulholland Dr. and Hollywood Blvd., West Hollywood, 323-654-8583

The Palm 9001 Santa Monica Blvd. bet. Doheny Dr. and Robertson Blvd., West Hollywood, 310-550-8811

Real Food Daily 414 N. La Cienega Blvd. bet. Melrose Ave. and Beverly Blvd., West Hollywood, 310-289-9910

Spago 1114 Horn Ave. at Sunset Blvd., West Hollywood, 310-652-4025

Wolfgang Puck Café 8000 Sunset Blvd. at Crescent Heights Blvd., West Hollywood, 323-650-7300

third/beverly

Antica Pizzeria, 8022 3rd St. bet. La Cienega and Crescent Heights Blvds., Los Angeles, 323-658-7607

Canter's 419 N. Fairfax Ave. bet. Melrose Ave. and Beverly Blvd., Los Angeles, 323-651-2030

Cava 8384 3rd St. bet. La Cienega and Crescent Heights Blvds., Los Angeles, 323-658-8898

El Coyote 7312 Beverly Blvd. bet. Fairfax and La Brea Aves., Los Angeles, 323-939-2255

Itacho 7311 Beverly Blvd. bet. Fairfax and La Brea Aves., Los Angeles, 323-938-9009

King's Road Café 8361 Beverly Blvd. bet. La Cienega and Crescent Heights Blvds., Los Angeles, 323-655-9044

Kokomo Café Farmer's Market, 6333 3rd St. at Fairfax Ave., Los Angeles, 323-933-0773

Mishima 8474 3rd St. bet. La Cienega and Crescent Heights Blvds., Los Angeles, 323-782-0181

Quality Food & Beverage 8030 3rd St. bet. La Cienega and Crescent Heights Blvds., Los Angeles, 323-658-5959

Red 7450 Beverly Blvd. bet. Fairfax and La Brea Aves., Los Angeles, 323-937-0331

Sushi Roku 8445 3rd St. Los Angeles, bet. La Cienega and Crescent Heights Blvds., 323-655-6767

Swingers 8020 Beverly Blvd. bet. Crescent Heights Blvd. and Fairfax Ave., Los Angeles, 323-653-5858

Who's on 3rd 8369 3rd St. bet. La Cienega and Crescent Heights Blvds., Los Angeles, 323-651-2928

Zen Grill 8432 3rd St. bet. La Cienega and Crescent Heights Blvds., Los Angeles, 323-655-9991

hollywood

Astro Burger 5601 Melrose Ave. at Gower St., Hollywood, 323-469-1924

A Votre Santé 345 N. La Brea Ave. bet. Melrose Ave. and Beverly Blvd., Hollywood, 323-857-0412

Caffé Luna 7463 Melrose Ave. bet. Fairfax and La Brea Aves., Hollywood, 323-655-8647

Catalina Bar & Grill 1640 Cahuenga Blvd. bet. Hollywood and Sunset Blvds., Hollywood, 323-466-2210

Hampton's Hollywood Café 1342 N. Highland Ave. bet. Sunset and Santa Monica Blvds., Hollywood, 323-469-1090

Hollywood Hills Coffee Shop 6145 Franklin Ave. bet. Vine and Gower Sts., Hollywood, 323-467-7678

In-N-Out Burger 7009 Sunset Blvd. bet. La Brea and Highland Aves., Hollywood, 800-786-1000

Kruang Tedd 5151 Hollywood Blvd. bet. Western and Normandie Aves., Hollywood, 323-663-9988

Les Deux Café 1638 Las Palmas Ave. bet. Hollywood and Sunset Blvds., Hollywood, 323-465-0509

Lucy's El Adobe Café 5536 Melrose Ave. bet. Gower St. and Wilton Pl., Hollywood, 323-462-9421

Miceli's 1646 Las Palmas Ave. bet. Hollywood and Sunset Blvds., Hollywood, 323-466-3438

Musso & Frank 6667 Hollywood Blvd. bet. Highland Ave. and Cahuenga Blvd., Hollywood, 323-467-7788

Pink's 709 N. La Brea Ave. at Melrose Ave., Hollywood, 323-931-4223

Roscoe's House of Chicken 'n' Waffles 1514 Gower St. bet. Hollywood and Sunset Blvds., Hollywood, 323-466-7453

Sanamluang 5176 Hollywood Blvd. bet. Western and Normandie Aves., Hollywood, 323-660-8006

Sunset Room 1430 Cahuenga Blvd. bet. Sunset Blvd. and Fountain Ave., Hollywood, 323-463-0004

Village Coffee Shop 2695 Beachwood Dr. nr. Franklin Ave., Hollywood, 323-467-5398

Zankou Chicken 5065 Sunset Blvd at Normandie Ave., Hollywood, 323-665-7842

los feliz/silver lake

Astro Family Restaurant 2300 Fletcher Dr. at Glendale Blvd., Silver Lake, 323-663-9241

Café Stella 3932 Sunset Blvd. at Santa Monica Blvd., Silver Lake, 323-666-0265

Eat Well 3916 Sunset Blvd. at Santa Monica Blvd., Silver Lake 323-664-1621

El Cid 4212 Sunset Blvd. bet. Fountain Ave. and Santa Monica Blvd., Silver Lake, 323-668-0318

Electric Lotus 4656 Franklin Ave. at Vermont Ave., Los Feliz, 323-953-0040

Fred 62 1850 N. Vermont Ave. bet. Franklin Ave. and Sunset Blvd., Los Feliz, 323-667-0062

Home 1760 Hillhurst Ave. bet. Franklin Ave. and Sunset Blvd., Los Feliz, 323-664-1624

Marouch 4905 Santa Monica Blvd. bet. Normandie and Vermont Aves., Silver Lake, 323-662-9325

Mexico City 2121 Hillhurst Ave. bet. Los Feliz Blvd. and Franklin Ave., Los Feliz, 323-661-7227

Millie's Diner 3524 Sunset Blvd
bet. Hyperion Ave. and Silver Lake
Blvd., Silver Lake, 323-664-0404

koreatown/mid-city

Atlas Bar & Grill 3760 Wilshire
Blvd. at Western Ave., Koreatown,
213-380-8400

Cassell's 3266 6th St. bet. Normandie
and Vermont Aves., Koreatown,
213-387-5502

El Cholo 1121 S. Western Ave. bet.
Olympic and Pico Blvds., Koreatown,
323-734-2773

Guelaguetza 3337 8th St. bet.
Western and Normandie Aves.,
Koreatown, 213-427-0601

La Boca del Conga Room 5364
Wilshire Blvd. bet. Fairfax and La Brea
Aves., Los Angeles, 323-938-1696

Lowenbrau Keller 3211 Beverly Blvd.
bet. Hoover St. and Rampart Blvd.,
Koreatown, 213-381-5723

Marla's Jazz Supper Club 2323
W. Martin Luther King, Jr. Blvd.
bet. Arlington and Wester Aves.,
Leimert Park, 323-294-8430

Nyala 1076 S. Fairfax Ave. bet.
Olympic and Pico Blvds., Los Angeles,
323-936-5918

Papa Cristos 2771 Pico Blvd.
at Normandie Ave., Koreatown,
323-737-2880

Shibucho 3114 Beverly Blvd. bet.
Hoover St. and Rampart Blvd.,
Koreatown, 213-387-8498

Soot Bull Jeep 3136 8th St.
bet. Normandie and Vermont Aves.,
Koreatown, 213-387-3865

Taylor's Prime Steaks 3361 8th St.
bet. Western and Normandie Aves.,
Koreatown, 213-382-8449

Tommy's 2575 Beverly Blvd.
at Rampart Blvd., Los Angeles,
213-389-9060

Vito's 814 N. Vermont Ave. bet.
Santa Monica Blvd. and Melrose Ave.,
Los Angeles, 323-667-2723

Versailles 1415 S. La Cienega Blvd.
at Pico Blvd., Los Angeles,
310-289-0392

downtown/east la

Ciudad 445 S. Figueroa St. at 5th St.,
Downtown, 213-486-5171

Clifton's 648 S. Broadway bet. 6th and
7th Sts., Downtown, 213-627-1673

Cole's P.E. Buffet 118 E. 6th St. bet.
Spring St. and Central Ave., Downtown,
213-622-4090

eating out

Empress Pavilion 988 N. Hill St. bet. Bernard and College Sts., Chinatown, 213-617-9898

Gallo's Grill 4533 Cesar E. Chavez Ave. at Ford Blvd., East LA, 323-980-8669

King Taco No. 2 4504 E. 3rd St. at Ford Blvd., East LA, 323-264-4067

Langer's Deli 704 S. Alvarado St. at 7th St., Downtown, 213-483-8050

La Serenata de Garibaldi 1842 E. 1st St. bet. Boyle Ave. and State St., Boyle Heights, 323-265-2887

Manuel's El Tepeyac 812 N. Evergreen bet. Wabash and Cesar E. Chavez Aves., East LA, 323-267-8668

McCormick & Schmick's Library Tower, 633 W. 5th St. at Grand Ave., Downtown, 213-629-1929

Original Pantry Café 877 S. Figueroa St. at 9th St., Downtown, 213-972-9279

Pacific Dining Car 1310 6th St. bet. Alvarado and Figueroa Sts., Downtown, 213-483-6000

Phillipe the Original 1001 N. Alameda St. at Main St., Chinatown, 213-628-3781

R-23 923 E. 3rd St. bet. Alameda St. and Santa Fe Ave., Downtown, 213-687-7178

Suehiro 337 E. 1st St. bet. Spring and Alameda Sts., Little Tokyo, 213-626-9132

farther afield

Bahooka's Ribs and Grog 4501 N. Rosemead Blvd. at Lower Azusa Rd., Rosemead, 818-285-1241

Bob's Big Boy, 4211 W. Riverside Dr. at Alameda Ave., Burbank, 818-843-9334

Ca' del Sole 4100 Cahuenga Blvd. bet. Moorpark St. and Lankershim Blvd., North Hollywood, 818-985-4669

Casa Bianca 1650 Colorado Blvd. bet. Eagle Rock Blvd. and Figueroa St., Eagle Rock, 323-256-9617

Caioti Pizza Café 4346 Tujunga Ave. bet. Moorpark St. and Ventura Blvd., Studio City, 818-761-3588

Chameli 8752 Valley Blvd. bet. Walnut Grove Ave. and Rosemead Blvd., Rosemead, 626-280-1947

Clearman's North Woods Inn 7247 N. Rosemead Blvd. bet. Huntington Dr. and Duarte Rd., San Gabriel, 626-286-4022

Damon's 317 N. Brand Blvd. bet. Ventura Fwy. and Broadway, Glendale, 818-507-1510

Donut Hole 15300 Amar Rd. bet. Unruh Ave. and Hacienda Blvd., La Puente, 626-968-2912

Joe Peep's 12460 Magnolia Blvd. bet. Coldwater Canyon Ave. and Laurel Canyon Blvd., North Hollywood, 818-506-4133

Krispy Kreme 1801 W. Imperial Highway at Beach Blvd., La Habra, 562-690-2650; 7249 Van Nuys Blvd., Van Nuys, 818-908-9113

Pie 'n' Burger 913 E. California Blvd. at Lake Ave., Pasadena, 626-795-1123

Rubin's Red Hot 15322 Ventura Blvd. at Sepulveda Blvd., Sherman Oaks, 818-905-6515

Sushi Nozawa 11288 Ventura Blvd. bet. Tujunga and Vineland Aves., Studio City, 818-508-7017

Sushi on Tap 11056 Ventura Blvd. bet. Tujunga and Vineland Aves., Studio City, 818-985-2254

index by type of venue or food

breakfast
Blueberry
Canter's
Eat Well
Figtree's Café
Fred 62
Gladstone's 4 Fish Malibu
Hollywood Hills Coffee Shop
Home
Hugo's
John O'Groats
King's Road Café
Kokomo Café
Mel's Drive-In
Omelette Parlor
Original Pantry Café
Phillipe the Original
Quality Food & Beverage
Rose Café
Swingers
Village Coffee Shop
Who's on 3rd

carnivores
Apple Pan
Astro Burger
Bahooka's Ribs and Grog
Bob's Big Boy

Cassell's
Clearman's North Woods Inn
Damon's
In-N-Out Burger
Lowenbrau Keller
Morton's
Musso & Frank
Original Pantry
Pacific Dining Car
The Palm
Phillipe the Original
Pie 'n' Burger
Pink's
Reign
Soot Bull Jeep
Taylor's Prime Steaks
Tommy's

chinese/dim sum
Empress Pavilion

delis
Canter's
Johnnie's
Langer's Deli
Nate 'n' Al's

diners/coffee shops
Apple Pan
Astro Family Restaurant
Eat Well
Fred 62
Hampton's Hollywood Café
Hollywood Hills Coffee Shop
Home
King's Road Café
Kokomo Café
Mel's Drive-In
Millie's Diner
Original Pantry
Swingers
Village Coffee Shop
Who's on 3rd

eastside scenesters
Café Stella
Canter's
Eat Well
Electric Lotus
Fred 62
Hollywood Hills Coffee Shop
Home
Mexico City
Millie's Diner
R-23
Vito's

fast food
Astro Burger
Bob's Big Boy
Cassell's
Donut Hole
In-N-Out Burger
King Taco No. 2
Krispy Kreme

Manuel's El Tepeyac
Mulberry Street Pizza
Phillipe the Original
Pie 'n' Burger
Pink's
Rubin's Red Hot
Tommy's
Zankou Chicken

greek
Papa Cristos

indian
Chameli
Electric Lotus
Pradeeps

industry scenesters
Cava
Dominick's
Hal's Bar & Grill
Hollywood Hills Coffee Shop
Itacho
Les Deux Café
Lucques
Musso & Frank
Newsroom Café
Pacé
Red
Sushi Roku
Swingers
Who's on 3rd
Zen Grill

japanese
Ginza Sushiko
Itacho
Matsuhisa
Mishima
R-23
Shibucho
Suehiro
Sushi Nozawa
Sushi on Tap
Sushi Roku

late night
Astro Family Restaurant
Caffé Luna
Canter's
Electric Lotus
Fred 62
Mel's Drive-In
Original Pantry
Pacific Dining Car
Pink's
Roscoe's House of Chicken 'n' Waffles
Shibucho
Suehiro
Swingers
Tommy's

mexican
Border Grill
El Cholo
El Coyote

Gallo's Grill
Gardens of Taxco
Guelaguetza
King Taco No. 2
La Serenata de Garibaldi
Lucy's El Adobe Café
Manuel's El Tepeyac
Mexico City

pizza

Antica Pizzeria
Caioti Pizza Café
California Pizza Kitchen
Casa Bianca
Joe Peep's
Mulberry Street Pizza
Vito's

thai

Kruang Tedd
Sanamluang

vegetarian

A Votre Santé
Chameli
Figtree's Café
Inn of the Seventh Ray
Jack Sprat's Grille
Newsroom Café
Nyala
Pradeeps
Real Food Daily

index by price

$

Apple Pan
Astro Burger
Astro Family Restaurant
Blueberry
Bob's Big Boy
Casa Bianca
Cassell's
Chameli
Clifton's
Cole's P.E. Buffet
Donut Hole
Eat Well
El Coyote
Figtree's Café
Firehouse
Fred 62
Gallo's Grill
Guelaguetza
Hampton's Hollywood Café
Hollywood Hills Coffee Shop
Home
In-N-Out Burger
Joe Peep's
Johnnie's
King's Road Café
King Taco No. 2
Kokomo Café
Krispy Kreme
Kruang Tedd

Langer's Deli
Lucy's El Adobe Café
Manuel's El Tepeyac
Mel's Drive-In
Mishima
Mulberry Street Pizza
Nyala
Omelet Parlor
Original Pantry
Papa Cristos
Phillipe the Original
Pie 'n' Burger
Pink's
Roscoe's House of Chicken 'n' Waffles
Rubin's Red Hot
Sanamluang
Swingers
Tommy's
Versailles
Village Coffee Shop
Vito's
Who's on 3rd
Zankou Chicken

$$

Antica Pizzeria
A Votre Santé
Bahooka's Ribs and Grog
Border Grill
Ca' del Sole
Café Stella
Caffé Luna
Caioti Pizza Café

California Pizza Kitchen
Canter's
Cava
Clearman's North Woods Inn
Damon's
El Cholo
Electric Lotus
Empress Pavilion
Flint's
Gardens of Taxco
Hugo's
Jack Sprat's Grille
La Serenata de Garibaldi
Lowenbrau Keller
Marouch
McCormick & Schmick's
Mexico City
Miceli's
Milky Way
Millie's Diner
Musso & Frank
Nate 'n' Al's
Neptune's Net
Newsroom Café
Quality Food & Beverage
Pacé
Pradeeps
Real Food Daily
Red
Rose Café
Soot Bull Jeep
Suehiro
Taylor's Prime Steaks

Wolfgang Puck Café
World Café
Zen Grill

$$$

Ago
Atlas Bar & Grill
Belvedere
Canal Club
Catalina Bar & Grill
Ciudad
Coconut Club
Continental
Dominick's
El Cid
Gardens
Ginza Sushiko
Gladstone's 4 Fish Malibu
The Grill
Hal's Bar & Grill
Inn of the Seventh Ray
Itacho
James' Beach
La Boca del Conga Room
Les Deux Café
Lucques
Maple Drive
Marla's Jazz Supper Club
Matsuhisa
Morton's
Osteria Romana Orsini
Pacific Dining Car
The Palm
Polo Lounge
Primi
R-23
Reign
Shibucho
Spago
Spago Beverly Hills
Stevie Joe's Lounge and Supper Club
Sushi Nozawa
Sushi on Tap
Sunset Room
Sushi Roku

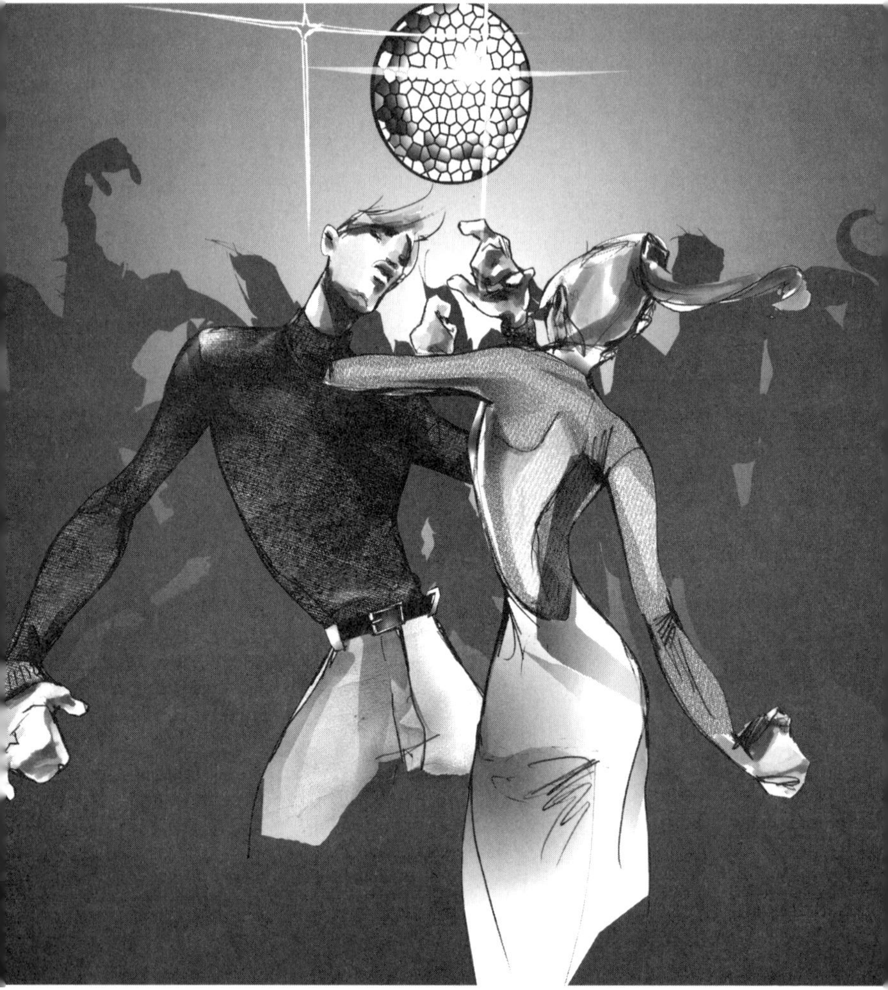

nightlife

when the sun goes down, Los Angeles reveals itself to be a tantalizing array of mini-universes. Go out at night and you'll see why this town is renowned for its vastness and diversity. Whether it's turntable stars, chic glitterati, Sunset star-seekers, new-glam operatives, sultry salseros, drag temptresses, or blue-haired indie kids, most are looking for one thing: to be noticed. ■ Pick an era; select an alter ego. Since almost everyone is starting from scratch here, there's nothing to hold a clubgoer back from realizing his or her most twisted or elegant fantasy. Remember, this is a city built on pretend and playing dress-up, so count on some fierce competition. Because memories are short and nostalgia runs high, you can slink into a noirish '40s nightclub and swig blue Lolitas or complete a space-rave marathon by staying out dancing until morning rush-hour traffic is on the wane.

After a history of making tabloid headlines and movie society mags — converging on the Sunset Strip in the '60s and '70s, and then dipping into gritty Downtown for the blowout '80s — LA's club life seemed snuffed out in the early '90s. Thanks to creative promoters like Joseph Brooks (whose glam club Makeup! is the talk of the town), Mitchell Frank (whose Spaceland captures Silver Lake's iconoclastic energy), and Marc Smith (owner of North, Three Clubs, and Vynyl), we are now entering a new club renaissance.

nightlife tips to get you going

» The alcohol stops flowing at 2am. This tends to chafe out-of-towners accustomed to a later curfew, but for Angelenos, it means you prick up your ears around 1:30 and hop on a bandwagon to the next party. Or, better yet, throw your own.

» Smoking is not appreciated in the vast majority of bars and clubs in LA, as a statute has forbidden smoking virtually anywhere inside in California. Some sympathetic owners turn a blind eye, but don't assume that because someone else is smoking that you can too.

» Life revolves around the car. If you're not taking a taxi, pack parking money (around $5-7 for each club you hit) and a good road map (essential for getting around — and getting unlost). And do yourself a huge favor and designate a driver. Driving drunk is never a good idea, but super-tough LA drunk driving laws will make you very, very sorry if you get careless.

» Call first. If someone answers, find out how crowded they expect to be or whether a live show is sold out. If you're not on the list (or, sometimes, even if you are), plan to get there early. A phone call is also a good way to find out if the club's hosting a private party, which happens every now and then (film wrap parties have been known to shut the doors of more than a few cool places).

» Carry ID. Unless you've found one of the few under-21 clubs in town, you'll be asked to show it. Even the greatest sob story on the planet won't get you in without one.

» Get a good day's sleep. Most clubs don't get going until 11pm.

getting good press

Since the nightlife scene is always revolving, it's a good idea to read up before stepping out. A little research can go a long way toward saving you precious time and gas money. Clubs come and go rapidly, and promoters move and change nights and venues on a whim. Make the trek to any decent record store and you'll usually find an alcove or two packed with flyers for particular shows or clubs to guide your way, especially if you're into a particular scene. Any good bookstore will carry more than its share of alternative magazines and newspapers. And local magazines will usually spotlight a club that's become a real scene-stealer — just remember that good press can often pack and ruin a good underground club, so it's best to ask around, too.

» *LA Weekly's* "Scoring the Clubs" section is good for week-to-week coverage of live shows, and the paper's dance club listings are the best and most reliable in town.

» For bigger concerts, check both the "7 Days in LA" section and the music section in *New Times Los Angeles*.

» The *LA Times* runs spotlights and listings on live club shows in their Thursday calendar; the paper's club coverage in "Club Buzz" is cooler than you'd expect for a mainstream rag.

>> **If you're interested** in a particular scene, it's best to pick up a publication with more focus. For the hip-hop/rave scene, go to one of the rave-centric record shops on Melrose and search for flyers or check out *Urb* magazine, which usually highlights one or two elemental spots. Also, try logging on to the site for promoter Green Galactic (*www.greengalactic.com*), who usually has something forward and futuristic going on.

>> **The gay scene** in Los Angeles takes on all different guises, from Silver Lake/Los Feliz (with its businesses based on Hyperion and Silver Lake Boulevards) to West Hollywood (Santa Monica Boulevard). Most of the free, gay-centric mags will give you an idea of the hot spots, but *Edge* and *Frontiers* are the most comprehensive.

>> **As always**, check out the CityTripping website (*www.citytripping.com*) to take you off the beaten path and to places you didn't know existed.

coping with the velvet rope

The overriding rule is, if you're not on the list, you're going to wait your turn in line — so just be patient. Above all, treat the doorman with the utmost respect. If he becomes your momentary buddy, he might let you know what your prospects are. Some clubs call themselves "members only" so that they can pick and choose, but in general things tend to be much looser and more accepting here than in the New York scene. Still, it helps to know and follow a few ground rules.

» **Don't be a slob.** "California casual" might mean you can wear jeans to swank eateries, but clubs expect you to show imagination and style. Every place has its own different fashion rules. Streetwear — baggy jeans, T-shirts, hats, and bandanas — is fine for rave or hip-hop clubs, but don't try it in Beverly Hills. Do your research to figure out if you should squeeze into Sky Bar chic (black is a safe bet) or your Day-Glo wig and black boa.

» **Don't be shy.** Call in advance and ask how people usually dress.

» **Go with the flow.** If it's a theme club, it's a good idea to be done up in the flavor of the evening — go glamorously ghoulish (black on black, with appropriately nocturnal skin coloring) for goth clubs, burst out all over for glam clubs (don't be afraid of a little latex), and go for nostalgic touches if you're heading to one of the many retro lounges popping up all over. If you're still unsure and you're in the neighborhood, just check out the line outside the club.

» **Don't assume** that just because you're hanging in a crowd, you're out of the running. You can generally guess within five or ten minutes whether you should stay or hit the road.

bars and lounges

BAR MARMONT *8171 Sunset Blvd. at Crescent Heights Blvd., West Hollywood, 323-650-0575; Hours: Mon-Sat 6pm-2am; Sun 7pm-2am; no cover*

Cozy and attitude-free, Bar Marmont is that rare bar on the Sunset Strip that attracts A-list celebrities yet doesn't overwhelm you with Hollywood snobbery. It helps that this is the bar of the landmark Chateau Marmont Hotel, a former down-at-the-heels resting place which has seen its share of rock-star glamour and Hollywood scandal (it's the place where John Belushi

OD'd). The Marmont has recently been renovated as a chic palace of bungalows (yes, Leo has slept here), and the Bar Marmont takes in both spillover from the hotel and an off-the-street clientele. As low-key as a celebrity-friendly martini lounge can get, the Marmont is a nice antidote to Sky Bar's arch atmosphere.

BIGFOOT LODGE *3172 Los Feliz Blvd. bet. Riverside Dr. and San Fernando Rd., Atwater Village, 323-662-9227; Hours: nightly 8pm-2am; no cover*
The Bigfoot Lodge is probably the only bar in Los Angeles where one can look at home wearing duck boots. The large rectangular room is completely lined with buffed pine beams. A brown and tan "Saskatchewan" road sign — the kind you see in national forests — separates the bar proper from the seating areas in the back. The aesthetic and ambience at Bigfoot work in uncanny ways. Local artists, club kids, guys in zoot suits, and glam girls all mingle here, padded by the anonymous throng of twentysomethings that keep any bar in business. Grab one of the whimsical cocktail menus and choose between a Girl Scout Cookie (creme de cacao and peppermint schnapps), a Toasted Marshmallow (Stoli Vanilla and Frangelico), and a Dudley Do-Right (made with — what else? — Canadian Club).

CAT CLUB *8911 Sunset Blvd. at San Vicente Blvd., West Hollywood, 310-657-0888; Hours: nightly 6pm-2am; no cover*
The Cat Club is the bad baby of Stray Cats drummer Slim Jim Phantom and a bunch of club promotion veterans, so it's likely to stick around longer than the

average club on the strip. Within its first two weeks it made a name for itself with club-watchers when new patrons spotted Eddie Vedder playing pool and Dr. Dre and Johnny Ramone surveying the scene. Composing a great rock 'n' roll evil triplet, the club — with a black awning tipping guests off to the sinfully dim lighting inside — cozies up between Duke's Coffee Shop and rock landmark the Whisky. Inside, the Cat Club is waiting for Betty Page reincarnate: It's all dungeon black and leopard-print. It's also remarkably free of star-kissed attitude, and there are dollar drinks till nine, which seems like a very decent and starving-rocker thing for the club to do.

DADDY'S *1610 N. Vine St. bet. Hollywood and Sunset Blvds., Hollywood, 323-463-7777; Hours: nightly 9pm-2am; no cover*
A welcome anomaly, Daddy's is a lounge-lizard oasis tucked in one of the grittier corners of Hollywood. The giveaway is the retro neon sign (*LA Confidential* meets new Hollywood), which beckons with a noirish allure. Inside, it's a chic, low-lit lounge that has been decorated with soothing curves and a saucy black-and-red motif. The new bar where the Lucky Seven used to be, Daddy's attracts various Hollywood players, usually residing somewhere in the middle of the industry food chain, all of whom look like they've been trucked in from Santa Monica. (Think sleek women with red lipstick and thin guys in black.) It's a good place to linger over conversation and martinis, provided you hit it on a weeknight. A nicely stocked jukebox (Barry White stands out), and clear, cool drinks in tall glasses makes Daddy's a small, elegant bar with a little extra soul.

THE DRESDEN ROOM *1760 N. Vermont Ave. bet. Franklin Ave. and Hollywood Blvd., Los Feliz, 323-665-4294; Hours: daily 11:30am-1:30am; no cover*

Mixing old-school kitsch with new lounge swing, the Dresden Room has been a prime destination for the city's many retro enthusiasts for years. Originally established in the '60s as a cocktail den for suave and heavily-lacquered lounge lizards, it was rediscovered in 1990 as a cozy and campy alternative to the hipper-than-thou bars around town. In the kind of fast city synergism that made Melrose Avenue, the area around it has become hip central recently, attracting a mix of '90s cool and old-fashioned kitsch that, these days, the Dresden management banks on. The bar and restaurant's main draw are husband and wife musical duo Marty and Elayne, a pair of camp-savvy glitter twins who have become famous for their matching pantsuits and their performance in the film *Swingers*. The couple's over-the-top takes on jazz standards and Captain & Tenille make the Dresden an experience not to be missed.

ENCOUNTER *Los Angeles International Airport, 201 World Way, 310-215-5151; Hours: daily 11am-2am; no cover*

What a smart move to take a creaking '70s restaurant with a fantastic external design (it used to be called the "Proud Bird") and turn it into an atomic spacelounge with a real sense of humor. Encounter is the kind of place that Austin Powers would dream up on Mars. Both a restaurant and a bar, Encounter beckons to tired travelers lured by food and drink, but it's also a regular destination for locals who crave a little futuristic space-age flash. DJ Señor Amor spins '60s-lounge discs regularly, and there's live music on Saturday nights. Everyone from rave kids to go-go addicts, design freaks to lounge mavens will get a kick out of this stilt-legged lounge. Like a UFO that accidentally touched down in the middle of LAX's traffic-control central, Encounter should not be missed.

FORMOSA CAFÉ *7156 Santa Monica Blvd. bet. Fairfax and La Brea Aves., Hollywood, 323-850-9050; Hours: Mon-Fri 4pm-1:30am; Sat-Sun 6pm-1:30am; no cover*

Two words: *LA Confidential*. You know the score — with lovely, old-Hollywood tabloid glamour and a faint spice of exclusivity, the Formosa is the kind of place where Raymond Chandler might trade gritty stories and down whiskey sours with James Ellroy. It seems that the Formosa is one of the first destinations for newly arrived industry punks, so these days it has a just-released-from-Yale vibe that puts a slight damper on the den-of-sin aura. Don't let that dissuade you; just try to avoid weekend nights. The Formosa has an indoor bar that's the perfect place for a clandestine meeting; there's an enclosed patio area in the back, and a romantic rooftop bar. You want star power? Elvis, Ava, Humphrey, and Marilyn all drank here.

NORTH *8029 Sunset Blvd. bet. Crescent Heights Blvd. and Fairfax Ave., West Hollywood, 323-654-1313; Hours: nightly 6pm-2am; no cover*

Painstakingly anonymous, North announces itself right in the flashy heart of the Sunset Strip with the strong anti-statement of a bland rock exterior (if you're circling the block, it's the place under that blue neon sign that says "spirits, dining"). Don't expect a bland experience, however, because North — both a burnished

nightlife

lounge and great restaurant — is run by Marc Smith, who brought Hollywood the very popular Three Clubs and the newly opened Vynyl. If that's not enough name-dropping for you, its designer created Swingers' diner flair and the Standard Bar's low-key cool. And nearly every rich, beautiful, and famous person in this city has graced the backdoor stairwell, so you've probably guessed by now that it's not for populists, communists, or the Birkenstock crowd. Nope, this is a place where Hollywood's caste system is in full effect. If you're just a simple being looking for Hollywood thrills, get there early — unless you can convince them that you're somebody you're not, or you look very, very tasty. Our final advice: Play it cool, or you'll quickly be found out.

SKY BAR *8440 Sunset Blvd. at La Cienega Blvd., West Hollywood, 323-650-8999; Hours: nightly 4pm-2am; no cover*

What's made this bar at the sleek, chic Mondrian Hotel so famous is that it's nearly impossible to get in without an advance reservation (which is impossible to get), unless you're a guest at the Mondrian. Good luck, kids, because if you do brush past that actor-in-training doorman (bronze, jawline to die for, copping his implacable pose from Oscar himself) and gates-of-heaven entrance, you're in the land of the fabulous. Movie stars, rock stars, star directors, star hairdressers, and star producers all schmooze in this movie set of a bar. If you do get in, you're in Hollywood. You simply can't get any closer without being it.

bars and lounges

DIVE BARS

The only bad thing about dive bars in LA is that none of them are undiscovered, though that shouldn't dissuade you from sampling their musky air and stained booths. (Some of the best dives in the world, after all, are in Hollywood — a dive in itself.) The best dive on the Eastside is **The Smog Cutter** *(864 N. Virgil Ave., Los Angeles, 323-667-9832)*, where famous literary bruiser Charles Bukowski used to tipple — though these days, karaoke rules. Moving west, check out the ever-popular punk-rock watering hole (and hole-in-the-wall) **The Frolic Room** *(6345 Hollywood Blvd., Hollywood, 323-462-5890)*, which has been immortalized in scores of films. Toward the Strip's "Rock Walk," **The Coach and Horses** *(7617 Sunset Blvd., Hollywood, 323-876-6900)* is a dark dive that's played host to Quentin Tarantino and where battling boozers take it outside.

GLITZY JOINTS

Here are the haunts of the jet set and others who pay double for cocktails and inspired settings. If you're a Hollywood nobody, you'd better arrive early to **Barfly** (*8730 Sunset Blvd., West Hollywood, 310-360-9490*), because after a certain point in the evening, it's strictly reservations only. Think purple velvet, Prada, and on-the-double bar sushi. Set apart from its eating quarters, the **Sunset Room** (*1430 Cahuenga Blvd., Hollywood, 323-463-0001*) has an ambient lounge that serves martinis to a hip, young industry crowd. Take your drink to a lush, wraparound booth or out to the airy patio. The club becomes a living Gap ad Thursday through Saturday nights, offering everything from swing to funk. The bar and restaurant for the deco-fabulous Argyle Hotel, **Fenix** (*8358 Sunset Blvd., West Hollywood, 323-654-2464*) recalls Old Hollywood — what better lure do you need for the Young Turks on Friday and Saturday nights? With a beautiful, natural outdoor patio for dining upstairs and a sultry little jazz and cocktail bar tucked into the back, **Rix** (*1413 5th St., Santa Monica, 310-656-9688*) is as unpretentious as an upscale bar can get. The crowd is a mix of young and old, and it's definitely not a pickup scene. The great old — and very elegant — Polynesian grandpa, **Trader Vic's** (*9876 Wilshire Blvd., Beverly Hills, 310-274-7777*) has weathered trend upon trend and remained a whimsical place with its potent signature Mai Tais, which are rumored to be a house invention. The multitudes who have been turned away from Sky Bar have cheered themselves at the Mondrian's other restaurant and bar with died-and-gone-to-heaven decor: **Asia de Cuba** (*8440 Sunset Blvd., West Hollywood, 323-848-6000*) is loaded with couples sheathed in black sipping rum and exotic cocktails while contemplating their next stab at gaining entrance next door. And for those who want a hotel bar with a sleek, retro atmosphere, try **The Standard** (*8300 Sunset Blvd., West Hollywood, 323-650-9090*). The mod décor may

nightlife

be pre-1970, though the clientele is anything but.

GO RETRO

Grab a fat stogie and pretend it's 1955; the fact that it's not will be made perfectly clear when you're asked to smoke it on the sidewalk. Nevertheless, Los Angeles is loaded with great retro bars to help you go back in time. Some are creaky, forgotten old taverns rediscovered by Art Center students (to the amusement of barkeeps and regulars); others are made-for-hipster lounges emanating the aura of yesteryear. If you lean toward German barmaids, plastered regulars belting out beer songs, and skyscraper beer glasses, the stein-parlor **Red Lion Tavern** *(2356 Glendale Blvd., Silver Lake, 323-662-5337)* is a favorite with local indie musicians. Try not to be too smitten by the **Tiki Ti** *(4427 Sunset Blvd., Los Feliz, 323-669-9381)* with its lush Polynesian theme and tons of kitsch knickknacks. The ship-ahoy-themed **HMS Bounty** *(3357 Wilshire Blvd., Los Angeles, 213-385-7275)* is a great, homey relic, with old-salt bartenders and a mix of art students and old-timers. If the ghost of Charles Bukowski could choose a place to haunt, he would have to pick his favorite old stomping ground, the stately, otherworldly **Musso and Frank Grill** *(6667 Hollywood Blvd., Hollywood, 323-467-5123)*. Musso's is the oldest restaurant in Hollywood and the place where Faulkner and Fitzgerald dined and drank. With the lounge craze hitting hard, young upstarts have begun sculpting new bars to play on the chic nostalgia of the '40s and '50s: **Jones Hollywood** *(7205 Santa Monica Blvd., Hollywood, 323-850-1727)* is a much more elegant place around 3pm, before the crush; for beautiful blue drinks in elegant Stork Club glasses, try **Liquid Kitty** *(11780 Pico Blvd., West LA, 310-473-3707)*. Rumored to be an inspiration for *Pulp Fiction*, the **Lava Lounge** *(1533 N. La Brea Ave., Hollywood, 323-876-6612)*, is a swank bar with parasols in the drinks and a lounge-rat-gone-to-Polynesia theme. For a little French chinoiserie filtered through New Hollywood, there's **The Good Luck Bar** *(1514 Hillhurst Ave., Los Feliz, 323-666-3524)*, which serves up glam elegance for the new millennium.

MARTINI NATION

The martini craze is still alive, well, and living in Los Angeles. **Kane** *(5574 Melrose Ave., Hollywood, 323-466-6263)* is at its most pleasant immediately after work, when the dark room with vinyl booths and leopard-print stools makes your Manhattan seem that much smoother. Across Melrose, you can sip your highball atop the roof deck at **The Martini Lounge** *(5657 Melrose Ave., Hollywood, 323-467-4068)*, or you can hang around inside for a good selection of tunes. Finally, **Lola's** *(945 N. Fairfax Ave., West Hollywood, 323-736-5652)* serves more apple martinis per capita than any bar in the world. This WeHo spot still packs 'em in as its rivals have become dreadfully passe.

PUB CRAWLING

Once you start checking out the multitude of pubs in this town, you may wonder if everyone just got off the plane from Manchester or Dublin. Here are a few of them (there are also a few listed in the Dive Bars section). Around the Third Street

Promenade in Santa Monica, quite a few pubs cater to out-of-town types: the **King's Head** *(116 Santa Monica Blvd., Santa Monica, 310-451-1402)* is a brightly lit bar with a centerpiece dartboard populated by lots of beachy, good-looking couples. **Britannia Inn** *(318 Santa Monica Blvd., Santa Monica, 310-458-5350)* appeals to nightclub types with its dark interior, loud music, tale-telling (and toasted) patrons smoking at the door, and an ever-so-slight pickup vibe (you can bet the dark brews go first here). **O'Brien's** *(2226 Wilshire Blvd., Santa Monica, 310-829-5303)* is probably the most popular Westside pub, so it's best to go there on weekdays — it's a favorite with journalists and other creative types. Farther east, the **Cat 'N' Fiddle** *(6530 Sunset Blvd., Hollywood, 323-468-3800)*, with a great courtyard right in the heart of Hollywood, might be the best way to get a little flora late at night. A couple of local bars are even better known for their live shows than for their beer and Irish whiskey: **Genghis Cohen** *(740 N. Fairfax Ave., West Hollywood, 323-653-0640)* is taken very seriously by A&R types and rock critics for its singer-songwriters, and **Molly Malone's Irish Pub** *(575 S. Fairfax Ave., Los Angeles, 310-935-1577)* is a neighborhood bar with a tendency toward a little brogue in its rock acts. College football alums gather at **Dublin's Irish Whiskey Pub** *(8240 Sunset Blvd., West Hollywood, 323-656-0100)* Saturday mornings in autumn to cheer on their alma maters and stuff their faces with heavy bar food while slinging darts. The lounge upstairs, Above Dublin's, has a cheesy — but utterly unpretentious — college dance bar feel.

clubs

THE DERBY *4500 Los Feliz Blvd. at Hillhurst Ave., Los Feliz, 323-663-8979, www.the-derby.com; Hours: nightly 5pm-2am; Admission: $5-7*
The stately old lady of nightclubs, the Derby used to be one of the famous Brown Derby chain restaurants (Lucy went there for some typical starstruck hijinks) and then was treated to an awesome refurbishment. Shortly thereafter, it began attracting the cool kids in droves. These days, swing culture and the Derby are basically synonymous, and not only does the Derby factor heavily in the movie *Swingers*, but the place is practically its muse: Director Jon Favreau parked it there regularly before he made a name for himself. Sadly, the swing scene peaked a couple of years ago in LA, and its trendiness has made old landmarks like the Derby seem, well, a little out-of-date. The place, however, is still worth visiting: cozy, curvy, and beautifully restored, the Derby has a small dance floor in the room with its tremendous centerpiece bar and pool tables, and another room simply for dancing. It's the perfect place to go if you're a die-hard swing dancer or just want to shoot a few games of pool and have a Cosmopolitan chaser.

THE PLAYROOM *836 N. Highland Ave. bet. Santa Monica Blvd. and Melrose Ave., Hollywood, 323-460-6630; Hours: Mon, Thu-Sat 10pm-3am; Admission: varies*
A Goliath of a club, the Playroom has a pretty typical disco interior: purple, black, and mirror balls. What makes it stand out, however, is its promotions, many of which have reignited LA clublife. On Wednesdays, Goth club Coven 13 takes over, and for the boys, there's Icon on Saturday nights. The big event is Cherry on Fridays, when the club gets a '70s overhaul and throbs to DJs Mike Messex and Joseph Brooks, who never align themselves with any particular

decade. The tight male and female go-go dancers don't hurt, either. The place is a big star-magnet: Leonardo DiCaprio, Vince Vaughn, and many others have warmed up the dance floor, and Counting Crows launched a tour here. The velvet rope can be daunting; try to get on the list by calling ahead or you may find yourself stuck in line.

SPACELAND *1717 Silver Lake Blvd. bet. Glendale and Sunset Blvds., Silver Lake, 213-833-2843, www.clubspaceland.com; Hours: Mon-Fri 6pm-2am, Sat-Sun 7pm-2am; Admission: varies*

The young club upstart which brought tons of attention to LA's indie-rock scene is beginning to show a few wrinkles, but it's still a great space, and one of the only spots on the Eastside to see perpetually cool live rock acts. Over the past few years, Spaceland has gotten a few facelifts, from the pool table lounge in back with its soda can pop-top decorations and *Logan's Run* motorcycle vibe to the removal of all mirrors and chrome (signs of its past glory as a Top 40 disco). Now the club has the industry crowd trekking over for a taste of the Eastside all the time. Manager Mitchell Frank recently separated from the Dust Brothers and their Ideal Records partnership; now he's back in full force as a booker with nearly impeccable taste in music. So Spaceland's no longer a hideout for the superhip and industry-phobic. What other club is there where Magnetic Fields, Elliott Smith, and Ben Lee really *want* to play?

VIPER ROOM *8852 Sunset Blvd. bet. San Vicente and La Cienega Blvds., West Hollywood, 310-358-1880, www.viperroom.com; Hours: nightly 9pm-2am; Admission: varies*

With its absinthe-and-pearls renovation, Johnny Depp's Viper Room has graduated from chic diamond in the rough (and place where River Phoenix bid his final farewell) to a real club gem. The Viper

Room is not the best place to go if you can't get on a guest list, especially if a top-billed band is playing. Though the club's bookers were some of the first to embrace the rampant lounge craze, they've recently turned their spotlight on the DJ/electronica scene with the great Tuesday club Atmosphere (past DJ sets have been by Crystal Method and Afrika Bambaataa). Rockers like the star-friendly space for warming up or showing off their new wares: Courtney Love and Hole played the splashy debut of the club's new look, and Stone Temple Pilots reintroduced themselves to the world there after their long hiatus. Who Johnny Depp knows has made him a real contender in the club world — which makes the Viper the most quintessentially Hollywood act in town.

DANCE CLUBS

Many of the great live-music clubs moonlight as dance clubs by adding bumping beats and moving bodies. Do some research before hitting the streets, as many of these have rotating theme nights. Formerly a Korean dance club, **Club Lingerie** *(6507 Sunset Blvd., Hollywood, 323-466-8557)* has been blessed with the bass and now plays party to a steamy go-go intimacy, with a good range of hip-hop, deep-house, and rare-groove DJs. Another rock club that opens its doors for dancing late at night, **Dragonfly** *(6510 Santa Monica Blvd., Hollywood, 323-466-6111)* has a cozy, funky hot Medina feel and spins a mix of hip-hop and old-school funk. Far south in Central LA, **Fais Do-Do** *(5257 W. Adams Blvd., Los Angeles, 323-269-9480)* is a renovated, architecturally intriguing former bank building that hosts some attention-getting theme clubs, including the mod dance party Solid (with discounts for those who come by scooter) and even a rare country-western DJ on Honky Tonk Sundays. **Goldfingers** *(6423 Yucca St., Hollywood, 323-962-2913)* is tucked into the tiny Yucca corridor space of the late Maxx's and is a small but mighty contender. Its best night is Friday, when Daniel Ash of Bauhaus and Love & Rockets takes control of the turntable. Run by the legendary Pierre (who used to run both the landmark boho Lhasa Club and the Club Largo), the boutique dance club **LunaPark** *(665 N. Robertson Blvd., West Hollywood, 310-652-0611)* is the chi-chi big sister gone uptown, a multi-tiered experience with dancing and live shows in the basement lounge. Just down the way, **The Factory/Ultra Suede** *(652 La Peer Ave./661 N. Robertson Blvd., West Hollywood, 310-659-4551)* has taken over the space formerly known as Love Lounge/Axis. The two autonomous spaces are combined as one dance emporium on Saturdays. The bohemian grotto **Opium Den** *(1605 Ivar Ave., Hollywood, 323-466-7800)* is exotic enough to live up to its name. One of the only megaclubs in town, the **Key Club** (*9030 Sunset Blvd., West Hollywood, 310-274-5800*) has taken over the massive Billboard Live and turned it into a huge dance club that spins a wild mix of everything from Top 40 and funk to edgy speed-garage. And **Vynyl** (*1650 Schrader Blvd., Hollywood, 323-465-7449*) might be a newer kid on the block, but it's owned by nightlife veteran Marc Smith. In a ski lounge-gone-rave club atmosphere, turntable wizards in the front room keep crowds nodding all night.

DRAG REVUES

If you're in the mood to put on a little lipstick and powder — or just watch a few gorgeous and daunting Amazonian queens get real — there are quite a few special club nights for you. **Dragstrip 66** at **Rudolpho's** (*2500 Riverside Dr., Silver Lake, 323-969-2596*) is put on by Silver Lake DJ Paul V on the second Saturday of each month. It might be the best party in town (Drew Barrymore and Perry Farrell seem to agree). There's always a theme ("Me Tarzan, Me Jane," "Victor/Victoria's Secret"), so call ahead. Drag mavens are made to feel at home at **Club 7969** (*7969 Santa Monica Blvd., West Hollywood, 323-654-0280*), on the edge of boys town. Club 7969 offers two separate events for ladies of the night: Queen's Throne on Monday and Illusion on Friday. And finally, for years the Thai restaurant **Tommy Tang's** (*7313 Melrose Ave., Hollywood, 323-937-5733*) has made its name with more than its great noodles. On Tuesday nights there's a show-stopping revue with drag waitresses. It's an old standard not to be missed.

GAY AND LESBIAN

Industrious gay newcomers can find the main hangouts within a day or two simply by asking around. In an often-changing scene, word of mouth is the rule, but here are a few places to get yo started. Most of these places are i

West Hollywood, also known as "boys town," which — with its beautiful kids from Ohio digging a vibrant gay scene for the first time — can be trying after awhile (for an artier and grittier scene, check out the Silver Lake and Los Feliz area). Longtime storefront bar on the boulevard with great videos (think Cyndi Lauper and Menudo), **Revolver** *(8851 Santa Monica Blvd., West Hollywood, 310-659-8851)* is a good place to start off for the guys. The crowd usually makes its way to **Rage** *(8911 Santa Monica Blvd., West Hollywood, 310-652-7055)*, an always-packed club with DJs playing everything from hard alternative to bright house. **Circus** *(6655 Santa Monica Blvd., 323-462-1291, Hollywood)* brings the boys out with a mix of occasional drag shows and tight Latin and house music. Guys from Silver Lake and Los Feliz who have more affinity for Courtney Love than for Deborah Cox prefer **Akbar** *(4356 Sunset Blvd., Silver Lake, 323-665-6810)* as their neighborhood haunt. Girl bars come and go, but **The Palms** *(8572 Santa Monica Blvd., West Hollywood, 310-652-6188)*, with its beer hall in front and disco in back, keeps on drawing them in with a mixed crowd. **Girl Bar**, a spectacular lesbian dance night, has been revived on Fridays at **The Factory** *(652 La Peer Ave., West Hollywood, 310-659-4551)*. A risqué treat, **Michelle's XXX Topless Revue** at **Club 7969** *(7969 Santa Monica Blvd., West Hollywood, 323-654-0280)*, a dance club for women, brings out topless dancers at the witching hour every Tuesday night.

GLAMORAMA

If any one recent turn of events could be responsible for LA's club revival, it would be the proliferation of exotic and erotic glam clubs. Though there are certainly naughtier events in town, these clubs are not for the prudish or mousy — people dress to impress, confuse, or shock. Start the weekend on Thursday night at **Vibrator** at **Club 7969** *(7969 Santa Monica Blvd., West Hollywood, 323-654-0280)* the raucous rock 'n' roll strip club

nightlife

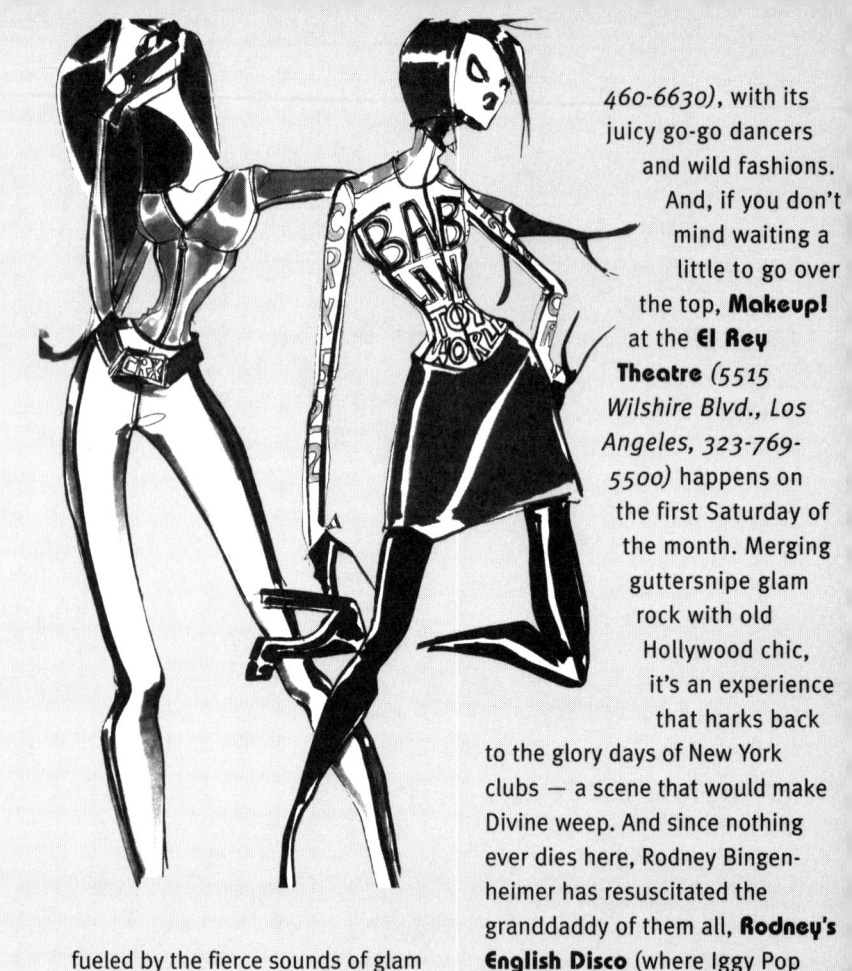

fueled by the fierce sounds of glam rock and live performances that begin around midnight. The outrageous **Cherry** happens every Friday night at **The Playroom** (*836 N. Highland Ave., Hollywood, 323-460-6630*), with its juicy go-go dancers and wild fashions. And, if you don't mind waiting a little to go over the top, **Makeup!** at the **El Rey Theatre** (*5515 Wilshire Blvd., Los Angeles, 323-769-5500*) happens on the first Saturday of the month. Merging guttersnipe glam rock with old Hollywood chic, it's an experience that harks back to the glory days of New York clubs — a scene that would make Divine weep. And since nothing ever dies here, Rodney Bingenheimer has resuscitated the granddaddy of them all, **Rodney's English Disco** (where Iggy Pop and David Bowie used to rub shoulders on the Strip) at **Fais Do-Do** (*5257 W. Adams Blvd., Los Angeles, 323-954-8080*).

100 | nightlife

GOTHIC FETISH

Do you love things that go bump in the night? Are Edgar Allen Poe, Anne Rice, and Winona Ryder's *Beetlejuice* malcontent your role models? Is black the only color on your fashion palette? You're not alone, because more and more goth clubs are springing up to serve the children of the night. An old barfly-punk standard, **Boardner's** *(1652 Cherokee Ave., Hollywood, 323-462-9621)* is a bar that draws the thin and translucent out of their lairs on Saturday nights for Bar Sinister, a gothic-industrial-fetish club with a dance floor, chill-out room, and "Dark Lounge." The dance club **Tempest** *(7323 Santa Monica Blvd., West Hollywood, 323-850-5115)* plays host to Absinthe, a Sunday night goth-industrial club for the spooky set. The old Las Palmas Theatre's great indigo-themed club, **Blue** *(1642 Las Palmas Ave., 323-462-7442)*, doubles your inky pleasures with two gothic nights each week: Nocturne, a witchy evening of dark wave on Monday, and Ministry, which throbs with industrial goth on Wednesday.

LATIN FLAVOR

If the inner salsera in you is aching to break out, there are a number of sultry Latin-flavored clubs for you. (Before you hit the dance floor, do yourself a favor and dig out your fancy dress; females go strappy and bare, while males go old-school elegant.) On Monday nights, **El Floridita** *(1253 Vine St., Hollywood, 323-871-8612)*, a little restaurant tucked into a minimall, turns electric with an 11-piece band. There's always a huge line of gorgeous people at the **The Conga Room** *(5364 Wilshire Blvd., Los Angeles, 323-938-1696)*, a sultry dance emporium financially blessed by Jimmy Smits and Jennifer Lopez that heats up with all forms of Latin dance: tango, salsa, mambo, you name it. The big downtown dance temple at **The Mayan** *(1038 S. Hill St., Downtown, 213-746-4287)* is the place to go on Friday and Saturday nights. It's all salsa, and they're out for converts: The place offers free salsa lessons with the cost of admission early in the evening. And **Rudolpho's** *(2500 Riverside Dr.,*

nightlife

Silver Lake, 323-669-1226) hosts Salsa de Noche on the first Saturday of every month, which is a packed, steamy gay salsa night.

LIVE MUSIC

Since most bands eventually have to make a pit stop in LA (to sign contracts and yawn through meetings with lawyers), they usually get their kicks by playing at night. These are some tried-and-true live venues, from the historically interesting oldsters to the innovative upstarts. The legendary **Doug Weston's Troubadour** (9081 Santa Monica Blvd., West Hollywood, 310-276-6168) is the best place for live music, as its dark wood walls make for amazingly warm acoustics. The Troubadour went from hosting a baby-faced Elton John (and that famous John Lennon sanitary napkin episode) to being Axl Rose's whiskey hang; now it's hosting an inspired range of hot young acts. These days, the **Whisky a Go-Go** (8901 Sunset Blvd., West Hollywood, 310-652-4202), seems to be resting on the laurels of its history as an old standard for tourists since Jim Morrison made his name on the stage (and a few groupies made theirs in the green room). **The Roxy** (9009 Sunset Blvd., West Hollywood, 310-276-2222) is an old industry standard — sleek, yet usually packed — and has the roped-off VIP area to prove it. The grand dames of the bunch are **The Palace** (1735 Vine St., Hollywood, 323-462-3000), a large concert venue with a huge rococo chandelier, dance floor, and balcony with stadium seating, and the **Hollywood Palladium** (6215 Sunset Blvd., Hollywood, 323-962-7600), a massive concert ballroom that used to be grunge central but now leans toward both Alanis and reliving its WWII roots with swing dance parties. **The House of Blues** (8430 Sunset Blvd., West Hollywood, 323-848-5100), or Disneyland by way of the Delta, is not a bad place for live shows if you don't mind the flashy security and loud patrons. An art deco boutique of a club, the Miracle Mile landmark **El Rey Theatre** (5515 Wilshire Blvd., Los Angeles, 323-

936-6400) has been selected by Beck and Bob Dylan for small shows because of its dark, romantic aura. Downtown in the Artists' District, **Al's Bar** *(305 S. Hewitt St., Downtown, 213-625-9703)* is a scrappy, graffiti-covered, boho-punk dream that will never die, and is probably the nearest thing to New York's CBGB. Along those lines, but with a rockabilly vibe, is **The Garage** *(4519 Santa Monica Blvd., Silver Lake, 323-662-6166)*, where on Sundays the most famous punk-friendly drag queen in LA, Vaginal Davis, treats you to the always-eventful Club Sucker. A blues barn plopped in the middle of Hollywood, **Jack's Sugar Shack** *(1707 Vine St., Hollywood, 323-466-7005)* caters to the rockabilly and Cali-country crowd. For something really intimate, the borscht-belt lounge **Largo** *(432 N. Fairfax Ave., West Hollywood, 323-852-1073)* has become a famous place for sophisticated jams: Jon Brion's famous rock free-for-all happens every Friday; E from the Eels, Grant Lee Phillips of Grant Lee Buffalo, and husband-wife team Aimee Mann and Michael Penn grace the stage often. Did you see *Buena Vista Social Club*? The man behind the group, Ry Cooder, got his love for stringed instruments by hanging out at **McCabe's** *(3101 Pico Blvd., Santa Monica, 310-828-4403)*, an audiophile's guitar shop which features acoustic-friendly shows in a small back room and has lately been hosting erratic little shows by cutting edge artists like Cat Power.

RAVE ON

Just as glam is breaking out all over, rave culture is becoming a contender, with some great clubs of its own. Some run into the wee hours, so get your beauty rest beforehand. Out in Santa Monica, the breakbeat/world-groove movement seems to have taken a firm hold with **Sugar** *(814 Broadway, Santa Monica, 310-899-1989)*, a club with a hip, futuristic design, a huge fish tank, and a penchant for beat culture of all eras, from chocolate-city soul to old-school breakdance culture, drum 'n' bass, and European trance. **Gabah**

(4658 Melrose Ave., Hollywood, 323-664-8913) may be housed in the old punk-rock stomping grounds of the Anticlub and run by people from the famous grunge-crib Raji's, but it's exorcising those demons for the millennium by evolving into a vital dance-culture venue (stars like Breakbeat Era play often). And many rock clubs are beginning to host tasty electronic nights: The thrash-metal haven **Coconut Teaszer** *(8117 Sunset Blvd., West Hollywood, 323-654-4773)* leads the pack with the late-late night, 3am-10am party, Does Your Mama Know? (let's hope not). **Spaceland's Koncrete Jungle** *(1717 Silver Lake Blvd., Silver Lake, 213-833-2843)* and the **Viper Room's Atmosphere** *(8852 Sunset Blvd., West Hollywood, 310-358-1880)* are also beginning to make names for themselves in the dance world.

STRIP CLUBS

Since sex and money seem to be on everyone's minds, there are a number of strip clubs for those seeking bare flesh. Some are upscale, while others are dives; here are a few of both to assist you in your randy moments. The closest a strip club gets to a rock 'n' roll dive, **Jumbo's Clown Room** *(5153 Hollywood Blvd., Hollywood, 323-666-1187)* is the minimall club known as the place where Courtney Love used to strip when she was terrorizing Hollywood. On a grander scale, there's **Cheetah's** *(4600 Hollywood Blvd., Los Feliz, 323-660-6733)*, where serious dancers moonlight as serious strippers — and get pretty creative with those poles. These days Cheetah's dominates as the Hollywood hang (Drew Barrymore, Sofia Coppola, and Dave Grohl have been spotted here). In between the two is **The Body Shop** *(8250 Sunset Blvd., West Hollywood, 323-656-1401)*, an old standard for celebs that's best known for its Monday amateur night. **Crazy Girls** *(1433 N. La Brea Ave., Hollywood, 323-969-0055)* features babes in high platforms doing fancy pole work, pool tables, and (of course) sports on the telly. If a little wet-and-dirty action turns

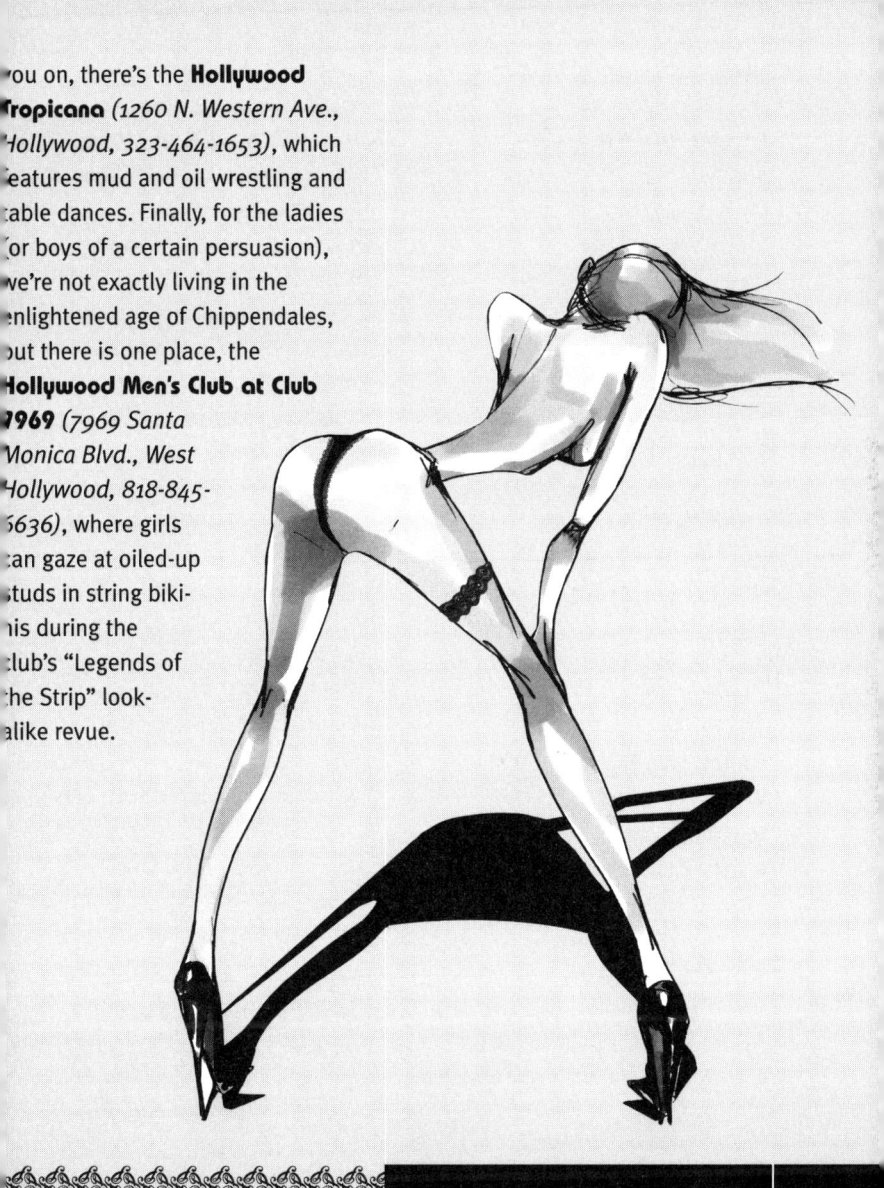

You on, there's the **Hollywood Tropicana** *(1260 N. Western Ave., Hollywood, 323-464-1653)*, which features mud and oil wrestling and table dances. Finally, for the ladies (or boys of a certain persuasion), we're not exactly living in the enlightened age of Chippendales, but there is one place, the **Hollywood Men's Club at Club 7969** *(7969 Santa Monica Blvd., West Hollywood, 818-845-5636)*, where girls can gaze at oiled-up studs in string bikinis during the club's "Legends of the Strip" lookalike revue.

nightlife | 105

index by neighborhood

santa monica/venice

Britannia Inn 318 Santa Monica Blvd. bet. 3rd and 4th Sts., Santa Monica, 310-458-5350

King's Head 116 Santa Monica Blvd. bet. Ocean and 2nd Sts., Santa Monica, 310-451-1402

McCabe's 3101 Pico Blvd. at 31st St., Santa Monica, 310-828-4403

O'Brien's 2226 Wilshire Blvd. bet. 22nd and 23rd Sts., Santa Monica, 310-829-5303

Rix 1413 5th St. at Santa Monica Blvd., Santa Monica, 310-656-9688

Sugar 814 Broadway at Lincoln Blvd., Santa Monica, 310-899-1989

brentwood/westwood/west la

Liquid Kitty 11780 Pico Blvd. at Barrington Ave., West LA 310-473-3707

beverly hills

Trader Vic's 9876 Wilshire Blvd. at Santa Monica Blvd., Beverly Hills, 310-274-7777

west hollywood

Asia de Cuba Mondrian Hotel, 8440 Sunset Blvd. at La Cienega Blvd. West Hollywood, 323-848-6000

Bar Marmont 8171 Sunset Blvd. at Crescent Heights Blvd., West Hollywood, 323-650-0575

Barfly 8730 Sunset Blvd. bet. San Vicente and La Cienega Blvds., West Hollywood, 310-360-9490

The Body Shop 8250 Sunset Blvd. bet. La Cienega and Crescent Heights Blvds., West Hollywood, 323-656-1401

Cat Club 8911 Sunset Blvd. at San Vicente Blvd., West Hollywood, 310-657-0888

Club 7969 7969 Santa Monica Blvd. bet. Crescent Heights Blvd. and Fairfax Ave., West Hollywood, 323-654-0280

Coconut Teaszer 8117 Sunset Blvd. at Crescent Heights Blvd., West Hollywood, 323-654-4773

Doug Weston's Troubadour 9081 Santa Monica Blvd. at Doheny Dr., West Hollywood, 310-276-6168

Dublin's Irish Whiskey Pub 8240 Sunset Blvd. bet. La Cienega and Crescent Heights Blvds., West Hollywood, 323-656-0100

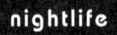

The Factory/Ultra Suede 652 La Peer Ave./661 N. Robertson Blvd. bet. Santa Monica Blvd. and Melrose Ave., West Hollywood, 310-659-4551

Fenix Argyle Hotel, 8358 Sunset Blvd. bet. La Cienega and Crescent Heights Blvds., West Hollywood, 323-654-2464

Genghis Cohen 740 N. Fairfax Ave. nr. Melrose Ave., West Hollywood, 323-653-0640

The House of Blues 8430 Sunset Blvd. nr. La Cienega Blvd., West Hollywood, 323-848-5100

Key Club 9030 Sunset Blvd. bet. Doheny Dr. and San Vicente Blvd., West Hollywood, 310-274-5800

Largo 432 N. Fairfax Ave. bet. Melrose Ave. and Beverly Blvd., West Hollywood, 323-852-1073

Lola's 945 N. Fairfax Ave. bet. Santa Monica Blvd. and Melrose Ave., West Hollywood, 323-736-5652

LunaPark 665 N. Robertson Blvd. bet. Santa Monica Blvd. and Melrose Ave., West Hollywood, 310-652-0611

North 8029 Sunset Blvd. bet. Crescent Heights Blvd. and Fairfax Ave., West Hollywood, 323-654-1313

The Palms 8572 Santa Monica Blvd. bet. San Vicente and La Cienega Blvds., West Hollywood, 310-652-6188

Rage 8911 Santa Monica Blvd. at San Vicente Blvd., West Hollywood, 310-652-7055

Revolver 8851 Santa Monica Blvd. bet. San Vicente and La Cienega Blvds., West Hollywood, 310-659-8851

Roxy 9009 Sunset Blvd. bet. Doheny Dr. and San Vicente Blvd., West Hollywood, 310-276-2222

Sky Bar Mondrian Hotel, 8440 Sunset Blvd. at La Cienega Blvd., West Hollywood, 323-650-8999

The Standard 8300 Sunset Blvd. bet. La Cienega and Crescent Heights Blvds., West Hollywood, 323-650-9090

Tempest 7323 Santa Monica Blvd. bet. Fairfax and La Brea Aves., West Hollywood, 323-850-5115

Viper Room 8852 Sunset Blvd. bet. San Vicente and La Cienega Blvds., West Hollywood, 310-358-1880

Whisky a Go-Go 8901 Sunset Blvd. bet. Doheny Dr. and San Vicente Blvd., West Hollywood, 310-652-4202

third/beverly

Molly Malone's Irish Pub 575 S. Fairfax Ave. nr. 6th St., Los Angeles, 310-935-1577

hollywood

Blue 1642 Las Palmas Ave. bet. Hollywood and Sunset Blvds., 323-462-7442

Boardner's 1652 Cherokee Ave. bet. Hollywood and Sunset Blvds., Hollywood, 323-462-9621

Cat 'N' Fiddle 6530 Sunset Blvd. bet. Highland Ave. and Cahuenga Blvd., Hollywood, 323-468-3800

Circus 6655 Santa Monica Blvd. bet. Highland Ave. and Cahuenga Blvd., Hollywood, 323-462-1291

Club Lingerie 6507 Sunset Blvd. bet. Highland Ave. and Cahuenga Blvd., Hollywood, 323-466-8557

The Coach and Horses 7617 Sunset Blvd. bet. Fairfax and La Brea Aves., Hollywood, 323-876-6900

Crazy Girls 1433 N. La Brea Ave. bet. Sunset Blvd. and Fountain Ave., Hollywood, 323-969-0055

Daddy's 1610 N. Vine St. bet. Hollywood and Sunset Blvds., Hollywood, 323-463-7777

Dragonfly 6510 Santa Monica Blvd. bet. Highland Ave. and Cahuenga Blvd., Hollywood, 323-466-6111

El Floridita 1253 Vine St. at Fountain Ave., Hollywood, 323-871-8612

Formosa Café 7156 Santa Monica Blvd. bet. Fairfax and La Brea Aves., Hollywood, 323-850-9050

The Frolic Room 6345 Hollywood Blvd. at Vine St., Hollywood, 323-462-5890

Gabah 4658 Melrose Ave. nr. Normandie Ave., Hollywood, 323-664-8913

Goldfingers 6423 Yucca St. nr. Cahuenga Blvd., Hollywood, 323-962-2913

Hollywood Palladium 6215 Sunset Blvd. bet. Vine and Gower Sts., Hollywood, 323-874-9649

Hollywood Tropicana 1260 N. Western Ave. nr. Fountain Ave., Hollywood, 323-464-1653

Jack's Sugar Shack 1707 Vine St. at Hollywood Blvd., Hollywood, 323-466-7005

Jones Hollywood 7205 Santa Monica Blvd. bet. Fairfax and La Brea Aves., Hollywood, 323-850-1727

Jumbo's Clown Room 5153 Hollywood Blvd. bet. Western and Normandie Aves., Hollywood, 323-666-1187

Kane 5574 Melrose Ave. at Gower St., Hollywood, 323-466-6263

Lava Lounge 1533 N. La Brea Ave. at Sunset Blvd., Hollywood, 323-876-6612

The Martini Lounge 5657 Melrose Ave. bet. Vine and Gower Sts., Hollywood, 323-467-4068

Musso and Frank Grill 6667 Hollywood Blvd. bet. Highland Ave. and Cahuenga Blvd., Hollywood, 323-467-5123

Opium Den 1605 Ivar Ave. bet. Hollywood and Sunset Blvds., Hollywood, 323-466-7800

The Palace 1735 Vine St. at Hollywood Blvd., Hollywood, 323-462-3000

The Playroom 836 N. Highland Ave. bet. Santa Monica Blvd. and Melrose Ave., Hollywood, 323-460-6630

Sunset Room 1430 Cahuenga Blvd. bet. Sunset Blvd. and Fountain Ave., Hollywood, 323-463-0001

Tommy Tang's 7313 Melrose Ave. bet. Fairfax and La Brea Aves., Hollywood, 323-937-5733

Vynyl 1650 Schrader Blvd. nr. Hollywood Blvd., Hollywood, 323-465-7449

los feliz/silver lake/atwater village

Akbar 4356 Sunset Blvd. at Fountain Ave., Silver Lake, 323-665-6810

Bigfoot Lodge 3172 Los Feliz Blvd. bet. Riverside Dr. and San Fernando Rd., Atwater Village, 323-662-9227

Cheetah's 4600 Hollywood Blvd. bet. Vermont and Hillhurst Aves., Los Feliz, 323-660-6733

The Derby 4500 Los Feliz Blvd. at Hillhurst Ave., Los Feliz, 323-663-8979

The Dresden Room 1760 N. Vermont Ave. bet. Franklin Ave. and Hollywood Blvd., Los Feliz, 323-665-4294

The Garage 4519 Santa Monica Blvd. at Virgil Ave., Silver Lake, 323-662-6166

The Good Luck Bar 1514 Hillhurst Ave. at Sunset Blvd., Los Feliz, 323-666-3524

Red Lion Tavern 2356 Glendale Blvd. nr. Silver Lake Blvd., Silver Lake, 323-662-5337

Rudolpho's 2500 Riverside Dr. at Fletcher Dr., Silver Lake, 323-969-2596

Spaceland 1717 Silver Lake Blvd. bet. Glendale and Sunset Blvds., Silver Lake, 213-833-2843

Tiki Ti 4427 Sunset Blvd. bet. Hillhurst and Fountain Aves., Los Feliz, 323-669-9381

koreatown/mid-city

The Conga Room 5364 Wilshire Blvd. bet. Fairfax and La Brea Aves., Los Angeles, 323-938-1696

El Rey Theatre 5515 Wilshire Blvd. bet. Fairfax and La Brea Aves., Los Angeles, 323-769-5500

Fais Do-Do 5257 W. Adams Blvd. bet. Fairfax and La Brea Aves., Los Angeles, 323-269-9480

HMS Bounty 3357 Wilshire Blvd. bet. Normandie and Vermont Aves., Los Angeles, 213-385-7275

The Smog Cutter 864 N. Virgil Ave. bet. Santa Monica Blvd. and Melrose Ave., Los Angeles, 323-667-9832

downtown/east la

Al's Bar 305 S. Hewitt St. at E. 3rd St., Downtown, 213-625-9703

The Mayan 1038 S. Hill St. bet. Olympic Blvd. and 11th St., Downtown, 213-746-4287

farther afield

Encounter Los Angeles International Airport, 201 World Way, 310-215-5151

index by type

dance clubs
Blue
Circus
Club Lingerie
Club 7969
Conga Room
The Derby
Dragonfly
Fais Do-Do
El Floridita
The Factory/Ultra Suede
Goldfingers
Key Club
LunaPark
Makeup! at El Rey
The Mayan
Opium Den
The Playroom

Rudolpho's
Sugar
Vynyl

dives
Al's Bar
Boardner's
The Coach and Horses
The Frolic Room
HMS Bounty
Red Lion Tavern
The Smog Cutter
Tiki Ti

gay/lesbian
Akbar
Circus
Club 7969
Club 836 at The Playroom
Dragstrip 66 at Rudolpho's
The Factory/Ultra Suede
The Palms
Rage
Revolver
Salsa de Noche at Rudolpho's

glam
Cherry at The Playroom
Makeup! at El Rey Theatre
Rodney's English Disco at Fais Do-Do
Vibrator at Club 7969

industry scenes
Asia de Cuba
Bar Marmont
Barfly
Cat Club
Daddy's
The Derby
The Dresden Room
Fenix, Argyle Hotel
Formosa Café
The Good Luck Bar
Jones Hollywood
Kane
Lava Lounge
Lola's
The Martini Lounge
Musso and Frank Grill
North
Rix
Sky Bar
The Standard
Sunset Room
Viper Room

latin
Conga Room
El Floridita
The Mayan
Rudolpho's

live music

Al's Bar
Coconut Teaszer
Conga Room
The Derby
Doug Weston's Troubadour
Dragonfly
El Floridita
El Rey Theatre
Fais Do-Do
The Garage
Genghis Cohen
Goldfingers
Hollywood Palladium
The House of Blues
Jack's Sugar Shack
Key Club
Largo
Lava Lounge
LunaPark
McCabe's
Molly Malone's Irish Pub
Opium Den
The Palace
Roxy
Spaceland
Sunset Room
Viper Room
Vynyl
Whisky a Go-Go

pubs

Britannia Inn
Cat 'N' Fiddle
Dublin's Irish Whiskey Pub
Genghis Cohen
King's Head
Molly Malone's Irish Pub
O'Brien's

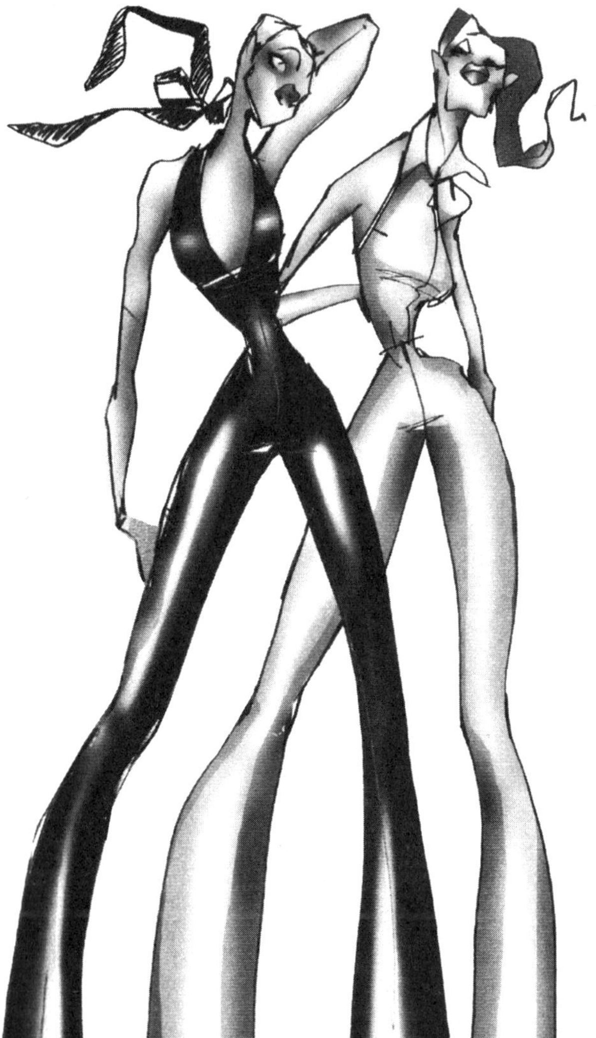

shopping

los angeles is among a small handful of cities in the world where one can shop for anything. Some say every*one* in Los Angeles is for sale; we know that every*thing* in LA is for sale — from Madonna's undergarments to an original Orson Welles manuscript. You just have to know where to look. ■ Whether you're a Chanel-clad pro drifting up Rodeo with dangling shopping bags or the vintage rat scouring Melrose for the perfect work boot, LA has an embarrassment of retail riches and countless specialty shops. Of course, shopping isn't limited merely to the act of purchasing. Browsing and window-shopping have been elevated to a sport in a city where most can only dream of spending at Bijan. "When I sell my first script" and "When I land my first role" are common proclamations outside such storefronts.

shopping tips to start you off

» Weather the trends. It's fun to wear the latest style, but you're smarter to invest in some versatile, timeless fashion staples that will have you looking fabulous for much longer.

» Call ahead for hours. Boutiques and smaller shops often don't open until noon.

» You have as much of a right to browse as the next person. Don't let a salesperson's flippant or dismissive attitude get you down.

» Be cautious of tricky return policies. To wit, never take the tag off something you've bought until you wear it.

» Beware of the impulse buy. Most stores will hold something for you. Think it over; you can always come back.

clothing

AMERICAN RAG *150 S. La Brea Ave. bet. Beverly Blvd. and 3rd St., Los Angeles, 323-935-3154; Hours: Mon-Sat 10am-10pm; Sun 12pm-7pm*

For trendsetters who straddle the line between vintage and modern fashion, American Rag, smack-dab on the La Brea strip, is the only place to shop. This vast, industrial-like store was the first to hawk both vintage and modern wear and has since expanded its stock to include housewares and a small café offering bistro fare. Although it's not as comprehensive as it once was, the secondhand selection is carefully chosen and not overly expensive. Perfect black cocktail dresses abound, and guys have loads of western and vintage shirts to choose from. Current designers taking up room on the racks include Anna Sui, Todd Oldham, Betsey Johnson, Stüssy, Diesel, Katherine Hamnet, and Mossimo. Accessorize your look perfectly with shoes — think Freelance, Espace, Puma — and eyewear from Diesel, Gucci, and Spy. Much of the gear at this self-styled department store is over $100, but there are still plenty of bargains to be found if you take thrill in the hunt.

CURVE *154 N. Robertson Blvd. at Beverly Blvd., West Hollywood, 310-360-8008; Hours: Mon-Sat 11am-7pm; Sun 12pm-6pm*
When New York fashion editors want to find out what's hip on the West Coast, they call Delia Seaman and Nevena Borisova, the twentysomething owners of Curve, an anchor of soigné on cutting-edge Robertson Boulevard. Curve keeps up with the latest international trends, so that customers like Cameron Diaz can keep up with New York style. Stocking up-and-coming New York-based designers like Fofo, Alpana Bawa, Beth Orduna, and Michelle Mason, Curve hawks only the edgiest pieces from each line — after all, who needs another pair of black pants? Since you'll find stuff here that you won't find anywhere else, vacationing New Yorkers, children of the rich and famous, and LA's wanna-be cool crowd clamor at Curve for one-of-a-kind pieces with a wacky edge. For those who are backsliding on fitness resolutions, beware: Curve only stocks sizes 2, 4, 6, and 8.

DECADES, INC. *8214 Melrose Ave. bet. La Cienega and Crescent Heights Blvds., Hollywood, 323-655-0223; Hours: Mon-Sat 11:30am-6pm*
Turning his sharp eye for vin-

tage fashion into the most heralded new shop in town, cabaret singer-turned-zeitgeist meister Cameron Silver sells only top-of-the-line vintage designer clothes at his Melrose Avenue store, which was dubbed the best vintage store in the country by *Harper's Bazaar*. Vintage fashion that looks modern is the store's self-proclaimed mantra, and Silver delivers in a storefront that he's dubbed the "Warhol Factory for the new millennium." The futuristic space has the high ceilings of an art gallery and the walls of an Hèrmes outlet. The dressing room is huge, and its outer-space decor invites flashbacks to Kubrick's *2001*. Hollywood's latest it girls flock here for mint-condition Halston, Rudi Gernreich, Lily Pulitzer, Gucci, Pucci, and Missoni pieces. ("Most favored shopper" status is conferred on regulars Tea Leoni, Courtney Cox, Rose McGowan, and her boy toy, Marilyn Manson.) Silver draws most of his merchandise from the '60s and '70s. Prices are high, but the pieces — all carefully selected by Silver himself — are in such good condition, you might mistake them for brand spanking new. Recently opened on the second floor is Decades Two Inc., a contemporary couture and designer resale boutique.

shopping

FRED SEGAL *8100 Melrose Ave. at Crescent Heights Blvd., West Hollywood, 323-651-4129; Hours: Mon-Sat 10am-7pm; Sun 12pm-6pm*

The corner of Melrose and Crescent Heights is ground zero for the best shopping in Los Angeles. Celebs and fashionistas flock to this complex of mind-bendingly cool boutiques for the fiercest fashions of the season. The block-long space is divided into small departments with the freshest gotta-get-it loot, from skin-tight jeans to jewelry to eyeglasses to shoes. Whatever the latest trend is — hip huggers, long dresses, knee-high boots — its first stop on any rack is at Fred Segal. A neophyte designer who sells well here is virtually guaranteed to rise to the top of the fashion heap. Parallel, Daryl K., and BCBG are examples of this phenomenon. Madonna, Drew Barrymore, Jennifer Love Hewitt, Helena Christensen, and the costume departments of hit TV shows all stock their closets at this reliably hip emporium. Exclusive makeup and fragrance lines and a shoe line round out the merchandise. For those without the bucks to burn, there's a twice-yearly sale, when everything is at least 50 percent off.

JANICE MCCARTY *912 Montana Ave. bet. 9th and 10th Sts., Santa Monica, 310-393-6858; 21 N. Fair Oaks Ave. at Colorado Blvd., Pasadena, 626-793-9130; Hours: Mon-Sat 11am-6pm*

This duo of eponymously named stores is known for its retro-inspired clothes designed by the Los Angeles-based Janice McCarty. Many of the clothes in her collection are made with antique fabrics (think quirky rayon prints) and buttons, evoking the timeless style of the '40s. Daryl Hannah, Melanie Griffith, and Susan Sarandon play at being glamorous movie stars in McCarty's sly re-creations of swinging calf-length dresses. McCarty will also alter her pieces any way you want-lengthening the sleeves or hemline, making the same piece in a different fabric, adding a pocket, whatever your fashionable little heart desires. Prices range from $50 to $300, but there are always a few good pieces on the sale rack. There is also a small selection of jewelry, housewares, and furniture.

LISA KLINE *136 S. Robertson Blvd. bet. Beverly Blvd. and 3rd St., Los Angeles, 310-246-0907; Hours: Mon-Sat 11am-7pm; Sun 12pm-5pm*
Svelte fashionistas frequent Lisa Kline's small boutique nestled on Robertson Boulevard for casualwear. One-stop shopping for the young and hip is the theme of the moment at this warm, inviting store; the staff is as friendly to Echo Park locals as it is to superstar customers like Claire Danes, Courtney Cox, and Jennifer Aniston, a custom which is not the norm. The store is a gold mine of formfitting tees, cuddly sweaters, perfectly cut jeans and pants, knee-length skirts, and comfy lingerie and sleepwear made by up-to-the-moment designers like Three Dots, Daisy Girl, Free Love, Cherry Pie, and Rebecca Danenberg. When Gwyneth Paltrow and Winona Ryder were dating pals Ben Affleck and Matt Damon, the gals bought matching Cherry Pie cherry-print pajamas here. Across the street is Lisa Kline Men, which outfits young celebs like Leonardo DiCaprio and Ben Lee with the latest fashions.

LURA STARR *7374 Beverly Blvd. bet. Fairfax and La Brea Aves., Los Angeles, 323-933-4704; Hours: Mon-Sat 11am-7pm; Sun 12pm-6pm*
This retro-themed retail outlet specializes in glamorous and alluring party dresses. Within its sunflower-yellow walls, you'll find racks of modern takes on the fashions of a more subtly sexual era — when all it took to incite a thrill was a peek of black stocking or a flash of bare shoulder. Mixing and matching from the '40s, '50s,

and '60s, the designers at Lura Starr have created a nostalgic hybrid. Pinup girls and lobby cards inspire you to dizzying heights of drop-dead glamour as you try on the formfitting frocks, strapless gowns, and beaded dresses. It's all in the details with these well-made clothes — silk linings, covered buttons, invisible zippers. You'll feel like Cinderella at the ball as you transform into a saucy sex goddess. Appropriately enough, former porn star Traci Lords is a Lura Starr devotee and occasionally models for the store.

MAXFIELD *8825 Melrose Ave. bet. Doheny Dr. and Robertson Blvd., West Hollywood, 310-274-8800; Hours: Mon-Sat 11am-7pm*
The austere concrete space and the complimentary bottles of Maxfield water say it all — Maxfield is *the* men's designer boutique in Los Angeles. In addition to the usual suspects (Gucci, Prada, Comme des Garçons), Maxfield carries more daring, lesser-known designers such as Rick Owens. The store's collection of men's antique accessories like pocket watches is worth a look, too.

NYSE *7385 Beverly Blvd. bet. Fairfax and La Brea Aves., Los Angeles, 323-938-1018; Hours: Mon-Sat 11am-7pm; Sun 12pm-6pm*
When über-hip fashionistas and style journos want to keep up with the latest trends, they hightail it over to NYSE, short for New York Style Exchange.

NYSE is always stocked with the togs that make it to the big fashion houses the next season. Black velvet paintings of insouciant nudes deck the walls, watching over you as you paw through the racks for something that screams your name. The friendly gals helming the store are helpful, giving invaluable advice in choosing which jeans flatter your butt the most. The prices here can get a little expensive, but each glamorous, well-made piece is worth every penny. Though this is a must-shop for girls who break the fashion mold, voluptuous women should take note that sizes 10 and 12 are few and far between.

OLIVER PEOPLES *8642 Sunset Blvd. bet. San Vicente and La Cienega Blvds., West Hollywood, 310-657-2553; Hours: Mon-Fri 10am-7pm; Sat 10am-6pm; Sun 12pm-6pm*
Few activities are more fun than sitting at a fitting desk at Oliver Peoples with a dozen eyeglass frames in front of you. After you've chosen the finalists from among a few hundred frames designed by Oliver Peoples and Paul Smith (the two lines that represent the bulk of the store's inventory), the process of elimination is more brutal than a Miss America pageant. The fashionable yet approachable staff will interject with its biases and aesthetic leanings. What rocks about Oliver Peoples, though, is that it's tough to go wrong.

PLANET FUNK *7571 Melrose Ave. bet. Fairfax and La Brea Aves., Hollywood, 323-655-2990; 126 Santa Monica Pl., entrance on Broadway at 3rd St., Santa Monica, 310-434-9778; Westside Pavilion, 10800 Pico Blvd. bet. Westwood Blvd. and Overland Ave., West LA, 310-441-5043; Hours: Mon-Fri 11am-7:30pm; Sat 10:30am-8pm; Sun 11:30am-7:30pm*
Planet Funk is one of the city's best-kept secrets, keeping up with the latest trends and selling 'em at much lower prices — think of it as a low-rent Fred

Segal. Planet Funk has joined forces with no-name fashion manufacturers from Europe to bring Euro style to the American masses. In keeping with the store's motto, "It's not what you know, it's what you wear," you'll find an eclectic collection of skirts, pants, jeans, dresses, and shirts in various styles made in quirky patterns and solids. These one-stop shops for the struggling trendoid are conveniently located in easy-access locations such as malls and on Melrose Avenue (who says a suburban girl can't look good?). If you wanna look fierce but don't have the checkbook to match, Planet Funk is always there to save the day.

POLKA DOTS AND MOONBEAMS *8367 3rd St. bet. La Cienega and Crescent Heights Blvds., Los Angeles, 323-651-1746; Hours: Mon-Sat 11am-6:30pm; Sun 12pm-5pm*
Don't call it a thrift shop. Polka Dots and Moonbeams hawks vintage finery from its small storefront space in the shadow of the Beverly Center. Though it may be a little pricey — there's not much merchandise under $50 — the prices are still within arm's reach, with most items clocking in at under $100. The store carries a stunning array of mint-condition rayon dresses, cashmere sweaters, and modest blouses on its jam-packed racks. Polka Dots also has one of the most affordably priced selections of vintage eyeglass frames and costume jewelry in town. A few doors down is Polka Dots and Moonbeams Modern, the store's new-clothes outpost; most of the merchandise takes its cue from the retro clothing down the street.

PRODUCT *134 S. Robertson Blvd. bet. Beverly Blvd. and 3rd St., Los Angeles, 310-860-9393; Hours: Mon-Sat 11am-7pm; Sun 12pm-6pm*
Within the stark white walls of this boutique are all the basics for a utilitarian yet subtly hip

wardrobe. The fashion-conscious throng here for the perfectly tailored, simply designed offerings. All the essentials are here — black pants in any cut, button-down shirts, leather coats, T-shirts, cargo pants, sundresses, and more. Product sells only its own line, which is designed by Korean-American local girl-made-good Elaine Kim. At its own stores, Product unveils special designs that aren't available anywhere else, some that are even one of a kind. There's also a good selection of belts, hats, shoes, and tights.

RE-MIX *7605 1/2 Beverly Blvd. bet. Fairfax and La Brea Aves., Los Angeles, 323-936-6210; Hours: Mon-Sat 12pm-7pm; Sun 12pm-6pm*
Step through the doorway at this modest shoe store on Beverly Boulevard and you'll feel as if you've entered a time capsule from an era when wingtips, two-tones, pumps, and saucy slingbacks shod the feet of every LA man and woman. Re-Mix will take you back to a time when shoes lasted more that a season, with durable double stitching, hand-glued soles, and comfortable leather uppers. Re-Mix's specialty is dead stock; in other words, the owners cull their merchandise from warehouses in every town from Podunk to

Poughkeepsie to find never-worn vintage shoes still in their original boxes. Gold spray-painted cow skulls and life-size painted burlesque girls line the walls, looking down on you as you vacillate between a sensible pair of '40s work boots and a snazzy set of gold lamé Lucite heels that would perfectly complete your desperate Hollywood starlet ensemble. Most of the shoes are available in a limited range of sizes, but the friendly owner will spend hours digging through his stock to find the pair that is destined for your peds. Prices are mostly in the $50-$100 range, and there is a small selection of vintage-reproduction clothes near the cash register.

SLOW 7474 Melrose Ave. bet. Fairfax and La Brea Aves., Hollywood, 323-655-3725; Hours: Sun-Fri 11:30am-8pm; Sat 11:30am-9pm
Looking for a sharp number to wear to that new club? Or how about a brightly colored pair of leather pants and a feather boa? Whatever decade you're most comfortable in, you'll find the togs to suit your look at Slow. Catering to the Japanese clubber and local struggling hipster populations, Slow is a treasure trove of vintage finds for clothes hounds. The vast concrete room is organized by color and style — with everything from that perfect '70s Iron Maiden T-shirt to a paisley housedress. In the back room is a huge selection of coats (rare for sunny Los Angeles), with leather, suede, faux fur, and polyester among the materials of choice. Slow also carries its own label of wacky creations — usually vintage garments spun into new inventions. Ravers take note: Slow has zillions of rave flyers on a rack near the entrance.

TRACEY ROSS 8595 Sunset Blvd. bet. San Vicente and La Cienega Blvds, West Hollywood, 310-854-1996; Hours: Mon-Sat 10am-7pm; Sun 12pm-5pm
A confessed shopaholic herself,

Tracey Ross knows what her fellow addicts want. Ross opened the store with her trust fund, after she used a big chunk of it to pay off her $75,000 in credit-card debt. Now scions of Hollywood royalty, the current crop of movie stars, new wave up-and-comers, and wannabes alike flock to this West Hollywood boutique for cashmere sweaters, summer dresses, perfect butt-sculpting pants, jewelry, and even silver giftware. Less self-consciously trendy than Fred Segal, this intimate and casual shop even has a daybed and ottomans for lounging during a hectic day of shopping, and Ross lets her regular customers bring their pooches. In the back, a manicurist does nails. This shop is for the beautiful, model-like set — you're lucky to find anything over a size 10 on the racks, and most of the clothes sell for $100-$500. But if you're addicted to the latest in fashion, it's a must-see.

URBAN OUTFITTERS *1440 3rd Street Promenade bet. Broadway and Santa Monica Blvd., Santa Monica, 310-394-1404; Hours: Mon-Thu 10am-10pm; Fri-Sat 10am-11pm; Sun 11am-8pm; 7650 Melrose Ave. bet. Fairfax and La Brea Aves., Hollywood, 323-653-3231; Hours: Mon-Fri 10am-9pm; Sat 10am-10pm; Sun 11am-8pm; 139 W. Colorado Blvd. bet. Pasadena and Fair Oaks Aves., Pasadena, 626-449-1818; Hours: Mon-Thu 11am-10pm; Fri-Sat 10am-11pm; Sun 12pm-8pm*
Teenage hipsters and the young at heart can get their gear at Urban Outfitters, where you can buy your subculture status for under $100 an outfit. With outlets across the country located in youth-oriented markets, this corporate chain suits the masses with all the accoutrements necessary for "alternative" status, which nowadays means an urban nomad look. Hip women's lines like Lip Gloss, Free People, Lush, Fresh Jive, and Dollhouse are staples here. Boys are represented, too, with work pants,

'70s T-shirts, and cute hoodies. Round out your bohemian lifestyle with the mishmash of funky housewares — think inflatable furniture, leopard faux-fur pillows, and paper lanterns — with which Urban Outfitters earned its moniker of "The Alternative Ikea." Wanna feed your head? There's also a selection of books that have earned their place on the hipster's short list.

VIN BAKER *132 1/2 S. La Brea Ave. bet. Beverly Blvd. and 3rd Sts., Los Angeles, 323-936-4001; Hours: Mon-Sat 11am-7pm, Sun 12pm-6pm*
Within the lime-colored walls of Vin Baker floats a sea of shoes — sandals, platforms, knee-high boots, and flats — to suit any mood. The store imports from Spanish and Italian factories funky fresh styles that can't be found anyone else. There's always a wide selection of shoes from the dependably hip French Robert Clergerie line, Vin Baker's own imprint, and other hard-to-find European designers. The well-crafted shoes are built to

last and never go out of style. Prices range from $100-$500, but half-price sales are frequent, with pairs available in virtually any size. TLC stocked up here on fur-lined boots for the MTV Music Awards.

WASTELAND *7428 Melrose Ave. bet. Fairfax and La Brea Aves., Hollywood, 323-653-3028; Hours: Mon-Sat 11:30am-8:30pm, Sun 12pm-8pm*
The clothes at the Wasteland scream with punk-rock exuberance, as local scenesters, taste-making fashionistas, and even a handful of celebrities — Drew Barrymore, Kate Moss, and Sofia Coppola among them — paw through the racks for the coolest retro threads. Even Anna Sui and Jean-Paul Gaultier have been spotted combing the selection for inspiration. The merchandise at this vintage superstore features everything from classic funk to vintage couture. Fashion-savvy boys throng here for a wide selection of '70s T-shirts, vintage denim, Hawaiiana, western, and workwear, while gals troll the decades for the perfect party dresses, cashmere sweaters, and Bakelite jewelry. There's also a designer resale area featuring current fashions, with bargain-priced pieces from Dries Van Noten, ABS, Anna Sui, and Betsey Johnson.

X-LARGE/X-GIRL *1766 N. Vermont Ave. bet. Franklin Ave. and Hollywood Blvd., Los Feliz, 323-666-3483; Hours: Mon-Sat 12pm-7pm; Sun 12pm-6pm*
Opened in 1991 in Los Feliz, long before Madonna moved there or *Los Angeles* magazine declared the neighborhood the "new Beverly Hills," X-Large was the first store in what is now the hippest neighborhood in town. Stocking all the essentials for the club set, X-Large has now merged with its sister store, X-Girl, expanding its hip-hop and skate-inspired wear to the sisters in the scene.

Partly owned by Mike D. of the Beastie Boys, the small boutique serves as the epicenter for neighborhood gossip and the lowdown on cool club scenes. The surprisingly friendly help have graduated from the icy-cold stares delivered by the staff in the early 90s. Skinny girls enjoy the affordable indigo jeans, A-line skirts, and baby tees, while guys can go baggy with ski pants, fleece separates, and retro logo-emblazoned T-shirts. Also preserved on a magazine rack are all the issues of the Beastie Boys' now-defunct *Grand Royal* magazine.

clothing

CELEBRITY-WORN

Everyone wants to be a star in Los Angeles. But even if you don't become a celebrity, you can at least dress like one. The city is home to several shops where you can purchase Hollywood's hand-me-downs at discount prices. **The Cinema Glamour Shop** (343 N. La Brea Ave., Hollywood, 323-933-5289) was the pioneer in discovering the gold mine of selling celebrity castoffs, donating all proceeds to the Motion Picture & Television Fund. There are no labels stating who wore what when, but Janet Leigh, Elizabeth Taylor, and Burt Reynolds have all made donations. **Baby Jane of Hollywood** (7985 Santa Monica Blvd., West Hollywood, 323-848-7080) sells celebrity underwear from the likes of Arnold Schwarzenegger and local heroine Angelyne. Baby Jane also does a swift business in paparazzi shots of your favorite celebrities nude. After the Northridge quake, it even sold rubble and broken items from celebrity homes, all carefully labeled in plastic bags. **It's a Wrap** (3315 Magnolia Blvd., Burbank, 818-567-7366) is a celebrity clothing clearinghouse, where wardrobe departments from TV shows unload last season's costumes. Most of the stuff here has been worn only once and is carefully sorted by show. More celebrity castoffs can be found at **Reel Clothes** (12132 Ventura Blvd., Studio City, 818-508-7762), where the merchandise is also identified by show, episode, and the star who wore it. Vintage store **Time After Time** (7245 Melrose Ave., Hollywood, 323-653-8463) has a small selection of celebrity clothing from the '30s, '40s, and '50s, from the likes of Natalie Wood and Marlon Brando.

CLUB CLOTHES

For a night of club-hopping, you gotta make sure you have the fabulous outfit to compete with the die-hards. To suit yourself up in knock-'em-dead garb from head to toe, hightail it over to Melrose Avenue. Stores open and close quickly on this hallowed street, but here are a few of the old stalwarts that can always be depended on for the perfect look. **Retail Slut** *(7308 Melrose Ave., Hollywood, 323-934-1339)* is a one-stop shop for suburban punks and goths, selling vinyl pants, cheap corsets, band T-shirts, fishnets, ghoulish makeup, Manic Panic products, and spiked collars since 1983. **Serious** *(7264 Melrose Ave., Hollywood, 323-936-5152)* stocks the latest clubwear from design duo Magnus and Hoochie, whose Serious line of clothing is sold at over 300 boutiques across the country. At their retail store on Melrose, the duo unleash their more outlandish creations, from an Evil Knieval-inspired pleather suit and sequined cowboy hat to a kitty cat hoodie. Mods converge at **Camden Lock** *(7021 Melrose Ave., Hollywood, 323-933-5752)* for all the gear that defines the mod aesthetic — three-button suits, knee-length skirts, and Fred Perry shirts. **Red Balls** *(7365 Melrose Ave., Hollywood, 323-655-3409)* stocks all the clubwear essentials, whether faux fur, vinyl, pleather, leopard print, or any fabric that's shiny or sparkly. Red Balls also has a notable selection of punk-rock footwear, from platforms to creepers. **The Sinister Store** *(1748 Vermont Ave., Los Feliz, 323-666-5100)* is the only place to get club gear (besides the vintage stores) on the Eastside of town. The unisex fashions range from corsets and bustiers to bondage pants and flame-embroidered shirts. You can embrace your inner goth at **Redemption** *(7300 Melrose Ave., Hollywood, 323-549-9128)*, with everything from frilly lace and velvet gowns to vinyl fetish gear. Finally, trashy fashion for both guys and gals can also be found at **Slave** *(1223

Abbot Kinney Way, Venice, 310-314-7016), which is unrivaled in its selection of leopard print clothing.

DESIGNER DUDS

Los Angeles style is giving New York a run for its money. As much as the rest of the world would like to think that the latest looks are born solely in Manhattan, Paris, and Milan, it's those venerable bastions of high fashion that are now taking their cues from the casually cool look of Tinseltown's finest. If a designer has his own Los Angeles retail outlet, celebrities can easily snag his latest creations off the rack, which translates into sales that are guaranteed to go through the roof. The epicenter of this high-fashion renaissance is the western end of Melrose Avenue. Down the street from the fashionista's fantasy-come-true store **Fred Segal** *(8100 Melrose Ave., West Hollywood, 323-651-4129; see main entry)*, **Miu Miu** *(8025 Melrose Ave., West Hollywood, 323-651-0073)* carries Miuccia Prada's younger, more playful line of clothes and serves as the sole U.S. outlet for her men's line. Because the store is filled with the designer's whimsical clothes and shoes in every style and every color, Prada converts will think they've died and gone to heaven. The London-based swimwear designer **Liza Bruce** *(7977 Melrose Ave., West Hollywood, 323-655-5012)* hawks her colorful swimwear and sportswear from her Melrose store, and also designs made-to-measure bathing suits. Sunset Plaza, along with Robertson Boulevard, is another essential fashion destination, with a bevy of leading designers' shops and a gaggle of sidewalk cafés to restore your senses. **D&G** *(8641 Sunset Blvd., West Hollywood, 310-360-7272)*, the younger, hipper, and cheaper arm of Dolce & Gabbana, carries the Sicilian duo's elegant, vintage-inspired clothing and accessories for men and women. **Anna Sui** *(8669 Sunset Blvd., West Hollywood, 310-360-6224)* sells her quirky takes on retro glamour with accessories, shoes, and jewelry to all the party girls in town. **Kenneth Cole** *(8752 Sunset Blvd., West Hollywood, 310-289-5085)* has brought his funky shoe line to Los Angeles and has since shod celebs like Brooke Shields in his classic designs. **Nicole Miller's** *(8633 Sunset Blvd., West Hollywood, 310-652-1629)* playful fashions have also long held court on the Strip. At the Beverly Center, **DKNY** *(Beverly Center, 131 N. La Cienega Blvd. at Beverly Blvd., West Hollywood, 310-289-9787)* unveils its sporty men's and women's wear. **Prada Men** *(343 N. Rodeo Dr., Beverly Hills, 310-385-5959)* is frequented by Hollywood heart throbs like Leonardo DiCaprio, who love the funky-cool shoes and clothes. Armani's comparatively affordable boutique, **Emporio Armani** *(9533 Brighton Way, Beverly Hills, 310-271-7790)*, is just around the corner. On Robertson Boulevard, Los Angeles' hottest shopping street, are **Kate Spade's** *(105 S. Robertson Blvd., Los Angeles, 310-271-9778)* classically urban bags and **Cynthia Rowley's** *(112 S. Robertson Blvd., Los Angeles, 310-276-9020)* retro-inspired, reasonably-priced party dresses.

Richard Tyler *(7290 Beverly Blvd., Los Angeles, 323-931-6769)* has outfitted actresses like Julia Roberts for award shows at his Beverly Boulevard boutique, ensconced in an art deco building. Also on Beverly, **Eduardo Lucero** *(7378 Beverly Blvd., Los Angeles, 323-933-2778)* doles out his body-conscious fashions to celebs like Jennifer Lopez. And British designer **Andrew Dibben** *(1618 Silver Lake Blvd., Silver Lake, 323-662-9189)* is pushing the vanguard east with his new boutique and workshop selling his cutting-edge sportswear in Silver Lake.

LINGERIE AND BEYOND

Frederick's of Hollywood *(6608 Hollywood Blvd., Hollywood, 323-466-8506)* was the world's first lingerie department store, and a motley crew of Japanese teenyboppers, lovesick twentysomethings, cornfed midwesterners, and burly transvestites converge here to find the perfect fuck-me pumps, push-up bras, and naughty negligees. If you need to nip and tuck a few unsightly bulges, corsets, and girdles are also available. Don't forget to soak up the history of restrictive undergarments in the Lingerie Museum in the back room. Further down Hollywood Boulevard is **Playmates** *(6438 Hollywood Blvd., Hollywood, 323-464-7636)*. Gwen Stefani and Courtney Love have both unleashed their inner harlot here. Pasties, seamy stockings, feather boas, garter belts, and crotchless panties — it's a one-stop shop for any erotic emergency. Head to the Sunset Strip to Larry Flynt's sex emporium **Hustler Hollywood** *(8920 Sunset Blvd., West Hollywood, 310-860-9009)*. Don't be disappointed at the lack of blackened windows and shuttered door: Hustler Hollywood is more of a Barnes & Noble-style sex shop, with supermarket-style aisles filled with hard-core videos, magazines, and a small selection of naughty lingerie. For those whose tastes run to the wilder side, **Dream Dresser** *(8444 Santa Monica Blvd., West Hollywood, 323-848-3480)* offers all the accoutrements for the fetish lifestyle, with harnesses, collars, and latex fashions. Owned and operated by two women, the **Pleasure Chest** (*7733 Santa Monica Blvd., West Hollywood, 323-650-1022*) is the preeminent sex-toy shop in town. The clerks won't bat an eye as you compare and contrast dildos and inflatable dolls. To clothe your most secret desires, you'll also find a small selection of leather and latex garments. Behind closed doors in the heart of an Orthodox Jewish neighborhood lies the self-proclaimed leader of latex rubber couture, **Syren** (*7225 Beverly Blvd., Los Angeles, 323-936-6693*). Besides catering to the local fetish community, the small storefront operation makes costumes for the film industry, like the full-body rubber suit for *Batman*. Drag queens should take note of the **Jim Bridges Boutique** (*12457 Ventura Blvd. #103, Studio City, 818-761-6650*), which specializes in full-blown transformations with clothing, makeup, wigs, corsets, and shoes, and **Lydia's TV Fashions** (*13837 Ventura Blvd., Sherman Oaks, 818-995-7195*), which also carries clothes, shoes, and undergarments for the girl with something extra.

MALLS

To some, the mall is the definition of pure hell, a virtual shopping prison. The same stores pop up again and again at these oversized cement boxes — Gap, Banana Republic, Contempo Casuals, Rampage, Ann Taylor, Express, the Limited, Victoria's Secret, Guess?. Most LA malls also have multiplexes and a fast-food court, as well as a handful of fine dining establishments. The hulking gray monolith known as the **Beverly Center** *(8500 Beverly Blvd., Los Angeles, 310-854-3432)* is the mall most loved by the well-heeled Westside crowd. This trendy shopping center is home to Bloomingdale's and Macy's, as well as Betsey Johnson, Club Monaco, and M.A.C. Cosmetics. If you can't bear the grub at the food court, there's the Hard Rock Café and Nobu Matsuhisa's Ubon on the street level. The open-air setting of the **Century City Shopping Center** *(10250 Santa Monica Blvd., Century City, 310-277-3898)* takes advantage of LA's year-round mild weather. Built on a former studio backlot of Twentieth Century Fox, this fancy-schmancy mall has a Crate & Barrel, a gourmet supermarket, and a bookstore where Monica Lewinsky signed her autobiography, as well as the usual chain outlets. Popular with the office-worker lunch crowd, Century City's impressive indoor-outdoor food court also houses the only LA outpost of New York's Stage Deli. Among the predictable crop of chain stores ensconced at the **Westside Pavilion** *(10800 Pico Blvd., West LA, 310-274-6255)* are BCBG and an art house multiplex. Designed by Frank Gehry, **Santa Monica Place** *(395 Santa Monica Pl., Santa Monica, 310-394-5451)* is the fave mall of the bratty overgrown cast of *Beverly Hills, 90210*. The usual stores hold court here, but it's worth stopping by if you need a quick shopping fix after visiting the Santa Monica Pier, which is just a block away. The grand dame of all Southern California malls is **South Coast Plaza** *(3333 Bristol St., Costa Mesa, 714-435-2000)*, also known as Rodeo Drive South. Some shopping-crazed Japanese tourists even make this mall their sole vacation destination. Not surprisingly, South Coast Plaza is the most profitable mall in the United States, with nine department stores that span the economic spectrum, from Barneys and Saks to Macy's and Sears. There are also a slew of big-time designer boutiques, including Gucci, Versace, Christian Dior, Ralph Lauren, Chanel, Calvin Klein, Tiffany, Hèrmes, Fendi, Armani, Cartier,

Prada, and Salvatore Ferragamo. Other highlights include the vast expanse of toys in FAO Schwarz, competing chocolate shops Ghiradelli and Godiva, restaurants like the Rainforest Café, and the celebrity-owned (Kevin Costner, Robert Wagner), golf-themed Clubhouse. There are also dueling day spas and an outpost of the Orange County Museum of Art. Just a few blocks from South Coast Plaza is perhaps the most disturbing mall of all: the **Anti-Mall** *(2930 Bristol St., Costa Mesa, 714-966-6660)*. Co-opting the rebel aesthetic to the nth degree is, according to its press release, this "iconoclast village of goods and consumables that feed the mind and the gut." Here you can purchase your rebel aesthetic at flagship stores Urban Outfitters and Tower Alternative. You can also chow down on countercultural home cooking at the The Gypsy Den, get your locks lopped off at the Crew Salon, relive Castro-era Cuba at the Habana Restaurant and Bar, try on Doc Martens and Creepers at Na Na, get vintage ephemera at Decor Delux and Stateside, and buy skatewear at Empire Sports. Like, fight the power, dude.

MELROSE STREETWEAR

Melrose Avenue between Fairfax and La Brea has long served young Angelenos as a youth axis with its never-ending selection of clubwear, used records, and kitschy novelties. For hip-hop streetwear with a tinge of disco, **Workmens** *(7280 and 7562 Melrose Ave., Hollywood, 323-933-2440)* leads the way on Melrose with a phat selection of oversized clothes that could outfit you and a friend in the same pair of pants. **No Problem** *(7601 Melrose Ave., Hollywood, 323-655-4740)* carries streetwear standbys Diesel and Suburban at reasonable prices. New York-based designer **Daryl K.** *(8125 Melrose Ave., West Hollywood, 323-651-2251)* has a storefront farther west on Melrose that shows off her hipster pants, comfortable nylon threads, and sensible, smart footwear. Finally, you'll always know what you're getting at **Urban Outfitters** *(7650*

Melrose Ave., Hollywood, 323-653-3231; see main entry) from household tchotchkes to grungy sweaters and industrial work shirts at prices that would make a true proletarian laugh.

RODEO DRIVE

Beverly Hills is home to the most exclusive row of shops in the world on the three blocks of Rodeo Drive between Wilshire and Santa Monica. If you can't afford the wares at shops like **Tiffany** *(210 N. Rodeo Dr., Beverly Hills, 310-273-8880)* and **Prada** *(343 N. Rodeo Dr., Beverly Hills, 310-385-5959)*, no one will sniff if you window-shop wistfully. Wealthy locals with money to burn descend from the hills to prowl these shops for luxury goods, dropping thousands without a second thought. Many of the stores require an appointment before you are allowed to even set foot in their hallowed halls. At **Bijan** *(420 N. Rodeo Dr., Beverly Hills, 310-273-6544)*, reputed to be the most expensive store in the world, the average shopper spends $100,000 in a single visit, and the cheapest item is a $50 pair of socks. An international array of designers have their Los Angeles stores on this gilded row, like **Armani** *(436 N. Rodeo Dr., Beverly Hills, 310-271-5555)* and its boutique counterpart, **Gucci** *(347 N. Rodeo Dr., Beverly Hills, 310-278-3451)*, **Christian Dior** *(230 N. Rodeo Dr., Beverly Hills, 310-859-4700)*, **Chanel** *(400 N. Rodeo Dr., Beverly Hills, 310-278-5500)*, **Louis Vuitton** *(295 N. Rodeo Dr., Beverly Hills, 310-859-0457)*, **Ralph Lauren** *(444 N. Rodeo Dr., Beverly Hills, 310-281-1500)*, and **Valentino** *(240 N. Rodeo Dr., Beverly Hills, 310-247-0103)*. The cobblestoned, curving thoroughfare dubbed Via Rodeo is really an outdoor shopping mall, with anchor tenants like Tiffany and **Cartier** *(220 N. Rodeo Dr., Beverly Hills, 310-275-5155)*. (Unfortunately, misguided tourists are now mistaking this Tinseltown creation as the real Rodeo Drive, posing for pictures at the bottom of the stairway.) McCormick and Schmick's on Via Rodeo is a good stop for the financially challenged;

its happy hour reigns supreme with Barneys salesgirls and industry assistants scarfing down $1.95 cheeseburgers, calamari, and bruschetta snacks with their after-work cocktails. Another cost-cutting secret is the free parking underneath Via Rodeo. Serious spenders also flock to the three swank department stores at the foot of Rodeo Drive. **Barneys New York's** *(9570 Wilshire Blvd, Beverly Hills, 310-276-4400)* only Los Angeles-area retail store is the hippest of the Beverly Hills department stores, offering the ultimate in deluxe glamour. The most up-to-the-minute fashions are for sale here, with collections from Vivienne Westwood, Dolce & Gabbana, and Calvin Klein. For a cheaper dose of glamour, stick to the first floor, where you'll find exclusive cosmetic lines like Nars, Poppy, and the retro-hip Body & Soul. **Neiman Marcus** *(9700 Wilshire Blvd., Beverly Hills, 310-550-5900)* is the old stalwart of the three, with high-end fashions from Versace, Chanel, and Armani, among others. Take a tip from the older set, who come out in droves for legendary end-of-season sales, with prices slashed up to 80 percent. **Saks Fifth Avenue** *(9600 and 9634 Wilshire Blvd., Beverly Hills, 310-275-4211)* is so massive that it's taken up residence in two buildings on this elegant stretch of Wilshire Boulevard. At Saks you'll find more designer clothing to please those with deep pockets, and an especially good collection of men's wear.

SCREW RETAIL

There are some who think that the more you pay for something, the better it is. And then there are the rest of us, who would rather die than pay retail. To really cop on to the thrill of the hunt, head to the Garment District, and come armed with cash, because many of these discount shops don't take credit cards. The core of this fashion district is the **California Mart** *(110 E. 9th St., Downtown, 213-630-3600)*. Normally closed to consumers, designers clean out their showrooms on the last Friday of each month at informal sample sales. Most of the sizes are 8 and under, but some believe the samples are better made than the mass-produced product. Five times a year there are Super Sale Saturdays, when the California Mart opens its huge exhibition hall to the public and manufacturers sell well below retail prices. **The Alley** *(alley between Santee St. and Maple Ave., from Olympic Blvd. to 12th St.)*, offers flea-market prices on new and trendy clothing, with some great shoe stores and leather shops, priced at 20 to 50 percent off retail prices. **The Cooper Building** *(860 S. Los Angeles St., Downtown, 213-622-1139)* was the first-ever factory outlet mall, with four floors of outlet stores, including Bloomingdale's, Rampage, and Guess?. Other deals on designer goods can be found in the stores on Los Angeles Street between 7th and 9th Streets. Garnering its stock from manufacturer overruns and unsold merchandise, **Loehmann's** *(333 S. La Cienega Blvd., Los Angeles, 310-659-0674)* sells off-price brand name merchandise for 30 to 65 percent below retail. The best deals are found in the back room, where top designers like Nicole Miller, Donna Karan, Ralph Lauren, and Jones New York are represented. If your life is not complete without a trip to an outlet mall, the **Citadel** *(5675 E. Telegraph Rd., Commerce, 323-?8-1220)* is just a few minutes ...heast of downtown LA in the ...Commerce, ...u can max out ...t card at ...3CBG, Betsey ...Old Navy, Joan & ...nd Esprit.

STREETWEAR ON LA BREA

The selection of streetwear found on La Brea has emerged as a bit more upscale and civilized than that found on Melrose. At **Union** *(110 S. La Brea Ave., Los Angeles, 323-549-6950)*, there's a terrific range of hip-hop tops for boys that'll entice even the more conservative dresser. **Stüssy** *(112 S. La Brea Ave., Los Angeles, 323-937-6077)* and **Suburban** *(126 S. La Brea Ave., Los Angeles, 323-933-1779)* have long been staples for street and clubwear; their storefronts here are sleek enough to warrant the considerable markup in price. Hoping to capitalize on hipster traffic, **Lucky Brand Dungarees** *(120 S. La Brea Ave., Los Angeles, 323-933-0722)* has also set up shop in this area.

While their naughtily cute ad campaigns can irritate even the most impervious consumer, they've found their niche with comfy, durable jeans. Finally, kudos to young designers Adriano Goldschmied and Patty Shelabarger of **8B** *(813 N. La Brea Ave., Hollywood, 323-935-6369)* for courageously opening a showroom in this high-rent area. Their lively, but not loud, fashions convey a lush quality that's a welcome shift from the muted sameness that's come to dominate much of the boutique scene.

VINTAGE THREADS

If you'd rather be caught dead than wear the same outfit as your arch nemesis, hightail it over to Los Angeles's coolest vintage shops for one-of-a-kind, knock 'em dead retro finery. Juliette Lewis, Kim Gordon, and Thurston Moore have all pawed through the racks at **Jet Rag** *(825 N. La Brea Ave., Hollywood, 323-939-0528)*, also a vintage emporium of choice for the struggling indie-rock set. Prices are cheap and the selection stretches over two floors, with an ample supply of leather jackets, '70s iron-on T-shirts, and '50s housedresses. On Thursdays and Sundays, the back room is home to Jet Rag's infamous $1 sale, where shoppers wade through knee-high piles of retro rags to find the perfect new outfit. **Aardvark's** *(7579 Melrose Ave., Hollywood, 323-655-6769; call for other locations)* has trained more than one budding hipster in the art of dressing vintage. Anchored on Melrose since the days before the strip was cool, Aardvark's has a huge selection of used Levi's, feather boas, gas-station attendant shirts, and beaded sweaters. You will have to look hard, since this old stalwart's selection has been picked over by the Melrose hordes. **Golyester** *(136 S. La Brea Ave., Los Angeles, 323-931-1339)* sells mint-condition cotton and rayon dresses worn by the everywoman from the '30s, '40s, and '50s and stocks enough cashmere sweaters, Bakelite jewelry, and killer pumps to satisfy even the most discerning vintage clothes hound. The pieces here are priced dearly, but every one of them's a gem — you won't find any stains or ripped seams on these clothes. If you have deep pockets and can stand the snotty staff at **Lily et Cie** *(9044 Burton Way, Beverly Hills, 310-724-5757)*, you'll go crazy over its luxe high-end fashions, including vintage haute couture pieces by Dior, Galanos, Poiret, Balenciaga, and Chanel. Slaves to style like Demi Moore, Winona Ryder, and Karl Lagerfeld all shop here regularly. Hunt hard and you'll find a handful of blouses and skirts under $100. The Hollywood and high-fashion elite also shop at **Paper Bag Princess** *(8700 Santa Monica Blvd., West Hollywood, 310-358-1985)*, whose owner, Elizabeth Mason, scours flea markets, thrift shops, and estate sales for vintage Pucci, Halston, Missoni, Diane Von Furstenberg, Pucci, and Gucci. The '60s and the '70s are the best-represented decades at this expensive shop. Men can also do well here, finding pieces by Lily Pulitzer, Don Loper, and Lily Dache. Across the street from vintage mainstay Polka Dots and Moonbeams, **Julian's** *(8366 3rd St., Los Angeles, 323-655-3011)* crams '40s, '50s, and '60s clothing and knickknacks into its small storefront space. The Russian owner of **Good Old Times** *(7739 Santa Monica Blvd., West Hollywood, 323-654-7103)* will follow you from room to room turning off lights while you rifle through this low-priced, hardly-touched mother lode of leather jackets, Hawaiian shirts, evening dresses, bowling shirts, and blouses. After hitting the tourist mecca that is the Venice Boardwalk, you can get your vintage fix at **Gotta Have It** *(1516 Pacific Ave., Venice, 310-392-5949)*, a consignment shop packed with a mismatched collection of coats, dresses, jackets, and plenty of stuff for guys, too. On the red-hot Eastside of town, hit **Ozzie Dots** *(4637 Hollywood Blvd., Los Feliz, 323-663-2867)*, which sells a fine crop of vintage duds in addition to its year-round selection of costumes, all at rock-bottom prices. The owners will help you complete your look with

shopping

their selection of fake hypodermic needles, stinky perfume, and glitter eyelashes. If you're broke but still want to update your wardrobe, at the small shop **Squaresville** *(1800 Vermont Ave., Los Feliz, 323-669-8464)*, you can get 40 percent cash and 60 percent trade-in for your tired threads. The selection is small, but good finds abound and are priced reasonably. **Pull My Daisy** *(3908 Sunset Blvd., Silver Lake, 323-663-0608)*, perched on what is fast becoming Silver Lake's main drag, stocks low-priced tchotchkes and small furnishings alongside its vintage finery.

glamour and grunge

BLACK WAVE TATTOO
118 S. La Brea Ave. bet. Beverly Blvd. and 3rd St., Los Angeles, 323-932-1900; Hours: Mon-Sat 11am-10pm; Sun 12pm-8pm

Leo Zulueta brought tribal tattooing to the States several years ago and continues to be regarded as the dean of the movement. He and his protégé Rory Keating design elaborate tribal tattoos, but they do custom work as well. If you're looking for something a little less permanent, the in-house artists can design a temporary henna or mendi tattoo for you. For the best experience, schedule an appointment at this $100-an-hour salon, which will soon also offer piercing.

HOUSE OF FREAKS
7353 Melrose Ave. at Fuller Ave., Hollywood, 323-655-1922, www.houseoffreaks.com; daily 1pm-8pm

Don't just stroll into McPiercings, slap down a ten, and let someone thrust a metal spear through the surface of your skin. Luckily, you can trust the intrepid gang at House of Freaks to provide you with a relaxed and easy — though not painless — body piercing experience. This hot spot for rockers and celebs has been in the piercing biz for five years now; whether your thing is a pierced septum (nose), tragus (inner cartilage of ear), or frenum (don't ask), House of Freaks can do the deed for you. Schedule an appointment to avoid a wait; prices start in the $20 range.

shopping | 145

VALERIE *460 N. Canon Drive at Little Santa Monica Blvd., Beverly Hills, 310-274-7348; Hours: Mon–Sat 10am–6pm*

When it comes to facial transformation, few can rival Valerie Sarnelle and her cosmetic boutique in the heart of the Beverly Hills retail district. From her bronzing fairy dusts that come in countless neutral tints to Lips Galore, her inexhaustible line of lip formulas, Valerie can glam up even the most fastidious fashion plate. The boutique's direct line has earned speed dial-status from a lineup of Hollywood starlets that includes Nicole Kidman, Charlize Theron, Halle Berry, Heather Locklear, and Tori Spelling, among countless others; Valerie herself is featured frequently as the role of savior on E!'s *Fashion Emergency*. Despite its celebrity reputation, with its friendly and instructive staff, Valerie's storefront is not an intimidating place to visit.

glamour and grunge

BEAUTY SCHOOL DROPOUT

For many Angelenos, stocking up on beauty supplies is almost as important as buying groceries. Inside boutique superstore Fred Segal, **Apothia** *(8100 Melrose Ave., West Hollywood, 323-651-0239)* carries a host of high-end products, ranging from Kiehl's lotions to Thymes Limited's home fragrance mist. You can help yourself to a tester of virtually every product and, in effect, come out of the store smelling like a human perfume bottle. The **Larchmont Beauty Center** *(208 N. Larchmont Blvd., Larchmont, 323-461-0162)* carries everything from aromatherapy to serious hair-care products. Once inside, you could spend an entire day drifting from the makeup artist to the colorist to the in-house masseuse. A cousin of the Larchmont store, the **Beverly Hills Beauty Center** *(350 N. Beverly Dr., Beverly Hills, 310-278-8815)* is packed to the rafters with all the necessary supplies, including (in one genre) lip crayons, lip balm, lip definers, lip gloss, lip glaze, and, that traditional favorite, lipstick.

BROWS AND NAILS

Eyebrow stylist to the stars **Anastasia** *(438 N. Bedford Dr., Beverly Hills, 310-273-3155)* has a five-month waiting list for the eponymous owner of the shop. Fortunately, Anastasia employs five assistants, any one of which will be happy to pluck you for $25. Inside hair salon Menage a Trois is **Pigments** *(8822 Burton Way, Beverly Hills, 310-858-7038)*, where Karen's precision with tweezers and a makeup brush has earned her a loyal following. Industry gals convene at **Lanny Nails** *(8300 3rd St., Los Angeles, 323-653-3370)*, where a team of Vietnamese women works on your hands and feet simultaneously. It's a steal: $14 for all 20 digits. At **Contempo Nails** *(333 S. Robertson Blvd., Beverly Hills, 310-855-8879)*, you'll rarely have to wait; Diane and her staff

shopping | 147

will get you in and out faster than you can slip off a mule. You can also get both neck and foot massages while your manicurist is at work, though these extra-manicurial services will cost you.

HAIR TODAY

Probably best known for Gwyneth Paltrow's short snip during her *Shakespeare In Love* period, **Privé Salon** *(8458 Melrose Pl., West Hollywood, 323-651-5045)* is the home of Eduardo Laurent and his long-standing reputation as the best stylist in town. While Laurent and his staff will make house calls to notable celebrities, the rest of us can book an appointment for an in-store visit at their digs on the quaint antique row of Melrose Place. If you're truly lucky, the staff will let you sit in Laurent's leopard skin chair. In Beverly Hills, Umberto holds rank as a veritable dean in the stylist community. One of the best-kept secrets, however, is **U** *(343 N. Camden Dr., Beverly Hills, 310-858-1178)*, where Umberto's stable of trainees will cut and blow-dry your hair for considerably reduced prices. The only caveat is that U will take appointments only one day in advance. For color, extensions, dreadlocks, or just your basic $40 men's cut, call Natalie Lynn or any of the gang at **Purple Circle** (1724 N. Vermont Ave., Los Feliz, 323-666-2965) for an appointment at this funkadelic hair salon that keeps its barber chairs filled morning, noon, and night. **Clark Nova** (8118 3rd St., Los Angeles, 323-655-1100) boasts the coolest interior, with old-style maroon barber chairs and sleek wood vanities over a polished concrete floor. Eusebio's work is impeccable — as are his twin English bulldogs, who will entertain you while you get your trim. At the Standard Hotel, **Rudy's Barbershop** (8300 Sunset Blvd., West Hollywood, 323-650-5669) offers $19 men's short cuts and a praiseworthy wall full of candy. Better yet, guys with unmanageable hair will applaud Rudy's for carrying Murray's pomade, that popular gunk that'll keep your hair in place for at least a month or two. For a real old-school experience, guys should take to **The Barber Shop Club** (6907 Melrose Ave., Hollywood, 323-939-4319), a throwback to the days when you could actually get a shave with your haircut while blues crackled from an old radio. On Thursday nights, the club hosts its Open Mic Night, with live music, poetry readings, and cigars.

SPA DAY

An afternoon at **Frederic Fekkai** (440 N. Rodeo Dr., Beverly Hills, 310-777-8700) mimics an escape to the Continent. Fekkai, whose work can be seen most prominently on Milan runways, has set a new standard for day spas in Los Angeles. The buttery walls and Tuscan decor give way to a procession of pampering services, including massages, facials, and full consultations. **Burke Williams** (8000 Sunset Blvd., West Hollywood, 323-822-9007) has been a day spa mainstay for several years. Star sightings in the whirlpool room and sauna are a favorite pastime of the clientele. The Detox-Calming Wrap is a favorite of stressed development execs who frequent the spa.

outfitting your pad

BLUEPRINT *8366 Beverly Blvd. bet. La Cienega and Crescent Heights Blvds., Los Angeles, 323-653-2439; Hours: Mon-Fri 10am-7pm; Sat 10am-6pm; Sun 12pm-5pm*
Much of the merchandise in this cavernous space parallels the contemporary styles at the more upmarket boutiques down the street, yet for functionality and reasonable prices, Blueprint can't be beat. A sleek bed of light cherry wood will run you less than $500; a retro-style chrome and Formica dining table with cool vinyl chairs won't clean you out, either, and will give your eating nook that diner look. Don't forget to go upstairs to check out the real bargains — full desks and workstations for a song. For those with dexterity issues (or busy schedules), Blueprint will send their guys to your house for full-service delivery and assembly, also reasonably priced.

ILAN DEI STUDIOS *1227 Abbot Kinney Way bet. Brooks and California Aves., Venice, 310-450-0999; Hours: Mon-Fri 9pm-5pm; Sat-Sun 12pm-6pm*
Ilan Dei recently opened this retail showroom "where lush minimalism and controlled anarchy meet," according to this Israeli designer, who began as a woodworking apprentice. Dei takes basic industrial materials and imbues them with contemporary flair; check out his Lizi Bed with its shapely, smooth headboard or the softer credenza with its curved edges and glass top. Dei also sells dozens of his affordable, contemporary accessories as original gifts, such as his popu-

lar lotus vase or whimsical Pandora's Box, a simple, elegant wood cylinder with an etched aluminum lid. It's no wonder that firms ranging from ICM to Oliver Peoples have hired Dei to design their spaces.

IN HOUSE *7370 Beverly Blvd. bet. Fairfax and La Brea Aves., Los Angeles, 323-931-4420; Hours: Mon-Fri 11:30am-5pm; Sat 11am-6pm*
At In House, you'll find the most comfortable and innovative furniture in town. Owners Mark Zuckerman and Monty Lawton's corian Circle 3 magazine table has found its way to the Baltimore Museum of Art as a revolutionary example of design blended with function. Each of the pieces, particularly the orderly couches and funky coffee tables, convey a sense of fragility without letting you forget that they are meant to be sat in and used. Though few can afford to outfit an entire house with this stuff, if you're looking for one pivotal showpiece, you can't do much better than a Tug Boat chair in a sensual crepe or a sleek Milky Way coffee table.

POSTOBELLO *7270 Beverly Blvd. bet. Fairfax and La Brea Aves., Los Angeles, 323-931-1899; Hours: Mon-Sat 11am-5pm*
Had enough cold, contemporary minimalism? You'll find Postobello a welcome haven. Unlike the mid-century modern showrooms down the street where a 1,000-square-foot floor displays all of eight pieces, Postobello packs dozens of armoires, chairs, and tables into its small store. The Tuscan-inspired furniture embodies a timeliness and versatility that would be equally suited to a Spanish hacienda in Larchmont or a brick-exposed Downtown loft. A gorgeous sleigh bed epitomizes the rich deep woods at work on this elegant yet warm design floor. If you decide to go with one of the smooth leather chairs, you may never leave the confines of your living room again.

ROSE BOWL FLEA MARKET

1001 Rose Bowl Dr., Pasadena, 323-560-7469; Hours: Second Sun of each month 9am-4:30pm

Before there was eBay, there were living, breathing swap meets. In that spirit, $6 grants you admission to one of the greatest spectacles of Americana around. Twenty thousand people stop by this flea market on the second Sunday of each month, the only time it's held. The layout can be overwhelming, as there's no way to see everything on one outing. Your best bet is to adopt one of two strategies: Resign yourself to browsing or limit yourself to a particular genre (such as antique skateboards or vintage lunch boxes) and doggedly pursue that one perfect item. Once you have a handle on things, trudging through the aisles becomes simultaneously exhilarating and exhausting. Just remember that folks can get pretty intense at a flea market, so maintain a level head when you start elbowing someone out of a Captain & Tenille LP.

SHABBY CHIC

1013 Montana Ave. bet. 10th and 11th Sts., Santa Monica, 310-394-1975; Hours: Mon-Sat 10am-6pm; Sun 12pm-5pm

If a Malibu beach house eloped with Victorian England, the offspring would be Shabby Chic, a store that has done more to define Santa Monica's relaxed, serene aesthetic than anyplace else. U.K. native Rachel Ashwell launched her business by rescuing old, damaged furniture and restoring it into pieces whose flaws — a dresser with a foggy mirror, for example — could be used to their advantage. For accompaniments such as slipcovers, linens, and various fabrics, Shabby Chic is a sensible place to start, particularly if your abode is more cozy than contemporary.

SHELTER

7920 Beverly Blvd. bet. Crescent Heights Blvd. and Fairfax Ave., Los Angeles, 323-937-3222; Hours: Mon-Sat 11am-7pm; Sun 12pm-5pm

Objets d'art abound at this boutique, whose simple, decorative items such as candleholders and sheep's-wool throw cushions blend the contemporary zeitgeist with the homey. The full deco-tinged pieces — particularly the clean leather sofas — will have you dreaming of your soon-to-be-built Neutra ripoff in the hills. And once you start handling the funky Kazak-sewn bed linens, it's impossible not to spin out of control. So do the sensible thing: Proceed to the design book table in the center of the store and buy one of the many volumes on modern design. It's a lot cheaper than overhauling your entire home in one spree.

SONRISA *7609 Beverly Blvd. bet. Fairfax and La Brea Aves., Los Angeles, 323-935-8438; Hours: Mon-Sat 11am-6pm*

Are you a storage fiend? This showroom celebrates mid-century steel-age functional simplicity. Take a close look at the basket lockers or standing laboratory medicine cabinets as stylish alternatives to a generic Ikea-born container. You'll know the spartan desks when you see them; it's that aluminum tanker of a desk that your homeroom teacher sat behind. If you don't care for the classic steel finish, Sonrisa can add a cool coat of sea-green to give your selections a bit of vitality. Though some of the items may seem dreadfully institutional, remember that icy steel is becoming cool again.

shopping | 153

outfitting your pad

CHAIN STORES

The number of housewares and furniture stores has exploded over the past decade as more Americans begin to pay closer attention to the decorative state of their abodes. Even the most unsuspecting slobs among us have been inspired to give their homes a more tasteful look. The Scandinavian lord of popular design, **Ikea** *(600 N. San Fernando Blvd., Burbank, 818-842-4532; call for other locations)*, can take some credit for the movement. Here, under one roof, you'll find all the necessities of home, from sleek light fixtures to affordable furniture, much of it in a smart, minimal style. Although the aesthetic can be a bit insipid, **Crate & Barrel** *(10250 Santa Monica Blvd., West LA, 310-551-1100; 75 W. Colorado Blvd., Pasadena, 626-683-8000)* is important to check for good-quality housewares that are versatile. The buyers at **Pottery Barn** *(Beverly Center, 131 N. La Cienega Blvd., Los Angeles, 310-360-1301; 10250 Santa Monica Blvd., West LA, 310-552-0170; call for other locations)* also do a conscientious job of keeping their merchandise fresh, particularly dinnerware and flatware. **Pier One Imports** *(3000 Wilshire Blvd., Santa Monica, 310-453-1559; call for other locations)* was doing home accessories long before Martha Stewart became an arbiter of household taste; for candleholders and the like, you could do a lot worse than one of their countless locations around town. Finally, don't turn your nose up at **Target** *(10820 Jefferson Blvd., Culver City, 310-839-5200; call for other locations)*. They've updated — and upgraded — their merchandise, particularly in the cookware section. Dare we say that their exclusive line of Michael Graves-designed items, such as teapots, papertowel holders, and salt and pepper shakers, are downright funky?

shopping

MID-CENTURY MODERN

Charles and Ray Eames are alive and well at **Modernica** *(7366 Beverly Blvd., Los Angeles, 323-933-0383)*, where clean postwar furnishings sit on the concrete showroom floor. The Herman Miller-designed Eames prototypes are surprisingly well priced. Besides, where else can you find a white vinyl couch made to order? If you're looking for bargains, check out Modernica's vintage storefront two doors west of the main store. Even though Jeffrey Perry has moved his **Futurama** *(446 N. La Brea Ave., Los Angeles, 323-937-4522)* showroom from Beverly Boulevard to La Brea's emerging design row, he has maintained his mission of offering both mid-century and custom furnishings that are both reasonable and, in the case of his genie coffee table, unique. Because of the quick turnover in inventory (Perry has a knack for finding items that buyers snatch up), you should visit on a regular basis to find the perfect item. **Johnny B. Wood** *(1409 Abbot Kinney Way, Venice, 310-314-1945)* resells mid-century furnishings, with particular attention to Scandinavian masters such as Eero Saarinen and Danish architect and chair maven Arne Jacobsen. A classically Venice hybrid, **Empire Snowboards** *(1639 Abbot Kinney Way, Venice, 310-450-4114)* is half board 'n' skate joint, half vintage furniture showroom. A visit here can yield a dining set and a matching snowboard.

ORIENTAL

If you'd like your home to look like a Southeast Asian colonial hotel, stop by **Not So Far East** *(160 S. La Brea Ave., Los Angeles, 323-933-8900)* for sensual wood furniture from the Pacific Rim. In addition to full bedroom sets on the main floor and armoires and large pieces upstairs, the store carries some stylishly sleek dinnerware with strong Asian accents. **Espiritu de Vida** *(5913 Franklin Ave., Hollywood, 323-463-0281)* specializes in home accessories and Buddha gear. Check out the delicate wall posters of Asian cigarette ads featuring robed beauties; teapots, sake sets, and statuettes also grace the cluttered store. Beautiful mosaic tables can be found at **Further** *(4312 Sunset Blvd., Silver Lake, 323-660-3601)*, along with rich Indonesian furniture and an assortment of accessories such as incense holders. Finally, the tastefully designed floor displays at **Chestnuts and Papaya** *(459 1/2 S. La Brea Ave., Los Angeles, 323-937-8450)* are sure to have you thinking East. With a touch of New York style and a worldly sensibility, Chestnuts is every Angeleno's Oriental dream.

POSTER HEAVEN

Any self-respecting Angeleno drawn to the city's cinematic history must display the obligatory movie poster. For sheer aesthetics, the **Jason Vass Gallery** *(1210 Montana Ave., Santa Monica, 310-395-2048)* has an impeccable collection of imported European posters from early-century cinema and advertisements, the Belle Epoque movement, and cultural events like the Louis Vuitton Expo. On the grungier side, **Back Lot** *(7278 Sunset Blvd., Hollywood, 323-876-6070)* is open only on Saturdays in a hard-to-find shack in an alley south of Sunset. The collection's owner will help you find whatever you're looking for in the cluttered yet inexhaustible collection of old posters, lobby cards, and glossy stills.

housewares and gifts

DAISY ARTS *1312 Abbot Kinney Way bet. Brooks and California Aves., Venice, 310-396-8463; Hours: Mon-Fri 9am-5pm*
For the mature gift — you know, when a Wonder Woman Pez dispenser or an Austin Powers action figure just won't do — nothing beats a timeless journal or photo album. Daisy Arts specializes in Italian leather-bound items, from calendars to diaries and beyond. On a funkier note, Day Glo felt handbags and packs from Italian-Japanese designers MH Way are sleek yet understated.

ILLUME *8302 3rd St. bet. La Cienega and Crescent Heights Blvds., Los Angeles, 323-782-0342; Hours: Mon-Sat 11am-6pm; Sun 12pm-5pm*
The moment you walk through the door at Illume, you'll be hit with the scents of over a thousand candles. Once you regain your senses, you'll have a difficult time choosing a single shape, size, or fragrance at this comprehensive emporium.

OZZIE & MOOSY *5439 6th St. nr. La Brea Ave., Los Angeles, 323-938-8886; Hours: Mon-Sat 10am-6pm*
Looking for a perfect gift for your little nephew? Friends of yours having a first-born? With professional backgrounds in child development, the owners of Ozzie & Moosy clearly care about kids, which is exactly what you'd want from a toy store. This pedantic mission is accomplished, however, with style, color, and panache. The store offers such necessities as jumbo toy chests and laundry baskets in natural fiber weaves and an adorable line of alpaca teddy bears. Hey, who says this stuff is just for kids?

SOOLIP *8646 Melrose Ave. bet. San Vicente and La Cienega Blvds., West Hollywood, 310-360-0545; Hours: Mon-Sat 11am-7pm; Sun 12pm-5pm*

shopping

Stop by Soolip's printing press in early fall to draw up your custom Christmas cards or, at the very least, choose some funky stationery. The prices tend toward the extravagant, but after taking one whiff of the scented ink, you'll be sold. Continue farther back past the main storefront to the small gallery space to check out works by local artists.

UNCLE JER'S *4459 Sunset Blvd. bet. Hillhurst and Fountain Aves., Los Feliz, 323-662-6710; Hours: Mon-Sat 11am-7pm; Sun 12pm-6pm*
You'll find far more than Buddha statuettes in Uncle Jer's selection of Asiana. In addition to the compulsory display of fragrant candles, Uncle Jer's sells saris, sumo-wrestler lunch boxes, and silk blouses with an Asian flair. And remember, as a sign posted under some South Asian knickknacks reads, "India is the new Santa Fe."

ZIPPER *8316 3rd St. bet. La Cienega and Crescent Heights Blvds., Los Angeles, 323-951-0620; Hours: Mon-Sat 11am-7pm; Sun 12pm-5pm*
Forget the registries at those department store mausoleums. Your newlywed friends (not to mention anyone else in your life with an occasion) will be far more grateful when they receive a gift of unparalleled spontaneity from Zipper. From kitsch such as Curious George housewares to haute mid-century design, Zipper has a wide range of stuff to fill your home from top to bottom.

housewares and gifts

KITSCH

Popular culture in America as we know it sprouted in Los Angeles. The Bradys' ranch spread, after all, is just over the hill in the San Fernando Valley, and motion pictures, television, car culture, and wrestling movies were all born in LA. That said, it'll come as no surprise that camp accessories, both past and present, are a major commodity in Los Angeles. Take **Soap Plant/Wacko** (*4633 Hollywood Blvd., Los Feliz, 323-663-0122*): Pop culture has never been displayed more comprehensively than it is at this huge storefront on the southern edge of Los Feliz. Kit-Cat wall clocks, Jackie O. magnets, inflatable loveseats, and books on virtually every important contribution to pop culture from Dr. Seuss to *Charlie's Angels* can be found here. That old-style wrestling mask can be picked up at **Y Que Trading Post** (*1770 Vermont Ave., Los Feliz, 323-664-0021*) along with Garbage Pail kids paraphernalia and flamingo string lights. On Melrose, **Off the Wall** (*7325 Melrose Ave., Hollywood, 323-930-1185*) operates more like a traditional antiques store, though its merchandise is anything but. Where else can you find a Spiro Agnew wall clock? **Ka-Boom** (*3816 Sunset Blvd., Silver Lake, 323-661-8697*) boasts one of the better antique Pez collections, as well as a line of lunch boxes and every piece of *E.T.* merchandise ever released. For a wide array of Elvis statuettes and an original Kentucky Fried Chicken ceramic bucket, go to **Chicken Little** (*1323 Abbot Kinney Way, Venice, 310-581-1676*). At **Firefly** (*1413 Abbot Kinney Way, Venice, 310-450-6288*), the quirky merchandise includes celebrity coasters, adorable sake sets, funky tops for women, and the indispensable "virgin/slut" soap kit.

foodstuffs

TRADER JOE'S *263 S. La Brea Ave. at 3rd St., Los Angeles, 323-965-1989; 7304 Santa Monica Blvd. bet. Fairfax and La Brea Aves., West Hollywood, 323-851-9782; 3212 Pico Blvd. at 32nd St., Santa Monica, 310-581-0253; call for other locations; Hours: daily 9am-9pm*
The mere mention of Trader Joe's among Angelenos elicits purring from grown adults. That's because Trader Joe's, with its several dozen locations, carries high-quality, innovative food at inexplicably low prices. Whether you're picking up one of their countless frozen delicacies — like spinach lasagna — that are custom-made for the store or scoring a respectable bottle of wine for a mere $7, Trader Joe's will have you fondling the groceries. Fresh pasta, dried fruit, fresh organic bread, natural fruit juices, and delicious cheeses are all regular items in these compact stores.

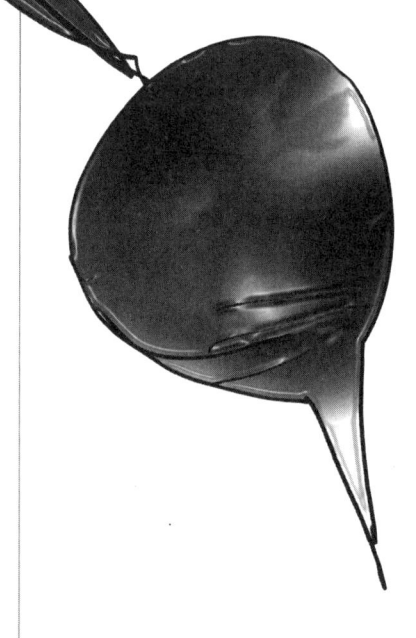

oodstuffs

ARMERS MARKETS

North of Los Angeles in California's Central Valley lies some of the most fruitful farmland in the world. Many small farmers travel into the city on a weekly basis to sell their homemade foods and produce to willing urbanites who are looking for a way to kill a weekend morning. For that hard-to-find fresh vegetable (okra or shitake mushrooms, anyone?), look no further than one of these bazaars.

The **Hollywood Farmers Market** takes over Ivar Street between Sunset and Hollywood each Sunday morning until about 1pm. Produce from all over the state is sold on Ivar, while prepared foods such as corn on the cob, tamales, and poultry sausages are on offer on Selma Avenue, the cross street. You'll find many of the same vendors on Saturdays at the **Santa Monica Farmers Market** on Arizona Avenue and 3rd Street. In addition, the **Beverly Hills Farmers Market** sets up shop on Canon Drive and Clifton Way on Sundays.

GOURMET FOOD

Cocktail and dinner parties, particularly in the hills, are common throughout the year as a pleasant nightlife alternative to fighting the traffic on Sunset while hopping from bar to restaurant to club. Sure, you're always safe bringing the customary bottle of wine, but to evoke true compliments on your originality, try something more creative. Few delicacies can match the succulence of **Al Gelato** *(860 S. Robertson Blvd., Beverly Hills, 310-659-8069)*. A couple of pints of their coffee crunch gelato and pear ice will earn you kudos from the entire party. For other creative dessert items, an honorable mention goes to the fruit tarts at **La Conversation** *(638 N. Doheny Dr., West Hollywood, 310-858-0950)*, rugelah from **Canter's** *(419 N. Fairfax Ave., Los Angeles, 323-651-2030)*, and anything and everything from the delectable **La Brea Bakery** *(624 S. La Brea Ave., Los Angeles, 323-939-6813)*. If hors

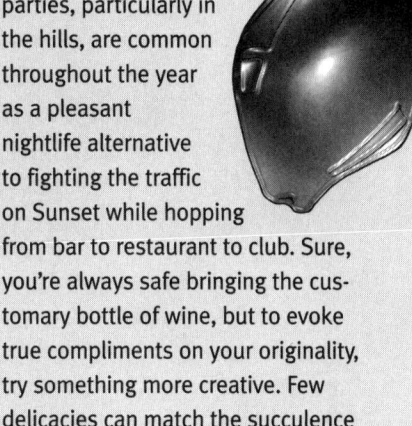

shopping

d'oeuvres are your assignment, fight the bustle to the deli counter at **Elat Market** *(8730 Pico Blvd., West LA, 310-659-0576)*, which prepares the best hummus in the city out of its kosher Sephardic kitchen. For an authentic Italian market, **Domingo's** *(17548 Ventura Blvd., Encino, 818-981-4466)* is worth the trip over the hill, whether you're looking for olives, cheeses, or Italian meats. Grilled vegetables from **Cuvee** *(145 S. Robertson Blvd., West Hollywood, 310-2714333)* will be a welcome addition to the spread among the health-conscious set. And there's only one place to go for the perfect baguette or country bread: the **Brentwood Bread Company** *(11640 San Vicente Blvd., Brentwood, 310-826-9400)*.

MARKETS

For the vegan and generally health-conscious, the aisles of **Erewhon's** *(7660 Beverly Blvd., Los Angeles, 323-937-0777)* are stocked with natural foods and holistically correct items such as herbs and vitamins. Slightly more appetizing for the ecumenical eater but still au naturel is **Wild Oats** *(1425 Montana Ave., Santa Monica, 310-576-4707; 8611 Santa Monica Blvd., West Hollywood, 310-854-6927)*, whose produce can match anyone's in town. For upscale supermarkets, **Gelson's** *(10250 Santa Monica Blvd., West LA, 310-277-4288; call for other locations)* continues to lead the pack with its combination of everyday staples and gourmet items. The prepared food counter will bail you out of last-minute dinner party preparations — and nobody will know it wasn't homemade. Smaller than Gelson's and a bit more expensive, but with a fiercely loyal clientele, **Bristol Farms** *(7880 Sunset Blvd., West Hollywood, 323-874-6301; call for other locations)* is another market not to be missed. On a good day, you can eat your way from aisle to aisle as you nosh on free samples. For a more interesting shopping excursion, try shopping at one of the countless ethnic supermarkets around the city. **H.K. Korean Supermarket** *(124 N. Western Ave., Koreatown, 323-469-8934)* has a mouthwatering array of prepared foods, such as kimchi, marinated anchovies, and soups, in addition to basic staples. **Elat Middle Eastern Market** *(8730 Pico Blvd., West LA, 310-659-7070)* is your best source for hummus, pita, flatbread, and Jewish delicacies. For the most authentic Los Angeles experience, head downtown to **Grand Central Market** *(317 S. Broadway, Downtown, 213-624-2378)* where an amalgam of cultures and languages meld in this culinary bazaar.

WINE AND ROSES

Wine may not flow here like it does up north, but Angelenos still appreciate a good bottle of cabernet when they see one. Finding what you're looking for is easy at **Epicurus** *(625 Montana Ave., Santa Monica, 310-395-1352)*, where, in addition to the friendly staff and descriptive recommendations, the shop hosts art shows from time to time. Purists trust Steve Wallace's **Wally's** *(2107 Westwood Blvd., Westwood, 310-475-0606)* to stock every significant wine on the market. Uncle Steve is more than willing to offer his opinion if you find yourself torn between a tannic merlot or a big Amarone. If you're a fan of single malts and Euro booze, **Du Vin** *(540 N. San Vicente Blvd., West Hollywood, 310-855-1161)* should pique your interest with its unusual and varied selection of wines and spirits, not to mention its charming cobblestone courtyard. As for flowers, **The Woods** *(11711 Gorham Ave., Brentwood, 310-826-0711)* has a spacious selection of blooms and gardening trinkets. Cute with a personable staff, **My Secret Garden** *(1865 N. Western Ave., Los Feliz, 323-469-1514)* serves the Eastside as a user-friendly neighborhood spot where you can pick up a few stems on your way home from work or en route to your date. If you need a more contemporary arrangement — something more Kurosawa than Merchant Ivory — get in touch with **Rita Flora** *(468 S. La Brea Ave., 323-938-3900)*, where you can sip an espresso while they prepare your design.

shopping | 163

books

BOOK SOUP *8818 Sunset Blvd. at Holloway Dr., West Hollywood, 310-659-3110; Hours: Mon-Thu 12pm-10pm; Fri 12pm-11pm; Sat 11:30am-11pm; Sun 11:30am-10pm*
You'd never think to look for one of the city's outstanding bookstores on a stretch of the Sunset Strip best known for the Whisky, the Viper Room, and other hard-rocking, heavy-boozing clubs. But those looking for an old-school neighborhood bookshop should proceed immediately to Book Soup. What they don't have among the pleasantly cluttered floor-to-ceiling shelves, the knowledgeable and friendly staff will score for you in a matter of days. Readings and signings are regular events; a sound newsstand that carries everything from the industry trades to foreign fashion glossies sits out front. The sidewalk tables at Book Soup's neighboring café are more notable for people watching than for the lackluster sandwiches on the menu.

MIDNIGHT SPECIAL *131 3rd Street Promenade bet. Arizona Ave. and Santa Monica Blvd., Santa Monica, 310-393-2923, www.msbooks.com; Hours: Mon-Thu 10:30am-11pm; Fri-Sat 10:30am-11:30pm; Sun 11am-11pm*
There's something reassuring about Midnight Special's continuing success on this high-rent stretch of the Promenade. This may be attributed to the fact that there isn't a better place to browse after a movie than at this large independent bookstore. Titles are meticulously organized by genre, including a large section dedicated to California and Los Angeles. Midnight Special has also recently added an inventory search of its 100,000 titles on its Web site, so you don't have to suffer the pain of landing a parking spot in Santa Monica for naught.

VROMAN'S *695 E. Colorado Blvd. bet. El Molino an Oak Knoll Aves., Pasadena, 626-449-5320; Museum Collection: 340 S. Lake Ave. at De Lacey Ave., Pasadena, 626-396-1670; Hours: Mon-Thu 9am-9pm; Fri-Sat 9am-10pm; Sun 10am-8pm*

Bookstore mavens will routinely mention the 106-year-old, 32,000-square-foot Vroman's at the top of their list of the best bookstores in the nation. For many notable authors making their rounds on the publicity circuit, Vroman's is ground zero for Los Angeles-area readings. As if 1.3 million titles weren't enough, you can drop into the stationery section for some new letterhead. For lovers of photography, architecture, and art books, Vroman's has also opened the Vroman's Museum Collection just around the corner.

books

NEIGHBORHOOD INDEPENDENTS

Skylight Books *(1818 N. Vermont Ave., Los Feliz, 323-660-1175)* is the kind of shop where you will actually seek out the staff's recommendations. In addition to marching in guest readings from notable culturalists such as Susan Faludi, Mike Davis, and cyberdaddy William Gibson, Skylight hosts monthly book groups. Sure, the big boys may be able to knock a buck off a hardback, but the folks at Skylight know their readers and their city. Neighborhood local Denis Dutton has been at it for years with his eccentrically independent bookshop, **Dutton's Brentwood Bookstore** *(11975 San Vicente Blvd., Brentwood, 310-476-6263)*. In addition to the books and an online newsletter loaded with criticism, Dutton's has a wide selection of classical, jazz, and film-soundtrack CDs and is known as a modern Bloomsbury of sorts for local writers. On a different bent, **Il-Literature** *(452 S. La Brea, Los Angeles, 323-937-3505)* is far from a well-rounded independent bookstore, but if you're looking to pick up a smart paperback for a weekend out of town, they carry a decent collection of novels-of-the-moment and a host of LA-based fiction such as the Black Sparrow Press titles, James Ellroy, and the like. At sister store Pulp, two doors south, you'll find a great selection of glossy design books.

SPECIALTY BOOKSTORES

Thank god for fetishists and junkies, because even the best bookstore can't be expected to stock everything. This being Hollywood, you have the inalienable right to purchase the script of your choice. The **Samuel French Theater & Film Bookshop** *(7623 Sunset Blvd., Hollywood, 323-876-0570)* has nearly every play and feature film script in print, and some that are out of print as well. The selection at **Larry**

Edmunds Cinema & Theater Bookshop *(6644 Hollywood Blvd., Hollywood, 323-463-3273)* may not be as extensive, but they have some other fun stuff, like memorabilia, stills, and posters. For the culinary artist and wine lover, **The Cook's Library** *(8373 3rd St., Los Angeles, 323-655-3141)* has several hundred cookbooks and a hypnotic rocking chair for your comfort. Next door, the **Traveler's Bookcase** *(8375 3rd St., Los Angeles, 323-655-0575)* has every travel guidebook under the sun. **A Different Light** *(8853 Santa Monica Blvd., West Hollywood, 310-854-6601)* serves the gay and lesbian community with a comprehensive selection of fiction, gender studies texts, and periodicals. And for the budding or working screenwriter and playwright, there isn't a better resource around than **The Writers' Store** *(2040 Westwood Blvd., Westwood, 310-441-5151)*. While they conduct much of their business online at *www.writersstore.com* and over the phone, there's a Westwood showroom where you can check out each of the competing script software programs.

SUPERSTORES

The nationwide **Barnes & Noble** *(10850 Pico Blvd., West LA, 310-475-4144; 1201 3rd Street Promenade, Santa Monica, 310-260-9110; call for other* *locations)* superstores have redefined book-selling and book-buying. Strangely (and some would argue fortunately), they have yet to open a location in the 323 area code. But you'll find their trademark combination of forest green carpet and oversized chairs all over the Westside and the valleys. What the store doesn't have in stock, they can procure for you within a matter of days; just don't expect a well-informed salesperson to engage you in a spontaneous conversation on whether Genet was a bastard or not. **Borders** *(330 S. La Cienega Blvd., Los Angeles, 310-659-4046; 1360 Westwood Blvd., Westwood, 310-475-3444)* does the megastore thing with the added benefit of a comprehensive music section, including an excellent selection of classical and jazz. The smaller chain storefronts of **Rizzoli** *(9501 Wilshire Blvd., Beverly Hills, 310-278-2247; 332 Santa Monica Blvd., Santa Monica, 310-393-0101)* are good places to browse and decompress from the wilds of the Beverly Hills retail district and the Third Street Promenade in Santa Monica.

USED BOOKS

There's something soothing about that decaying pulp smell in a used bookstore. You'll recognize that aroma at the well organized **CM Bookshop** *(2388 Glendale Blvd., Silver Lake, 323-913-9677)*, where you can bargain with Carl, then take your findings next door to the Silverlake Coffee Co. for a read. On the Westside, **Angel City Books** *(218 Pier Ave., Santa Monica, 310-399-8767)* has the finest collection of books on dadaism and surrealism, as well as Buddhism. Angel City is very serious about its craft; those books that aren't pristinely wrapped in cellophane will be in near-perfect condition. For an appraisal of what you believe to be a first edition Fitzgerald, drop into **W&V Dailey Rare Books** *(8216 Melrose Ave., West Hollywood, 323-658-8515)*. William will inspect your baby and give you an estimate.

music and video

VIRGIN MEGASTORE *8000 Sunset Blvd. at Crescent Heights Blvd., West Hollywood, 323-650-8666, www.virginmega.com; Hours: Mon 9am-12:30am; Tue-Thu 9am-12am; Fri-Sat 9am-1am; Sun 9am-12am*

Music stores, like bookshops, have gone the route of the superstore. Somehow, though, these behemoths have managed to avoid that charmless department-store aura. The Virgin Megastore, to wit, has used its mammoth size as an asset, not a hindrance. Founded by British popular culture proprietor Richard Branson, Virgin covers the entertainment gamut from music to video to books. On the ground floor, where you'll find the bulk of the music, dozens of listening stations line the perimeter, where you can sample tracks from a disc before you lay down $17 (they also have a section that includes tough-to-find imports). Upstairs you'll find videos, box sets, and classical selections. For music junkies, Monday nights after midnight are a must-shop time at Virgin; the store remains open an extra thirty minutes into Tuesday morning to allow fans to buy the week's new releases, which are available to the public on Tuesdays.

TOWER RECORDS *8801 Sunset Blvd. at Horn Ave., West Hollywood, 310-657-7300, www.towerrecords.com; Hours: daily 9am-12am*

Tower lacks the size, otherworldliness, and, at times, the consistent inventory of Virgin, but it can still serve as your first-stop option for most of your music needs. Folks who prefer to do their music shopping online will find that Tower makes life easy, with its retail store serving as an easy return/exchange outlet for stuff you purchase over the Web. In-store performances are more than a special occasion, and the listening stations are kept fresh with new stock as it arrives.

music and video

MUSIC AFFICIONADOS

Aron's Records *(1150 N. Highland Ave., Hollywood, 323-469-4700)* has such a comprehensive collection of music, ranging from trance and trip-hop to country, that it ought to be regarded as a public utility. The store's buyers can provide you with an armful of suggested titles for the listening station if you give them a general idea of what you like. The staff at **A-1 Record Finders** *(5629 Melrose Ave., Hollywood, 323-732-6737)* offer a unique service: they'll search high and low for anything on vinyl. Their in-house stock ain't too shabby, either. **Rockaway Records** *(2395 Glendale Blvd., Silver Lake, 323-664-3232)* has been around since the '70s. Their immense collection slants toward classic rock, but the percentages dictate that you're bound to find something you're looking for. **Prime Cuts** *(7758 Santa Monica Blvd., West Hollywood, 323-654-8251)* sounds like a barber shop, but it's actually a ground zero West Hollywood record shop for any dance spinner in Southern California. Whatever tracks they don't carry on disc, they're certain to have on 12-inch vinyl, and vice versa. For more obscure stuff like 7-inch, garage, punk, and ska, head down to **Destroy All Music** *(3818 Sunset, Silver Lake, 323-663-9300)*.

VIDEO AND MUNCHIES

Even the most ambitious night crawlers need an occasional evening of flannel pajamas and delivery fare. On nights like these, the last thing you need is the sensory overload of a Blockbuster

shopping

store-lights blaring like an arcade, kids with sticky fingers dodging your kneecaps, and, "Sorry, our only copy of your selection is out on a six-day rental, but could we interest you in *Look Who's Talking VII*?" Fortunately, when Kirstie Alley just won't cut it, there's somewhere to go. Whatever it is you're looking for, **Rocket Video** *(726 N. La Brea Ave., Hollywood, 323-965-1100)* probably has it. The staff organizes titles by genre, including a wall full of cult favorites and obscure television selections from the U.K. **Vidiots** *(302 Pico Blvd., Santa Monica, 310-392-8508)* offers a similarly comprehensive selection on the Westside. Moreover, they have a great range of pre-viewed copies for sale at low prices. Cinephiles in Los Feliz and points east croon over **Jerry's Video Room** *(1904 Hillhurst Ave., Los Feliz, 323-666-7471)*, which is, literally, just a room. Nevertheless, Jerry has every title imaginable and then some towering over you in the cramped space. Newcomer **Cinefile** *(11280 Santa Monica Blvd., West LA, 310-312-8836)* has taken the horror revival and run with it, stocking the most esoteric cult horror pictures along with everything else that's ever made its way to video. As for the munchies, **Pink Dot** *(800-PINK-DOT, www.pinkdot.com)* could only be a Los Angeles invention — a place that delivers everything from cigarettes to submarine sandwiches. Also on the Web, **Kozmo.com** *(www.kozmo.com)* is giving Pink Dot a run for its money. In addition to food and beverages, Kozmo offers videos, DVDs, game cartridges, books, and magazines in under an hour.

shopping

index by neighborhood

santa monica/venice

Angel City Books *218 Pier Ave. bet. Main and 2nd Sts., Santa Monica, 310-399-8767*

Barnes & Noble *1201 3rd Street Promenade at Wilshire Blvd., Santa Monica, 310-260-9110*

Chicken Little *1323 Abbot Kinney Way bet. Brooks and California Aves., Venice, 310-581-1676*

Daisy Arts *1312 Abbot Kinney Way bet. Brooks and California Aves., Venice, 310-396-8463*

Empire Snowboards *1639 Abbot Kinney Way bet. California Ave. and Venice Blvd., Venice, 310-450-4114*

Epicurus *625 Montana Ave. bet. 6th and 7th Sts., Santa Monica, 310-395-1352*

Firefly *1413 Abbot Kinney Way at California Ave., Venice, 310-450-6288*

Gotta Have It *1516 Pacific Ave. bet. Brooks Ave. and Venice Way, Venice, 310-392-5949*

Ilan Dei Studios *1227 Abbot Kinney Way bet. Brooks and California Aves., Venice, 310-450-0999*

Janice McCarty *912 Montana Ave. bet. 9th and 10th Sts., Santa Monica, 310-393-6858*

Jason Vass Gallery *1210 Montana Ave. bet. 12th and 13th Sts., Santa Monica, 310-395-2048*

Johnny B. Wood *1409 Abbot Kinney Way at California Ave., Venice, 310-314-1945*

Midnight Special *1318 3rd Street Promenade bet. Arizona Ave. and Santa Monica Blvd., Santa Monica, 310-393-2923*

Number One *1426 Montana Ave. bet. 14th and 15th Sts., Santa Monica, 310-656-2455*

Pier One Imports, *3000 Wilshire Blvd. bet. 26th St. and Bundy Dr., Santa Monica, 310-453-1559*

Planet Funk *126 Santa Monica Pl., entrance on Broadway at 3rd St., Santa Monica, 310-434-9778*

Rizzoli *332 Santa Monica Blvd., at 3rd St. Promenade, Santa Monica, 310-393-0101*

Santa Monica Farmers Market *Arizona Ave. at 3rd St.*

Santa Monica Place *395 Santa Monica Place at Broadway and 3rd St., Santa Monica, 310-394-5451*

shopping

Shabby Chic *1013 Montana Ave. bet. 10th and 11th Sts., Santa Monica, 310-394-1975*

Slave *1223 Abbot Kinney Way bet. Brooks and California Aves., Venice, 310-314-7016*

Trader Joe's *3212 Pico Blvd. at 32nd St., Santa Monica, 310-581-0253*

Urban Outfitters *1440 3rd Street Promenade bet. Broadway and Santa Monica Blvd., Santa Monica, 310-394-1404*

Vidiots *302 Pico Blvd. bet. 3rd and 4th Sts., Santa Monica, 310-392-8508*

Wild Oats *1425 Montana Ave. at 15th St., Santa Monica, 310-576-4707*

brentwood/west la/westwood

Barnes & Noble *10850 Pico Blvd. at Overland Ave., West LA, 310-475-4144*

Borders *1360 Westwood Blvd. bet. Wilshire and Olympic Blvds., Westwood, 310-475-3444*

Brentwood Bread Company *11640 San Vicente Blvd. nr. Bingham Ave., Brentwood, 310-826-9400*

Century City Shopping Center *10250 Santa Monica Blvd. at Ave. of the Stars, Century City, 310-277-3898*

Cinefile *11280 Santa Monica Blvd. bet. Barrington Ave. and Sawtelle Blvd., West L.A., 310-312-8836*

Crate & Barrel *Century City Mall, 10250 Santa Monica Blvd. bet. Avenue of the Stars and Century Park W., West LA, 310-551-1100*

Dutton's Brentwood Bookstore *11975 San Vicente Blvd. bet. Bundy Dr. and Montana Ave., Brentwood, 310-476-6263*

Elat Market *8730 Pico Blvd. bet. Robertson and La Cienega Blvds., West LA, 310-659-0576*

Gelson's *10250 Santa Monica Blvd. at Ave. of the Stars, West LA, 310-277-4288*

Pier One Imports, *10984 Santa Monica Blvd. at Veteran Ave., West LA, 310-478-6884*

Planet Funk *Westside Pavilion, 10800 Pico Blvd. bet. Westwood Blvd. and Overland Ave., West LA, 310-441-5043*

Pottery Barn *Century City Mall, 10250 Santa Monica Blvd. bet. Ave. of the Stars and Century Park W., West LA, 310-552-0170*

Ron Herman Sportswear *11677 San Vicente Blvd. at Barrington Ave., Brentwood, 310-207-0927*

Target *10820 Jefferson Blvd. bet. Sepulveda Blvd. and Overland Ave., Culver City, 310-839-5200*

Wally's *2107 Westwood Blvd. bet. Santa Monica and Olympic Blvds., Westwood, 310-475-0606*

Westside Pavilion *10800 Pico Blvd. at Westwood Blvd., West LA, 310-274-6255*

The Woods *11711 Gorham Ave. at San Vicente Blvd., Brentwood, 310-826-0711*

The Writers' Store *2040 Westwood Blvd. bet. Santa Monica and Olympic Blvds., Westwood, 310-441-5151*

beverly hills

Al Gelato *860 S. Robertson Blvd. bet. Wilshire and Olympic Blvds., Beverly Hills, 310-659-8069*

Anastasia *438 N. Bedford Dr. bet. Little Santa Monica and Wilshire Blvds., Beverly Hills, 310-273-3155*

Armani *436 N. Rodeo Dr. bet. Little Santa Monica and Wilshire Blvds., Beverly Hills, 310-271-5555*

Barneys New York *9570 Wilshire Blvd. bet. Santa Monica Blvd. and Rodeo Dr., Beverly Hills, 310-276-4400*

Beverly Hills Beauty Center *350 N. Beverly Dr. bet. Little Santa Monica and Wilshire Blvds., Beverly Hills, 310-278-8815*

Beverly Hills Farmers Market *Canon Dr. at Clifton Way*

Bijan *420 N. Rodeo Dr. bet. Little Santa Monica and Wilshire Blvds., Beverly Hills, 310-273-6544*

Cartier *220 N. Rodeo Dr. bet. Little Santa Monica and Wilshire Blvds., Beverly Hills, 310-275-5155*

Chanel *400 N. Rodeo Dr. bet. Little Santa Monica and Wilshire Blvds., Beverly Hills, 310-278-5500*

Christian Dior *230 N. Rodeo Dr. bet. Little Santa Monica and Wilshire Blvds., Beverly Hills, 310-859-4700*

Contempo Nails *333 S. Robertson Blvd. bet. Wilshire and Olympic Blvds., Beverly Hills, 310-855-8879*

Emporio Armani *9533 Brighton Way bet. Rodeo Dr. and Wilshire Blvd., Beverly Hills, 310-271-7790*

Frederic Fekkai *440 N. Rodeo Dr. bet. Little Santa Monica and Wilshire Blvds., Beverly Hills, 310-777-8700*

Gucci 347 N. Rodeo Dr. bet. Little Santa Monica and Wilshire Blvds., Beverly Hills, 310-278-3451

Lily et Cie 9044 Burton Way at Doheny Dr., Beverly Hills, 310-724-5757

Louis Vuitton 295 N. Rodeo Dr. bet. Little Santa Monica and Wilshire Blvds., Beverly Hills, 310-859-0457

Neiman Marcus 9700 Wilshire Blvd. bet. Santa Monica Blvd. and Rodeo Dr., Beverly Hills, 310-550-5900

Pigments 8822 Burton Way bet. Doheny Dr. and Robertson Blvd., Beverly Hills, 310-858-7038

Prada 343 N. Rodeo Dr. bet. Little Santa Monica and Wilshire Blvds., Beverly Hills, 310-385-5959

Ralph Lauren 444 N. Rodeo Dr. bet. Little Santa Monica and Wilshire Blvds., Beverly Hills, 310-281-1500

Rizzoli 9501 Wilshire Blvd. at Rodeo Dr., Beverly Hills, 310-278-2247

Saks 9700 Wilshire Blvd. bet. Santa Monica Blvd. and Rodeo Dr., Beverly Hills, 310-550-5900

Tiffany 210 N. Rodeo Dr. bet. Little Santa Monica and Wilshire Blvds., Beverly Hills, 310-273-8880

U 343 N. Camden Dr. nr. Wilshire Blvd., Beverly Hills, 310-858-1178

Valentino 240 N. Rodeo Dr. bet. Little Santa Monica and Wilshire Blvds., Beverly Hills, 310-247-0103

Valerie 460 N. Canon Drive at Little Santa Monica Blvd., Beverly Hills, 310-274-7348

west hollywood

A Different Light 8853 Santa Monica Blvd. nr. San Vicente Blvd., West Hollywood, 310-854-6601

Anna Sui 8669 Sunset Blvd. bet. San Vicente and La Cienega Blvds., West Hollywood, 310-360-6224

Apothia Fred Segal, 8100 Melrose Ave. at Crescent Heights Blvd., West Hollywood, 323-651-0239

Baby Jane of Hollywood 7985 Santa Monica Blvd. bet. Crescent Heights Blvd. and Fairfax Ave., West Hollywood, 323-848-7080

Book Soup 8818 Sunset Blvd. at Holloway Dr., West Hollywood, 310-659-3110

Bristol Farms 7880 Sunset Blvd. at Fairfax Ave., West Hollywood, 323-874-6301

Burke Williams 8000 Sunset Blvd. at Crescent Heights Blvd., West Hollywood, 323-822-9007

Curve 154 N. Robertson Blvd. at Beverly Blvd., West Hollywood, 310-360-8008

Cuvee 145 S. Robertson Blvd. bet. Beverly Blvd. and 3rd St., West Hollywood, 310-2714333

D&G 8641 Sunset Blvd. bet. San Vicente and La Cienega Blvds., West Hollywood, 310-360-7272

Daryl K. 8125 Melrose Ave. bet. La Cienega and Crescent Heights Blvds., West Hollywood, 323-651-2251

Decades, Inc. 8214 Melrose Ave. bet. La Cienega and Crescent Heights Blvds., West Hollywood, 323-655-0223

DKNY Beverly Center, 131 N. La Cienega Blvd. at Beverly Blvd., West Hollywood, 310-289-9787

Dream Dresser 8444 Santa Monica Blvd. bet. La Cienega and Crescent Heights Blvds., West Hollywood, 323-848-3480

Du Vin 540 N. San Vicente Blvd. bet. Melrose Ave. and Beverly Blvd., West Hollywood, 310-855-1161

Fred Segal 8100 Melrose Ave. at Crescent Heights Blvd., West Hollywood, 323-651-4129

Good Old Times 7739 Santa Monica Blvd. bet. Fairfax and La Brea Aves., West Hollywood, 323-654-7103

Hustler Hollywood 8920 Sunset Blvd. bet. Doheny Dr. and San Vicente Blvd., West Hollywood, 310-860-9009

Kenneth Cole 8752 Sunset Blvd. bet. San Vicente and La Cienega Blvds., West Hollywood, 310-289-5085

La Conversation, 638 N. Doheny Dr. bet. Sunset and Santa Monica Blvds., West Hollywood, 310-858-0950

Liza Bruce 7977 Melrose Ave. bet. Crescent Heights Blvd. and Fairfax Ave., West Hollywood, 323-655-5012

Maxfield 8825 Melrose Ave. bet. Doheny Dr. and Robertson Blvd., West Hollywood, 310-274-8800

Miu Miu 8025 Melrose Ave. bet. Crescent Heights Blvd. and Fairfax Ave., West Hollywood, 323-651-0073

Nicole Miller 8633 Sunset Blvd. bet. San Vicente and La Cienega Blvds., West Hollywood, 310-652-1629

Oliver Peoples 8642 Sunset Blvd. bet. San Vicente and La Cienega Blvds., West Hollywood, 310-657-2553

Paper Bag Princess 8700 Santa Monica Blvd. bet. San Vicente and La Cienega Blvds., West Hollywood, 310-358-1985

Pleasure Chest 7733 Santa Monica Blvd. bet. Fairfax and La Brea Aves., West Hollywood, 323-650-1022

Prime Cuts 7758 Santa Monica
Blvd. bet. Fairfax and La Brea Aves.
West Hollywood, 323-654-8251

Privé Salon 8458 Melrose Pl. nr.
La Cienega Blvd., West Hollywood,
323-651-5045

Rudy's Barbershop The Standard,
8300 Sunset Blvd. bet. La Cienega
and Crescent Heights Blvds.,
West Hollywood, 323-650-5669

Soolip 8646 Melrose Ave. bet. San
Vicente and La Cienega Blvds.,
West Hollywood, 310-360-0545

Tower Records 8801 Sunset Blvd.
bet. San Vicente and La Cienega Blvds.,
West Hollywood, 310-657-7300

Tracey Ross 8595 Sunset Blvd.,
bet. San Vicente and La Cienega Blvds,
West Hollywood, 310-854-1996

Trader Joe's 7304 Santa Monica
Blvd. bet. Fairfax and La Brea Aves.,
West Hollywood, 323-851-9782

Virgin Megastore 8000 Sunset
Blvd. at Crescent Heights Blvd.,
West Hollywood, 323-650-8666

W&V Dailey Rare Books
8216 Melrose Ave. bet. La Cienega
and Crescent Heights Blvds.,
West Hollywood, 323-658-8515

Wild Oats 8611 Santa Monica Blvd.
bet. San Vicente and La Cienega Blvds.,
West Hollywood, 310-854-6927

third/beverly

American Rag 150 S. La Brea Ave.
bet. Beverly Blvd. and 3rd St.,
Los Angeles, 323-935-3154

Beverly Center 8500 Beverly Blvd.
at La Cienega Blvd., Los Angeles,
310-854-3432

Black Wave Tattoo 118 S. La Brea,
bet. Beverly Blvd. and 3rd St.,
Los Angeles, 323-932-1900

Blueprint 8366 Beverly Blvd. bet.
La Cienega and Crescent Heights Blvds.,
Los Angeles, 323-653-2439

Borders 330 S. La Cienega Blvd.
bet. 3rd and 6th Sts., Los Angeles,
310-659-4046

Canter's 419 N. Fairfax Ave.
bet. Melrose Ave. and Beverly Blvd.,
Los Angeles, 323-651-2030

Chestnuts and Papaya 459 1/2
S. La Brea Ave. bet. 3rd and 6th Sts.,
Los Angeles, 323-937-8450

Clark Nova 8118 1/2 3rd St. bet.
La Cienega and Crescent Heights Blvds.,
Los Angeles, 323-655-1100

The Cook's Library 8373 3rd St.
bet. La Cienega and Crescent Heights
Blvds., Los Angeles, 323-655-3141

Cynthia Rowley 112 S. Robertson
Blvd. bet. Beverly Blvd. and 3rd St.,
Los Angeles, 310-276-9020

Eduardo Lucero 7378 Beverly Blvd. bet. Fairfax and La Brea Aves., Los Angeles, 323-933-2778

Erewhon 7660 Beverly Blvd. bet. Fairfax and La Brea Aves., Los Angeles, 323-937-0777

Futurama 446 N. La Brea Ave. bet. Melrose Ave. and Beverly Blvd., Los Angeles, 323-937-4522

Golyester 136 S. La Brea Ave. bet. Beverly Blvd. and 3rd St., Los Angeles, 323-931-1339

Il-Literature & Pulp 452-6 S. La Brea bet. 3rd and 6th Sts., Los Angeles, 323-937-3506

Illume 8302 3rd St. bet. La Cienega and Crescent Heights Blvds., Los Angeles, 323-782-0342

In House 7370 Beverly Blvd. bet. Fairfax and La Brea Aves., Los Angeles, 323-931-4420

Julian's 8366 3rd St. bet. La Cienega and Crescent Heights Blvds., Los Angeles, 323-655-3011

Kate Spade 105 S. Robertson Blvd. bet. Beverly Blvd. and 3rd St., Los Angeles, 310-271-9778

La Brea Bakery 624 S. La Brea Ave. bet. 6th St. and Wilshire Blvd., Los Angeles, 323-939-6813

Lanny Nails 8300 3rd St. bet. La Cienega and Crescent Heights Blvd., Los Angeles, 323-653-3370

Lisa Kline 136 S. Robertson Blvd. bet. Beverly Blvd. and 3rd St., Los Angeles, 310-246-0907

Loehmann's 333 S. La Cienega Blvd. at San Vicente Blvd., Los Angeles, 310-659-0674

Lucky Brand Dungarees 120 S. La Brea Ave. bet. Beverly Blvd. and 3rd St., Los Angeles, 323-933-0722

Lura Starr 7374 Beverly Blvd. bet. Fairfax and La Brea Aves., Los Angeles, 323-933-4704

Modernica 7366 Beverly Blvd. bet. Fairfax and La Brea Aves., Los Angeles, 323-933-0383

Not So Far East 160 S. La Brea Ave. bet. Beverly Blvd. and 3rd St., Los Angeles, 323-933-8900

NYSE 7385 Beverly Blvd. bet. Fairfax and La Brea Aves., Los Angeles, 323-938-1018

Ozzie & Moosy 5439 6th St. nr. La Brea Ave., Los Angeles, 323-938-8886

Polka Dots and Moonbeams 8367 3rd St. bet. La Cienega and Crescent Heights Blvds., Los Angeles, 323-651-1746

Postobello 7270 Beverly Blvd. bet. bet. Fairfax and La Brea Aves., Los Angeles, 323-931-1899

Pottery Barn Beverly Center, 131 N. La Cienega Blvd. at Beverly Blvd., Los Angeles, 310-360-1301

Product 134 S. Robertson Blvd. bet. Beverly Blvd. and 3rd St., Los Angeles, 310-860-9393

Re-Mix 7605 1/2 Beverly Blvd. bet. Fairfax and La Brea Aves., Los Angeles, 323-936-6210

Richard Tyler 7290 Beverly Blvd. bet. Fairfax and La Brea Aves., Los Angeles, 323-931-6769

Rita Flora 468 S. La Brea Ave. bet. 3rd and 6th Sts., 323-938-3900

Shelter 7920 Beverly Blvd. bet. Crescent Heights Blvd. and Fairfax Ave., Los Angeles, 323-937-3222

Sonrisa 7609 Beverly Blvd. bet. Fairfax and La Brea Aves., Los Angeles, 323-935-8438

Stüssy 112 S. La Brea Ave. bet. Beverly Blvd. and 3rd St., Los Angeles, 323-937-6077

Suburban 126 S. La Brea Ave. bet. Beverly Blvd. and 3rd St., Los Angeles, 323-933-1779

Syren 7225 Beverly Blvd. bet. Fairfax and La Brea Aves., Los Angeles, 323-936-6693

Trader Joe's 263 S. La Brea Ave. at 3rd St., Los Angeles, 323-965-1989

Traveler's Bookcase 8375 3rd St. bet. La Cienega and Crescent Heights Blvds., Los Angeles, 323-655-0575

Union 110 S. La Brea Ave. bet. Beverly Blvd. and 3rd St., Los Angeles, 323-549-6950

Vin Baker 132 1/2 S. La Brea Ave. bet. Beverly Blvd. and 3rd Sts., Los Angeles, 323-936-4001

Zipper 8316 3rd St. bet. La Cienega and Crescent Heights Blvds., Los Angeles, 323-951-0620

hollywood/hancock park/larchmont

A-1 Record Finders 5629 Melrose Ave. at Larchmont Blvd., Hollywood, 323-732-6737

Aardvark's 7579 Melrose Ave. bet. Fairfax and La Brea Aves., Hollywood, 323-655-6769

Aron's Records 1150 N. Highland Ave. bet. Fountain Ave. and Santa Monica Blvd., Hollywood, 323-469-4700

Back Lot 7278 Sunset Blvd. bet. Fairfax and La Brea Aves., Hollywood, 323-876-6070

The Barber Shop Club 6907 Melrose Ave. bet. La Brea and Highland Aves., Hollywood, 323-939-4319

Camden Lock 7021 Melrose Ave. bet. La Brea and Highland Aves., Hollywood, 323-933-5752

The Cinema Glamour Shop 343 N. La Brea Ave. bet. Melrose Ave. and Beverly Blvd., Hollywood, 323-933-5289

8B 813 N. La Brea Ave. bet. Santa Monica Blvd. and Melrose Ave., Hollywood, 323-935-6369

Espiritu de Vida 5913 Franklin Ave. bet. Gower St. and Western Ave., Hollywood, 323-463-0281

Frederick's of Hollywood 6608 Hollywood Blvd. bet. Highland Ave. and Cahuenga Blvd., Hollywood, 323-466-8506

Hollywood Farmers Market Ivar Street bet. Hollywood and Sunset Blvds.

House of Freaks 7353 Melrose Ave. at Fuller Ave., Hollywood, 323-655-1922

Jet Rag 825 N. La Brea Ave. bet. Santa Monica Blvd. and Melrose Ave., Hollywood, 323-939-0528

Larchmont Beauty Center 208 N. Larchmont Blvd. bet. Beverly Blvd. and 3rd St., Larchmont, 323-461-0162

Larry Edmunds Cinema & Theater Bookshop 6644 Hollywood Blvd. bet. Highland Ave. and Cahuenga Blvd., Hollywood, 323-463-3273

No Problem 7601 Melrose Ave. bet. Fairfax and La Brea Aves., Hollywood, 323-655-4740

Off the Wall 7325 Melrose Ave. bet. Fairfax and La Brea Aves., Hollywood, 323-930-1185

Pier One Imports 5711 Hollywood Blvd. bet. Gower St. and Western Ave., Hollywood, 323-466-3443

Planet Funk 7571 Melrose Ave. bet. Fairfax and La Brea Aves., Hollywood, 323-655-2990

Playmates 6438 Hollywood Blvd. bet. Highland Ave. and Cahuenga Blvd., Hollywood, 323-464-7636

Red Balls 7365 Melrose Ave. bet. Fairfax and La Brea Aves., Hollywood, 323-655-3409

Redemption 7300 Melrose Ave. bet. Fairfax and La Brea Aves., Hollywood, 323-549-9128

Retail Slut 7308 Melrose Ave. bet. Fairfax and La Brea Aves., Hollywood, 323-934-1339

Rocket Video 726 N. La Brea Ave. bet. Santa Monica Blvd. and Melrose Ave., Hollywood, 323-965-1100

Samuel French Theater & Film Bookshop 7623 Sunset Blvd. bet. Fairfax and La Brea Aves., Hollywood, 323-876-0570

Serious 7264 Melrose Ave. bet. Fairfax and La Brea Aves., Hollywood, 323-936-5152

Slow 7474 Melrose Ave. bet. Fairfax and La Brea Aves., Hollywood, 323-655-3725

Time After Time 7245 Melrose Ave. bet. Fairfax and La Brea Aves., Hollywood, 323-653-8463

Urban Outfitters 7650 Melrose Ave. bet. Fairfax and La Brea Aves., Hollywood, 323-653-3231

Wasteland 7428 Melrose Ave. bet. Fairfax and La Brea Aves., Hollywood, 323-653-3028

Workmens 7280 and 7562 Melrose Ave. bet. Fairfax and La Brea Aves., Hollywood, 323-933-2440

los feliz/silver lake

Andrew Dibben 1618 Silver Lake Blvd. bet. Glendale and Sunset Blvds., Silver Lake, 323-662-9189

CM Bookshop 2388 Glendale Blvd. nr. Silver Lake Blvd., Silver Lake, 323-913-9677

Destroy All Music 3818 Sunset Blvd. at Hyperion Ave., Silver Lake, 323-663-9300

Further 4312 Sunset Blvd. at Fountain Ave., Silver Lake, 323-660-3601

Jerry's Video Room 1904 Hillhurst Ave. at Franklin Ave., Los Feliz, 323-666-7471

Ka-Boom 3816 Sunset Blvd. at Hyperion Ave., Silver Lake, 323-661-8697

La Conversation 2118 Hillhurst Ave. bet. Los Feliz Blvd. and Franklin Ave., Los Feliz, 323-666-9000

My Secret Garden 1865 N. Western Ave. at Franklin Ave., Los Feliz, 323-469-1514

Ozzie Dots 4637 Hollywood Blvd. bet. Vermont and Hillhurst Aves., Los Feliz, 323-663-2867

Pull My Daisy 3908 Sunset Blvd. at Santa Monica Blvd., Silver Lake, 323-663-0608

Purple Circle 1724 N. Vermont Ave. bet. Franklin Ave. and Hollywood Blvd., Los Feliz, 323-666-2965

Rockaway Records 2395 *Glendale Blvd. nr. Silver Lake Blvd., Silver Lake, 323-664-3232*

Sinister Store 1748 *Vermont Ave. bet. Franklin Ave. and Hollywood Blvd., Los Feliz, 323-666-5100*

Skylight Books 1818 *N. Vermont Ave. bet. Franklin Ave. and Hollywood Blvd., Los Feliz, 323-660-1175*

Soap Plant/Wacko 4633 *Hollywood Blvd. bet. Vermont and Hillhurst Aves., Los Feliz, 323-663-0122*

Squaresville 1800 *Vermont Ave. bet. Franklin Ave. and Hollywood Blvd., Los Feliz, 323-669-8464*

Uncle Jer's 4459 *Sunset Blvd. bet. Hillhurst and Fountain Aves., Los Feliz, 323-662-6710*

X-Large/X-Girl 1766 *N. Vermont Ave. bet. Franklin Ave. and Hollywood Blvd., Los Feliz, 323-666-3483*

Y Que Trading Post 1770 *Vermont Ave. bet. Franklin Ave. and Hollywood Blvd., Los Feliz, 323-664-0021*

mid-city/koreatown

H.K. Korean Supermarket 124 *N. Western Ave. bet. Beverly Blvd. and 3rd St., Koreatown, 323-469-8934*

downtown

The Alley, *alley between Santee St. and Maple Ave., from Olympic Blvd. to 12th St.*

California Mart 110 *E. 9th St. at Los Angeles St., Downtown, 213-630-3600*

The Cooper Building 860 *S. Los Angeles St. bet. 8th and 9th Sts., Downtown, 213-622-1139*

Grand Central Market 317 *S. Broadway bet. 3rd and 6th Sts., Downtown, 213-624-2378*

farther afield

Anti-Mall 2930 *Bristol St. at Baker St., Costa Mesa, 714-966-6660*

Citadel 5675 *E. Telegraph Rd., Commerce, 323-888-1220*

Crate & Barrel 75 *W. Colorado Blvd. bet. Pasadena and Fair Oaks Aves., Pasadena, 626-683-8000*

Domingo's 17548 *Ventura Blvd. bet. White Oak and Louise Aves., Encino, 818-981-4466*

Ikea 600 *N. San Fernando Blvd. bet. Burbank and Magnolia Blvds., Burbank, 818-842-4532; 17621 Gale Ave. bet. Albatross and Fullerton Rds.,*

City Of Industry, 626-912-8788; 20700 Avalon Blvd. nr. San Diego Fwy., Carson, 310-527-4532

It's a Wrap 3315 Magnolia Blvd. bet. Hollywood Way and Buena Vista St., Burbank, 818-567-7366

Janice McCarty 21 N. Fair Oaks Ave. at Colorado Blvd., Pasadena, 626-793-9130

Jim Bridges Boutique 12457 Ventura Blvd. #103 nr. Whitsett Ave., Studio City, 818-761-6650

Lydia's TV Fashions 13837 Ventura Blvd. bet. Hazeltine and Woodman Aves., Sherman Oaks, 818-995-7195

Reel Clothes 12132 Ventura Blvd. nr. Laurel Canyon Blvd., Studio City, 818-508-7762

Rose Bowl Flea Market 1001 Rose Bowl Dr. nr. Arroyo Blvd., Pasadena, 323-560-7469

South Coast Plaza 3333 Bristol St. bet. Sunflower Ave. and San Diego Fwy., Costa Mesa, 714-435-2000

Urban Outfitters 139 W. Colorado Blvd. bet. Pasadena and Fair Oaks Aves., Pasadena, 626-449-1818

Vroman's 695 E. Colorado Blvd. bet. El Molino an Oak Knoll Aves., Pasadena, 626-449-5320

index by type

books
A Different Light
Angel City Books
Barnes & Noble
Book Soup
Borders
CM Bookshop
The Cook's Library
Dutton's Brentwood Bookstore
Il-Literature & Pulp
Larry Edmunds Cinema & Theater Bookshop
Midnight Special
Rizzoli
Samuel French Theater & Film Bookshop
Skylight Books
Traveler's Bookcase
Vroman's
W&V Dailey Rare Books
The Writers' Store

clothing: clubwear
Camden Lock
Red Balls
Redemption
Retail Slut
Serious
Sinister Store
Slave

clothing: designer

Andrew Dibben
Anna Sui
Armani
Bijan
Chanel
Christian Dior
Cynthia Rowley
D&G
DKNY
Daryl K.
Eduardo Lucero
8B
Emporio Armani
Gucci
Janice McCarty
Kate Spade
Kenneth Cole
Liza Bruce
Louis Vuitton
Lura Starr
Miu Miu
Nicole Miller
Prada
Ralph Lauren
Richard Tyler
Valentino

clothing: designer resale

American Rag
Decades, Inc.
Lily et Cie
Paper Bag Princess

clothing: discount

The Alley
California Mart
Citadel
The Cooper Building
Loehmann's
Target

clothing: fashion boutiques

American Rag
Chestnuts and Papaya
Curve
Fred Segal
Lisa Kline
Maxfield
NYSE
Product
Tracey Ross

clothing: vintage

Aardvark's
American Rag
Baby Jane of Hollywood
The Cinema Glamour Shop
Golyester
Good Old Times
Gotta Have It

shopping

Jet Rag
Julian's
Ozzie Dots
Polka Dots and Moonbeams
Pull My Daisy
Reel Clothes
Rose Bowl Flea Market
Slow
Squaresville
Time After Time
Wasteland

clothing: department stores

Barneys New York
Fred Segal
Neiman Marcus
Saks

clothing: lingerie and fetish

Dream Dresser
Frederick's of Hollywood
Hustler Hollywood
Jim Bridges Boutique
Lydia's TV Fashions
Playmates
Pleasure Chest
Syren

clothing: shoes and accessories

Cartier
Fred Segal Feet
Kate Spade
Kenneth Cole
Louis Vuitton
Miu Miu
Oliver Peoples
Prada
Re-Mix
Tiffany
Urban Outfitters
Vin Baker

clothing: streetwear

Lucky Brand Dungarees
No Problem
Planet Funk
Stüssy
Suburban
Union
Urban Outfitters
Workmens
X-Large/X-Girl

cosmetics/hair/body

Anastasia
Apothia
The Barber Shop Club
Beverly Hills Beauty Center
Black Wave Tattoo

Burke Williams
Clark Nova
Contempo Nails
Frederic Fekkai
House of Freaks
Lanny Nails
Larchmont Beauty Center
Number One
Pigments
Privé Salon
Purple Circle
Rudy's Barbershop
U
Valerie

florists

My Secret Garden
Rita Flora
The Woods

food and wine

Al Gelato
Beverly Hills Farmers Market
Brentwood Bread Company
Bristol Farms
Canter's
Cuvee
Domingo's
Du Vin
Elat Market
Epicurus
Erewhon
Gelson's
Grand Central Market
H.K. Korean Supermarket
Hollywood Farmers Market
La Brea Bakery
La Conversation
Pink Dot
Santa Monica Farmers Market
Trader Joe's
Wally's
Wild Oats

furniture

Blueprint
Chestnuts and Papaya
Crate & Barrel
Empire Snowboards
Further
Futurama
Ikea
Ilan Dei Studios
In House
Johnny B. Wood
Modernica
Not So Far East
Postobello
Pottery Barn
Rose Bowl Flea Market
Shabby Chic
Shelter
Sonrisa

gifts/home accessories
Back Lot
Blueprint
Chestnuts and Papaya
Chicken Little
Crate & Barrel
Daisy Arts
Espiritu de Vida
Firefly
Further
Illume
Ikea
Ilan Dei Studios
Jason Vass Gallery
Ka-Boom
Modernica
Not So Far East
Off the Wall
Ozzie & Moosy
Pier One Imports
Pottery Barn
Shelter
Soap Plant/Wacko
Soolip
Target
Uncle Jer's
Y Que Trading Post
Zipper

malls
Anti-Mall
Beverly Center
Century City Shopping Center
Santa Monica Place
South Coast Plaza
Westside Pavilion

music
A-1 Record Finders
Aron's Records
Destroy All Music
Prime Cuts
Rockaway Records
Tower Records
Virgin Megastore

video
Cinefile
Jerry's Video Room
Kozmo.com
Rocket Video
Vidiots

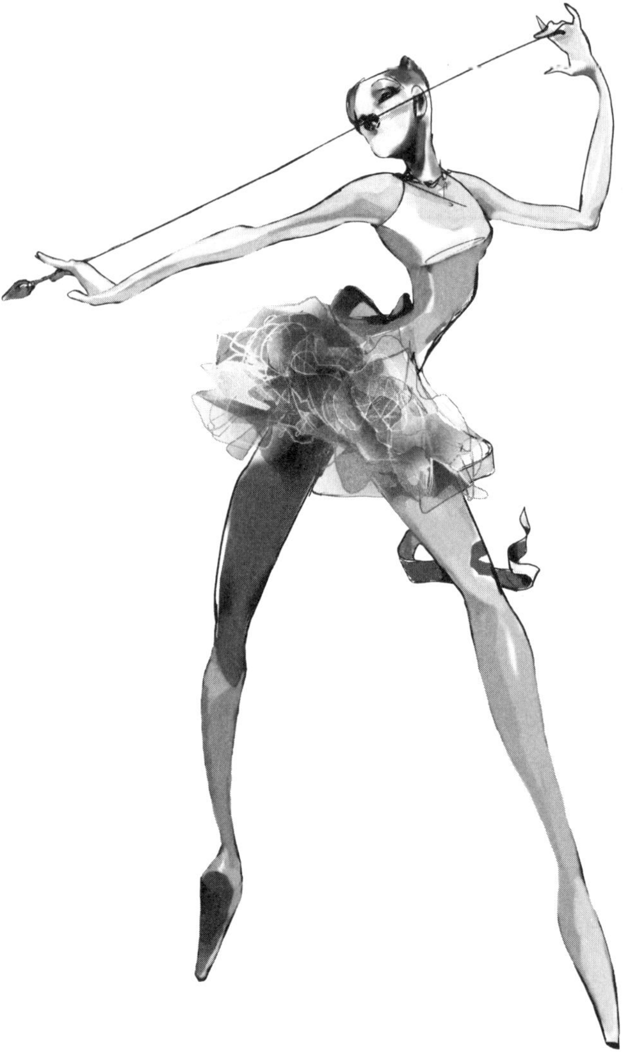

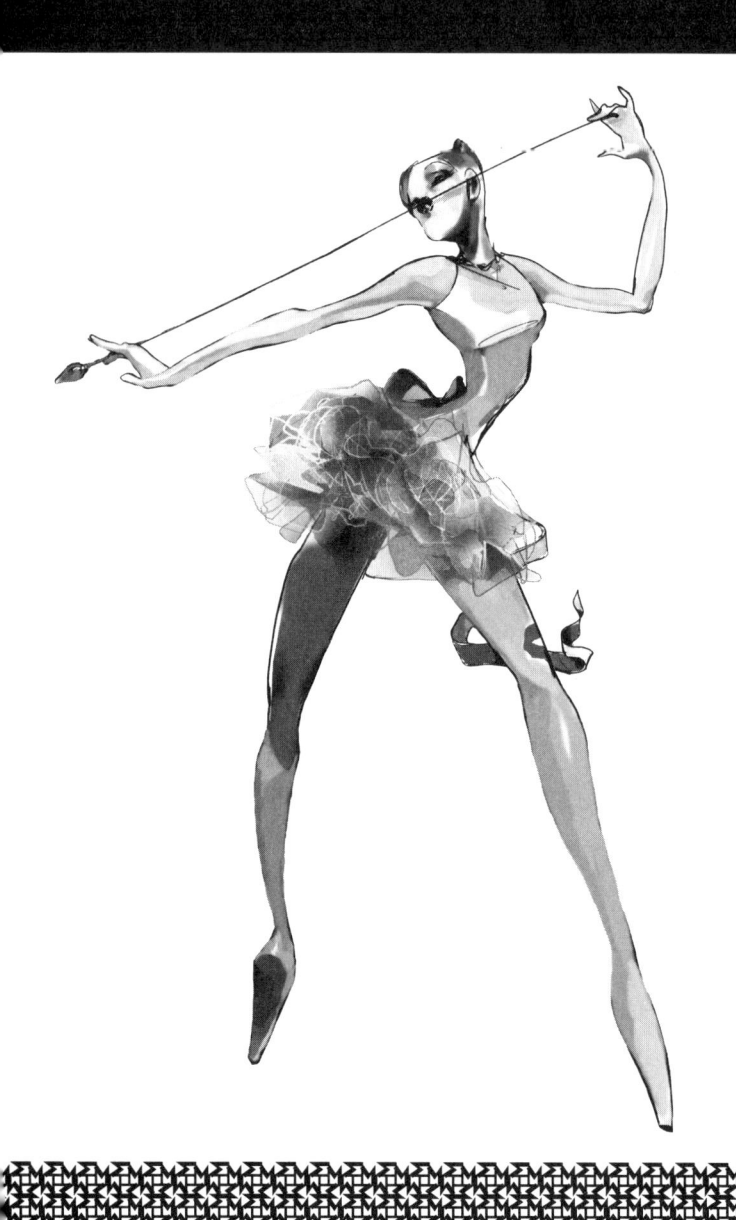

culture and the arts

woody allen once scoffed, "I don't want to live in a city where the only cultural advantage is that you can make a right turn on a red light." Surprise: He was talking about Los Angeles. Rest assured, however, that along with liberal traffic laws, Los Angeles has an inexhaustible number of cultural offerings. You're probably quite familiar with Los Angeles's prominent standing in the world of cinema, but you may be surprised that icons in the world of higher culture, from artist David Hockney to architect Frank Gehry, not only call Los Angeles home, but have created artistic styles in which the influence of LA as both city and idea are intrinsic.

Much of what's going on in the art world, be it film, galleries, museums, or performance, requires current updates. Check out the CityTripping.com Web site for up-to-date recommendations, as well as *Los Angeles* magazine, *Glue*, *LA Weekly*, and the *New Times* for detailed descriptions of what's going on week to week. The following listings are a good foundation for the city's cultural landscape and a great place to start.

film

If you plan to make it in the film world, you'd better school yourself in film history first, from special effects-riddled new releases to Tinseltown's timeless cinematic gems. Fortunately, as the consummate movie mecca, Los Angeles has so many cinemas, film museums, and festivals that even the most finicky cineast can get his film fix.

AMERICAN CINEMATHEQUE

Egyptian Theatre, 6712 Hollywood Blvd. bet. Highland Ave. and Cahuenga Blvd., Hollywood, 323-461-2020, www.americancinematheque.com

The preeminent organization in town devoted to the art of viewing films, the American Cinematheque brings fine cinema to the masses from its new digs at one of Hollywood's most famous historic theaters. The outrageously opulent Egyptian Theatre was built in 1922 by film impresario Sid Grauman, who was inspired architecturally by then newly discovered King Tut's tomb. Although today there are no monkeys in cages and the ushers no longer dress like Cleopatra, the theater has been faithfully restored to its former glory, replete with its original sunburst ceiling and open-air portico. The massive cinema was the first of Grauman's impressive movie palaces in Hollywood; he later opened the Chinese Theater across the street and owned a slew of theaters in downtown's venerable Broadway district. The Cinematheque now screens an inventive selection of films daily in the refurbished auditorium, leaning toward offbeat genre studies. Some of the highlights include a retrospective honoring the sex-crazed cinema of Russ Meyer, a Mods & Rockers Film Festival, and a program featuring Twisted Hollywood Shorts. The Alternative Screen is a bimonthly series that unveils the best of new undistributed American independent films.

film

DRIVE-INS

One of the last vestiges of Americana is the drive-in theater, with its tinny in-car speakers and huge, looming screens. Where else but in California can you watch a movie from the privacy of your own car? Because of our balmy climate, it's possible to catch a flick under the stars all year round. Although once there was a drive-in in every Los Angeles neighborhood, today there are only a few left operating. So go pay homage to the last of the dying breed, the single-screen drive-in, while you still can and indulge in your teenage make-out fantasies. On Route 66 in Azusa, the **Azusa Foothill Drive-in** (675 E. Foothill Blvd., Azusa, 626-334-0263) is a classic of the genre — and the only single-screen theater still operating in Southern California-with a vintage neon sign pointing the way to today's larger-than-life silver-screen stars. Multiscreen drive-ins in the Los Angeles area include the **Vineland Drive-in** (443 N. Vineland Ave., City of Industry, 626-961-9262), **Southbay 6 Drive-in** (Main St. bet. 405 and 110, Carson, 310-532-8811), and the **Fiesta Four Drive-in** (8462 E. Whittier Blvd., Pico Rivera, 562-948-3671).

FILM FESTIVALS

With countless filmmakers breezing through town hawking their latest work to the big studios, there's always an excuse for a film festival in LA. While you may find a diamond in the rough here, the festival circuit is not known for having consistent standards. Of the multitude, Los Angeles's most prestigious film event is **AFI's International Film Festival** (www.afionline.org), showing over 50 official selections drawn from current cinema from the U.S. and around the world. The **LA Short Film Festival** (www.lashortsfest.com) is held at Barnsdall Art Park in October, celebrating the best in new short films. **Outfest** (www.outfest.com), a two-week festival celebrating all things gay, lesbian, bisexual, and transgendered, takes place in July at the Directors Guild. In April, **The Los Angeles Independent Film Festival** *(323-937-9155, www.laiff.com)* unites the independent filmmaking community by showcasing the finest indie films from all over the country. **Doctober** *(www.documentary.org)* presents the best in short and feature-length documentaries every October, giving many Academy Award-nominated docs their only Los Angeles-area screenings. The **Angelus Awards Student Film Festival** *(800-874-0999, www.angelus.org)*, held every October at the Director's Guild, is dedicated to honoring student films of uncommon caliber that creatively explore the complexity of the human condition. Every July at the Disneyland Hotel, the **Anime Expo** *(www.anime-expo.org)* offers the latest and greatest in Japanese animation. A film festival for the truly independent, **Dances With Films** *(323-850-2929, www.danceswithfilms.com)* screens films by unknown up-and-coming directors, actors, and producers who have no star power whatsoever, every July. The **Hollywood Film Festival** and the **Hollywood Discovery Awards** *(310-288-1882, www.hollywoodawards.com)* try to bridge the gap between mainstream Hollywood and neophyte filmmakers. The **Resfest Digital Film Festival** *(www.resfest.com)* spotlights films created through the emerging media of digital video cameras and desktop editing systems every November. First held in smoky bars, the **Santa Monica Film Festival** *(310-289-7144, www.smff.com)* now screens international independent films monthly at the Aero and has its Moxie awards every February. Its mission is to showcase quality films without all the hype, media distractions, and prohibitive costs of most film festivals. The **Hollywood Black Film Festival** *(310-348-3942, www.hbff.org)* aims to enhance the careers of emerging and established black North American filmmakers through a public exhibition and competition every February. In May, the **Los Angeles Asian Pacific Film & Video Festival**

(213-680-4462 x68) offers a host of films and videos by people of Asian Pacific descent and by renowned Asian filmmakers who do not otherwise get a chance to have their work shown in the U.S. Exploring the complexity and diversity of worldwide black cinema, the **Pan African Film & Art Festival** *(323-295-1706, www.paff.org)* is the largest festival in the United States dedicated to the exhibition of black films, screening features, shorts, and documentaries from Africa and the African diaspora.

FILM SOCIETIES AND SMALLER FILM VENUES

If you think that the only films screening these days are bastard forms of entertainment aimed at the lowest common denominator, think again, because Los Angeles is home to a motley crew of film school geeks, foreign film buffs, genre fanatics, and just plain regular folks who support a rich network of quality film programming. The experts say there's a wider range of films on offer in Los Angeles than anywhere else in the world. To wit, most of the museums around town have screening rooms where they show films and videos related to their collections. **The Autry Museum of Western Heritage** *(Griffith Park, 4700 Western Heritage Way, Los Feliz, 323-667-2000)* regularly unfurls historic films and serials, such as a manic western/sci-fi hybrid called *Phantom Empire*, that celebrate the mythic West. To the delight of Hancock Park's blue-haired old ladies, Tuesday matinees at the LA County Museum of Art's **Bing Theater** *(5905 Wilshire Blvd., Los Angeles, 323-857-6010)* feature classic films from the Warner Brothers and Turner vault at classic prices (only $2 a pop). On Friday and Saturday nights, the Bing's programming is much bolder, ranging from lowbrow John Waters and Roger Corman retrospectives to more sophisticated series celebrating the films of cinematographer Vittorio Storraro and Krzystof Kieslowski's masterwork *The Decalogue*, for the more significant sum of $7. The **Museum of Contemporary Art** *(250 S. Grand Ave., Downtown, 213-621-2766)* usually screens experimental and other rarely seen films of an artistic bent on Thursdays. Cinema buffs flock to the Los Angeles Chapter of the **Key Sunday Cinema Club** *(Laemmle Monica Four-Plex, 1332 Second St., Santa Monica, 888-467-0404)*, where sneak previews screen every Sunday at 10am with a one-hour discussion following. The catch is that the film isn't announced ahead of time — but that's half the fun. The **Alex Film Society** *(216 N. Brand Ave., Glendale, 818-754-8250)* holds screenings of restored prints of classic feature films, cartoons, newsreels, and short subjects at the historic Alex Theatre in downtown Glendale. The **UCLA Film and Television Archives** *(James Bridges Theater, 405 Hilgard Ave., Westwood, 310-206-FILM)* embraces international art cinema, going beyond the usual Eurocentric film programs to present new films from Africa and Asia at their only U.S. screenings. Nightly programs run the gamut from Japanese anime to contemporary documentaries to a tribute to George Burns. The **Goethe Film Institute** *(5750 Wilshire Blvd., Ste. 100, Los Angeles, 323-525-3388)* offers anything and everything from German cinema, with such programs as New Animation from Germany and retrospectives on German filmmakers who are unknown to American audiences. An offshoot of the annual Outfest Film Festival, **Outfest at the Village** *(1125 N. McCadden*

culture and the arts | 195

Pl., Hollywood, 323-960-2394) takes over the Gay and Lesbian Center's Village every Wednesday to screen the latest films and videos by local and international gay, lesbian, and bisexual filmmakers. **Midnight Special** (1318 Third Street Promenade, Santa Monica, 310-393-2923), a bookstore with attitude, hosts Documental, a documentary and experimental film and video series. With two separate programs on the last Saturday of every other month, these free screenings show daring new pieces for free. Each of the film guilds in town also has its own theater, which are often open to the public for film festivals and special screenings and lectures. Call for information about the **Academy of Motion Picture Arts and Sciences** (8949 Wilshire Blvd., Beverly Hills, 310-247-3600), the **Writers Guild** (135 S. Doheny Dr., Beverly Hills, 323-951-4000) and the **Directors Guild** (7920 Sunset Blvd., West Hollywood, 310-289-2000). Bimonthly at übercool nightclub **Spaceland** (1717 Silver Lake Blvd., Silver Lake, 213-833-2843), **Flicker** brings short films, all shot on Super 8 or 16mm, to the masses. Every summer, the **Los Angeles Conservancy** (213-896-9114) shows kitschy classics like Forbidden Planet and It in Downtown's historic movie palaces lining Broadway. The weekly series hops from theater to theater, giving architecture junkies the chance to see many of these usually closed theaters in action. The **Friends of the Orpheum** (213-239-0949) have their annual Spookfest every Halloween season, and besides showing scary cinema like The Mummy and Freaks, they host the world's largest hearse procession and an accompanying burlesque show.

MOVIE HOUSES

The best places to look up current movie listings are the *LA Weekly* and the *Los Angeles Times*, but the following quality movie houses can always be depended upon for a good flick. The **Nuart** *(11272 Santa Monica Blvd., West LA, 310-478-6379)* is the Westside's bastion of alternative cinema and often the sole outlet for exclusive releases like *The Blair Witch Project* or *Run Lola Run*. It also shows documentaries, director's cuts, and newly restored prints of classics like *Blade Runner*. The **Laemmle** chain of movie theaters is the progenitor of independent cinema multiplexes, with outposts in West Hollywood *(8000 Sunset Blvd., 323-848-3500)*, Santa Monica *(1332 Second St., 310-394-9741)*, and Pasadena *(667 E. Colorado Blvd., 626-844-6500)*. In addition to hosting film series with themes like "New Chinese Cinema" and "Gay Cinema Invades Beverly Hills," the Laemmle theaters always offer the latest in newly released art-house cinema. For a taste of Tinseltown retro glamour, envision the throngs who once came to witness the star-studded premieres at the **Chinese Theater** *(6925 Hollywood Blvd., Hollywood, 323-464-8111)*, and match your hand and footprints with over 200 legendary screen idols, from Marilyn Monroe to C3PO. Don't neglect to appreciate the gaudy grandeur of this Chinese movie palace and its 69-foot-high jade-green bronze roof. The **Cinerama Dome** *(6360 Sunset Blvd., Hollywood, 323-466-3401)*, built in 1963, garnered its architectural landmark status by being the first and only geodesic dome ever

culture and the arts | 197

built in concrete. It was designed for three-camera projections of 70mm films and was curved to give a three-dimensional effect. Although it's slated to be remodeled as a multiplex (the horror!), it still shows first-run big-budget movies, so see this soon-to-be-ruined relic now. Perennial favorite **New Beverly Cinema** (*7165 Beverly Blvd., Los Angeles, 323-938-4038*) is the best revival house in town, with creative pairings like the "Bad-Gal Double Bill" and the "Sin and Salvation Double Header," showing nightly. Plus, it often unfurls retrospectives of influential directors, like Andrei Tarkovsky, Akira Kurosawa, Russ Meyer, and Wes Craven. **The Old Town Music Hall** (*140 Richmond St., El Segundo, 310-322-2592*) is home to the Mighty Wurlitzer Theater Pipe Organ. Before each classic flick, a man in red suspenders plays a short concert on the Wurlitzer. At least one silent film plays per month, along with classics starring yesteryear's molls and gangsters. Famed for its vast legroom (when remodeled, the owners pulled out every other row of seats), funky neighborhood theater **The Vista** (*4473 Sunset Dr., Los Feliz, 323-660-6639*) sells its tickets from a hieroglyph-covered gilded ticket booth for its quirky selection of first-run films. The newly plush auditorium's theme is ornate-retro Egyptian, complete with colorful murals, cylindrical glass chandeliers, and pharaohs lining the walls. Santa Monica's own single-screen neighborhood movie palace, **The Aero** (*1328 Montana Ave., Santa Monica, 310-395-4990*), was financed by aircraft mogul Donald Douglas in 1939, and is now in danger of closing. If it's still open (Robert Redford is rumored to be saving it), it shows discount double features of second-run films for $6, with freshly popped popcorn at each intermission. Known to most as the $2 theater, **Cineplex Odeon Fairfax** (*7907 Beverly Blvd., Los Angeles, 323-653-3117*), with three screens, is another budget theater, though its prices have ballooned to the ungodly sum of $2.75. Still, the excellent selection of films changes weekly. The ornately restored **El Capitan** *(6838 Hollywood Blvd., Hollywood, 323-467-7674)* only shows Disney movies (since Mickey Mouse and his friends forked over a lot of dough for the theater's extensive restoration), and usually has a pre-film floor show. On Broadway in downtown LA are the architectural gems of downtown's historic theater district. Only two theaters, the Palace and the Orpheum, still operate as cinemas today, with the rest housing swap meets, fundamentalist Christian churches, or squatters' paradises. The **Palace** *(630 S. Broadway, Los Angeles, 213-239-0959)* is the oldest continuously operating cinema on the West Coast, and the **Orpheum** *(842 S. Broadway, Downtown, 213-239-0937)* has a completely restored Wurlitzer organ that is used a few times a year for concerts. Both cater to Los Angeles's Latino population by showing double bills of the latest Hollywood blockbusters with Spanish subtitles. For a closer look at these architectural gems, take the **Los Angeles Conservancy Broadway Theaters Walking Tour** *(213-623-2489)*. Newly reopened after being dark for two years, the **Silent Movie Theatre** *(611 N. Fairfax Ave., 323-655-2520)* is the only silent cinema still operating in the United States, screening the best silent movies (and occasionally a classic talkie) from the '30s and '40s with live organ accompaniment. And if bigger is better, Los Angeles's premier **IMAX Theater** *(California Science Center, 700 State Dr., Downtown, 213-744-2014)* takes the cake. With its seven-story-high screen and 3-D capability, you can lose yourself in *Encounters in the Third Dimension* or *The Island of the Sharks*, just two of the many films showing indefinitely.

culture and the arts

live performance

Los Angeles may not seem like much of a live performance town, but with every waiter in town ready for his big break, there are plenty of ambitious, fledgling actors to fill up the many small theaters in town, just waiting for a high-profile casting agent to walk in and sign 'em for a film deal on the spot. You can also gawk at the occasional sitcom regular or small-time movie star exercising his or her acting chops, proving they can play meatier roles than a troubled high school student or neurotic corporate thirtysomething. For up-to-date reviews of what's currently playing on stages all around the city, check out the *LA Weekly* and the *New Times*, or log on to TheatreLA.org, as well as, of course, the weekly Hot Picks at CityTripping.com.

CENTER THEATER GROUP

135 N. Grand Ave. bet. Temple and First Sts., Downtown, 213-628-2772; www.taperahmanson

Officially part of the Music Center of Los Angeles, CTG is the premier theater company in Los Angeles. Its two venues, the Ahmanson Theater and the Mark Taper Forum, play host to big-name productions, with the cavernous Ahmanson the site of elaborate Broadway-style musicals and the more intimate Taper fashioning itself as a leading regional theater. The Taper prides itself on its commitment to new voices and will occasionally feature a work-in-progress, as it did in 1999 for Anna Deveare Smith's *House Arrest*, her collage of true-life characters and monologues surrounding the Clinton scandal. Make sure you check your seat location if you're heading over to the Ahmanson; the house is so enormous that you may need a telescope to recognize the players onstage.

GEFFEN PLAYHOUSE *10886 Le Conte Ave. nr. Westwood Blvd., Westwood, 310-208-6500 www.geffenplayhouse.com*
The Geffen Theater is a venue less rooted in the patrician arts community and more dedicated to humanistic, "thinking person's theater": that is, good character-driven stuff in an accessible setting. Connected with UCLA's School of Theater, Film, and Television, the Geffen sits on campus, and its homey, stone façade evokes a community Shakespeare festival. But don't let the quaintness fool you — the Geffen Playhouse is ground zero for important American theater, including Margaret Edson's Pulitzer Prize-winning *Wit* and seemingly annual installments from Jon Rabin Baitz.

HOLLYWOOD BOWL *2301 N. Highland Ave. bet. Mulholland Dr. and Franklin Ave., Hollywood, 323-850-2000; www.hollywoodbowl.org*
With its signature concert shell and nearly 18,000 seats, the Hollywood Bowl is the largest natural amphitheater in the world. To properly enjoy the Bowl as the perfect place for a cheap but elegant date, you must bring an elaborate, overflowing picnic basket and quaff a bottle or two of wine beforehand in the grassy knolls that surround the theater. The cheapest seats are only a dollar — though they're a little hard, so bring a cushion. The stack-style parking at the Bowl is brutal, but the local bus system offers park-and-ride services to different parts of the city for a pittance. In the summers, the Bowl is the home of the Los Angeles Philharmonic. But it's not all classical; the summer schedule also includes jazz, fireworks spectaculars, and big-screen movies-plus-music honoring master composer John Williams.

live performance

CABARET

If you enjoy drowning your sorrows in a stiff martini while a torch singer pours out her heart or a piano player tickles the ivories, check out these vintage lounges. **The Dresden Room** *(1760 N. Vermont Ave., Los Feliz, 323-665-4294)* opened its doors nearly 50 years ago and has been pouring near-lethal concoctions for neighborhood lowlifes ever since. (Be sure to try a Blood and Sand, the house drink.) Credited with relaunching the LA lounge scene, singers Marty and Elayne have been ensconced at the Dresden since the early '80s. With cocaine-plastered smiles on their faces, they belt out wacky renditions of the Bee Gees' "Staying Alive" and Frank Sinatra standards. For a more upscale vibe, the **Cinegrill** at the Hollywood Roosevelt Hotel *(7000 Hollywood Blvd., Hollywood, 323-466-7000)* hosts a revolving cast of top-dollar chanteuses. The intimate **Gardenia Club** *(7066 Santa Monica Blvd., Hollywood, 323-467-7444)* is traditional cabaret all the way, with an occasional comedy act thrown in. **Masquers Cabaret** *(8334 3rd St., Los Angeles, 323-653-4848)* serves up everything but the kitchen sink within its irreverent walls, from one-acts and one-man shows to sketch and stand-up comedy. On Saturdays at Hollywood's venerable Italian restaurant **Miceli's** *(1646 N. Las Palmas Ave., Hollywood, 323-769-5899)*, Ronny Mack's Swingin' LA pays homage to the Rat Pack with a night full of song, comedy, and improv. Drawing hipsters to Chinatown from all over is the live karaoke band at **Quon Brothers Grand Star** *(943 Sun Mun Way, Chinatown, 213-626-2285)*, which has become the birthday venue of choice for Silver Lake denizens. And at **Vitello's** *(4349 Tujunga Ave., Studio City, 818-769-0905)*, amateur opera singers belt out their own twisted lyrics to opera and show tunes, inspired by such timely topics as Viagra.

COMEDY

Los Angeles has all the usual mainstream comedy clubs, where old comics try to breathe life into old routines, but if you're after sidesplitting nirvana you'll do better at one of the alternative comedy nights around town or at one of LA's many improv theaters. The mainstream clubs have a cover, in addition to a two-drink minimum. But if you really want to burn a hole in your wallet just to hear a bunch of warmed-over comedic cliches, here's the 411. When it opened its doors in 1972, the **Comedy Store** *(8443 Sunset Blvd., West Hollywood, 323-656-6225)* was the only major comedy club in town. For years, starving comics worked the door and swept the floors until they earned their way to top billing. Jim Carrey, Sam Kinison, and Pauly Shore (his mom is the owner) all got their starts here. The New York-based **Improv** *(8162 Melrose Ave., West Hollywood, 323-651-2583)*, with its signature long brick wall, opened its LA doors a few years after the Comedy Store, and the two have been rivals ever since. The Improv often has surprise drop-in appearances from such favorite sons as Jerry Seinfeld and Robin Williams. The third dinosaur on the local comedy scene, the **Laugh Factory** *(8001 Sunset Blvd., West Hollywood, 323-656-1336)*, is probably most famous for the free Thanksgiving dinner it dishes out to struggling comics and actors every year, but it also features familiar TV-comedy-hour faces serving up the usual stand-up fare. If you normally can't bear watching stand-up comedy, the unique comics who pack the stage at many of the alternative nights around town have brains and talent, not to mention their own brand of brilliantly wicked, acerbic wit. Mondays at **Largo** *(465 N. Fairfax Ave., Los Angeles, 323-852-1073)* are heralded by many as the best in town. If you don't mind the snobbish staff with fancy headsets and the expensive drinks at **LunaPark** *(665 N. Robertson Blvd., West Hollywood, 310-652-0611)*, Sunday night's UnCabaret, hosted by the inimitable Beth Lapides, features four comics doing comedy-as-therapy-as-art monologues. A

culture and the arts

favorite stage of the local alternative comedy scene, UnCabaret has been the testing ground for Janeane Garofalo and Julia Sweeney's stand-up routines in progress. You can also find onstage goofballs and their hecklers at the many restaurants and coffeehouses around town. Some especially popular nights are Comedy at Bat, every Friday night at old-time Italian joint **Miceli's** (1646 Las Palmas Ave., Hollywood, 323-446-3438); Last Laughs Before the 101, at the **Hollywood Hills Coffee Shop** (6145 Franklin Ave., Hollywood, 323-467-7678); the **Kindness of Strangers Coffeehouse** (4378 Lankershim Blvd., North Hollywood, 818-752-9566) on their Friday and Saturday open mics; and Young Comics Exposed, every Wednesday at **Farfalla** (143 N. La Brea Blvd., Los Angeles, 323-954-2504). Finally, funny in itself is a trip to **Hustler Hollywood** (8920 Sunset Blvd., West Hollywood, 310-860-9009), Larry Flynt's porn superstore, but on Wednesdays its coffeehouse plays host to a selection of worthwhile comics.

IMPROV THEATERS

Improv theaters in LA serve as a rigorous boot camp for many of today's future sitcom stars. Most of these theaters have intense improv training classes, and only the most talented comics rise through the ranks to make it to the main stage for the anything-goes nightly performance. The granddaddy of them all is the **Groundlings** (7307 Melrose Ave., Hollywood, 323-934-9700), which has become a pipeline of comedy talent for both actors and writers to sitcoms and *Saturday Night Live*; Phil Hartman, Laraine Newman, and Lisa Kudrow all cut their teeth here. Paul Reubens created his Pee Wee Herman character here, and Conan O'Brien also spent time clowning on the stage. **The Improv Olympic West Theatre** *(6468 Santa Monica Blvd., Hollywood, 323-962-7560)*, the younger sibling to Chicago's Improv Olympic, has its own small, intimate space on Hollywood's Theater Row. Nightly sketches are often inspired by the audience's suggestions, with late shows on Fridays and Saturdays. In one of the more posh comedy spaces in town, **Acme Comedy Theater** *(135 N. La Brea Ave., Los Angeles, 323-525-0202)* is known for presenting top-notch, sidesplitting improv, spawning a few members of Fox's *MadTV*. Founded by émigrés from Chicago's renowned Second City troupe, **Bang Improv Studio** *(457 N. Fairfax Ave., West Hollywood, 323-653-6886)* is the wackiest improvisational theater around, with long-form experimental sketches in kitschy surroundings. Its superlow prices ($1-2, with free coffee!) only add to the charm. Set up a few years ago by HBO to serve as a training ground for funny neophytes, the **HBO Workspace** *(733 N. Seward St., Hollywood, 323-993-6099)* is becoming a popular venue for young, creatively minded comedians to ply their trade in front of an appreciative audience. Seating goes fast, so call ahead. And every Sunday, alumni from Chicago's Second City do improv at the **Jazz Bakery** *(3233 Helms Ave., Culver City, 310-271-9039)*.

NOHO THEATER SCENE

Despite its cutesy name, NoHo (short for North Hollywood) has a fledgling theater scene, with a handful of bare-bones stages showcasing irreverent, shoestring-budget productions of anything from experimental avant-garde to modern revivals. Half a dozen stages hover around NoHo's crossroads at Magnolia and Lankershim, and more are scheduled to open soon, making the East Valley a worthwhile destination for the independent theater supporter. **American Renegade Theatre Company** *(11136 Magnolia*

culture and the arts | 205

Blvd., North Hollywood, 818-763-4430) opened a new two-theater space after the Northridge earthquake demolished its former quarters. The work of the **Bitter Truth Theatre** (11050 Magnolia Blvd., North Hollywood, 818-755-7900) reflects its feminist bent, with plays that convey the joy and pain of being female. The **Raven Playhouse** (5233 Lankershim Blvd., North Hollywood, 818-509-9519) creatively executes one-acts and full-length plays in its cramped quarters next to the Eagle coffeehouse. Nearby, the **Actor's Forum's** (10655 Magnolia Blvd., North Hollywood, 818-506-0600) small, intimate theater has good sight lines and even a marquee. And at the **NoHo Actors' Studio** (5215 Lankershim Blvd., North Hollywood, 818-990-2324), in the neighborhood since the beginning, the plays are hit and miss, but often worth seeing for their inventive bent.

SPOKEN WORD

Los Angeles is a hotbed for book and poetry readings, mostly set in run-down coffeehouses in the farthest reaches of the city. But heads and shoulders above the rest is **Beyond Baroque Literary Arts Center** (681 Venice Blvd., Venice, 310-822-3006), the foremost serious literary venue in Los Angeles. Since 1968, Beyond Baroque has been training and showcasing local and visiting avant-garde poets and alternative literary artists. It also hosts an ongoing series of open poetry readings, gallery exhibitions, musical performances, and writing workshops, from which Tom Waits and Viggo Mortensen have graduated. **Glaxa** (3707 Sunset Blvd., Silver Lake, 323-663-5295), which stands for God's Love And eXcellent Adventure, hosts anything-goes open mics on Sundays, with Tuesdays as a singer-songwriter open mic. Greasers and their rockabilly chicks head to the **Barber Shop Club** (6907 Melrose Ave., Hollywood, 323-939-4319) for music and storytelling open mics every Thursday. Proud queers grab the mic on Tuesdays at **Stonewall Gourmet Coffee** (8717 Santa Monica Blvd., West

Hollywood, 310-659-8009). (As a side note, don't miss Thursdays at Stonewall, when drag queen bingo takes place.) The best spoken word in LA has also sunk its roots into the other side of the hill, in the San Fernando Valley. The **Kindness of Strangers** *(4378 Lankershim Blvd., North Hollywood, 818-752-9566)* has a storytelling open mic called Anything but Standup. The former owner of the legendary literary haunt Iguana Café now hosts an open mic on Sundays at his new store **Exile Books and Music** *(14925 Magnolia Blvd., Sherman Oaks, 818-986-6409)*. Deep in the West Valley, **Cobalt Café** *(22047 Sherman Way, Canoga Park, 818-348-3789)* also hosts a worthwhile open reading on Tuesdays. Bookstores are great venues to hear some of your favorite authors read when they breeze through town. **Book Soup, Skylight Books, Dutton's Brentwood, A Different Light**, and **Vroman's** (see bookstore section) get the best authors. Check the *LA Weekly* or the *New Times* for current listings.

THEATER ROW

On a two-block stretch of Santa Monica Boulevard between Cole and Hudson Avenues is Hollywood's Theater Row, a cluster of independently owned and operated theaters. Some of these holes in the wall seem no bigger than a rec room, but the talent far surpasses the modest surroundings. The **Hudson Theatre** *(6537 Santa Monica Blvd., Hollywood, 323-769-5858)* is the anchor of the street, with a quartet of snazzy 99-seat theaters, each with its own flavor. The Hudson Guild's troupe presents staid, traditional plays like *Hedda Gabler*, while the Hudson Main Stage presents venerable crowd pleasers like Neil Simon plays. The Hudson Avenue theater cooks up socially relevant fare, especially if it challenges the white-male corporate establishment, and the Hudson Backstage lends its space to any up-and-coming theater producers that'll fork over dough for rent, including *Reefer Madness: The New Hit Musical*. The **Attic Theater** *(6562 Santa Monica Blvd., Hollywood,*

323-469-3786), a smaller and more modest theater than its neighbor across the street, with only 46 seats, also presents everything from classic revivals from the literary canon to fictional self-help seminars.

THEATER AND PERFORMANCE ART

Glaxa *(3707 Sunset Blvd., Silver Lake, 323-960-1095)* is the Eastside's bastion of cutting-edge experimental theater and performance art. Home to the Fabulous Monsters performance-art troupe, the theater encourages Silver Lake's finest performers to make Glaxa their home base, also featuring live bands on off-nights and open mics on Sundays and Tuesdays. Grand opening night featured a transvestite version of Jean Genet's *The Maids*, which brilliantly set the tone for the stage. There is also a café that serves breakfast, lunch, and dinner, as well as all the froufrou coffee drinks you could want. **The Celebration Theater** *(7051B Santa Monica Blvd., West Hollywood, 323-957-1884)* is the queen of the gay theater scene, exclusively featuring plays by and about gays and lesbians. The main stage productions run on the weekends, while more experimental fare runs Mondays through Wednesdays. The **Actors Gang** *(6209 and 6201 Santa Monica Blvd., Hollywood, 323-465-0566)* was founded in 1981 by now-movie star Tim Robbins and several of his UCLA theater school friends, and it now specializes in creating high-energy, risk-taking theater. The **Interact Theater** *(11855 Hart St., North Hollywood, 818-773-7862)* is a true collective, owned and operated by its 50 members and producing any play that gets approved by the membership, ranging from Greek tragedies to modern-day musicals. In the summers, the **Will Geer Theatricum Botanicum** *(1419 Topanga Canyon Blvd., Topanga Canyon, 310-455-2322)* presents Shakespearean favorites like *Romeo and Juliet* and *A Midsummer Night's Dream* on a rustic outdoor stage under a canopy of trees. And yes, to answer your question, Will Geer was Grandpa Walton.

museums

For those of you looking for cultcha with a capital C, LA has more museums per capita than any other U.S. city. Check out the following venues for the cream of the crop.

ARMAND HAMMER MUSEUM OF ART 10899
Wilshire Blvd. at Westwood Blvd., West LA, 310-443-7000; www.hammer.ucla.edu; Hours: Tue-Wed 11am-7pm; Thu 11am-9pm; Fri-Sat 11am-7pm; Sun 11am-5pm

Reneging on his deal to donate his vast art collection to LACMA, Occidental petroleum magnate Armand Hammer instead built this museum to showcase the Impressionist and post-Impressionist masterpieces of his collection. The exhibits here are hit and miss, but some of the successful ones are much more adventurous and intriguing than what is seen at LACMA and MOCA, including a provocative survey of feminist art and an exhibition on how Disney's theme parks were built. The Armand Hammer also often hosts free jazz concerts and poetry readings. On Thursdays, the museum is free and open late.

GETTY CENTER 1200
Getty Center Dr., Brentwood, 310-440-7300; www.getty.edu; Hours: Tue-Wed 11am-7pm; Thu-Fri 11am-9pm; Sat-Sun 10am-6pm

For the only-in-LA file: entry to the Getty is free, but to be guaranteed admission you have to make a parking reservation, which will cost you $5. Regulars often reserve months in advance to see this new landmark. Designed by Richard Meier, the mammoth hillside museum and research center has a breathtaking panoramic view of Los Angeles and the Pacific Ocean. The Getty is packed to the gills on weekends, so it's better to go during the week if you can. Some say the Getty collection is too hodgepodge, but the five interconnected pavilions house changing exhibitions and the

culture and the arts

ever-expanding permanent collections of pre-20th century European paintings, drawings, illuminated manuscripts, sculpture, and decorative arts, and 19th- and 20th-century American and European photographs. The photography exhibits are particularly interesting, including a combined exhibition of Nadar and Warhol's photographic portraits and an exhibition on Sarah Siddons, the famous 19th-century British actress who cultivated her own celebrity. The original site of the museum, the Getty Villa in Malibu, will reopen in 2001 and house the ostentatious collection of J. Paul Getty's classical antiquities. The Getty also hosts gallery talks, lectures, film screenings, concerts, and poetry readings, which are getting pretty hip these days with Beth Lapides's UnCabaret and a Nadar/Warhol-inspired poetry reading featuring such local luminaries as esteemed drag performer Vaginal Davis.

GRIFFITH OBSERVATORY

2800 E. Observatory Rd. nr. Los Feliz Blvd., Los Feliz, 323-664-1191; www.griffithobservatory.org; Hours: summer daily 12:30pm-10pm; winter Tue-Fri 2pm-10pm; Sat-Sun 12:30pm-10pm

Familiar to most from *Rebel Without a Cause*, this 1934 art deco landmark is where the climactic moments of that bad-seed classic film were filmed. Check out the free public telescope (nightly, 7-10pm), be thrilled by the tesla coil's lightning bolts, and marvel at the Foucault pendulum. To stave off post-holiday weight-gain depression, jump on the altered scales to see what you'd weigh on the moon and the other eight planets. On clear days, you can get a close look at the Hollywood sign and a bird's-eye view of the Los Angeles basin. The planetarium is also the location for the pot smoke-filled institution known as the Laserium, where you can see laser light shows to your favorite Pink Floyd, Led

Zeppelin, or '80s new wave songs. Mind-altering substances are optional.

LOS ANGELES COUNTRY MUSEUM OF ART
5905 Wilshire Blvd. bet. Fairfax and La Brea Aves., Los Angeles, 323-857-6000; www.lacma.org; Hours: Tue-Thu 10am-5pm; Fri 10am-9pm; Sat-Sun 11am-6pm

The largest museum west of the Mississippi, the Los Angeles County Museum of Art features a comprehensive permanent collection spanning the history of Western art from the past to the present, with a significant collection of Asian and Near Eastern art as well. You could easily spend the whole day wandering between LACMA's diverse and comprehensive galleries, but instead of checking out the same Impressionists you see everywhere, be daring and explore some of the museum's more specialized collections, such as the Rifkin Collection of German Expressionism, with prints, drawings, and associated ephemera from Weimar Germany, and the Japanese Pavilion, which is the only building outside of Japan devoted solely to Japanese art. The museum also houses a large collection of contemporary California artists like David Hockney and Richard Diebenkorn. On Friday evenings, there is a free jazz series in the courtyard, with some of LA's best jazzbos and cocktails and hors d'oeuvres. Sundays offer chamber music concerts in the Bing Theater. And for all you cheapskates, there is free admission on the second Tuesday of every month, though you'll still have to pay for the big-time ticketed exhibitions.

MUSEUM OF CONTEMPORARY ART
250 South Grand Ave. at 3rd St., Downtown, 213-621-2766; The Geffen Contemporary, 152 North Central Ave. at W. 1st St., Little Tokyo; www.moca-la.org; Hours: Tue-Wed 11am-5pm; Thu 11am-8pm;

Fri-Sun 11am-5pm
Built so that the LA art world's well-heeled collectors could donate and show off their personal collections (not to mention get huge tax write-offs), the Museum of Contemporary Art is the preeminent venue for contemporary art in Los Angeles. Ensconced in California Plaza in a stark building designed by Japanese architect Arata Isozaki, MOCA's mission is to expose the public to the best art created after 1940. The museum displays rotating selections from its permanent collection and special exhibitions of contemporary pieces from all the modern-day heavyweights — John Cage, Cindy Sherman, and Karen Finley among them. Not limiting itself to the conventional forms of painting, drawings, and sculpture, MOCA also showcases video, photography, film, music, dance, performance, design, architecture, and whatever else an up-and-coming artist can convince the curators is art these days. Occasionally, the small auditorium in the basement hosts experimental films, live performances, and lectures. A free shuttle goes to the museum's satellite, the Geffen Contemporary, a cavernous warehouse-like space redesigned by Frank Gehry that housed the MOCA for several years while its permanent home was being con-

tructed. On Thursdays the museum is open late, with free admission, a cash bar, free hors d'oeuvres, and live music performances by artists like El Vez (the Mexican Elvis) and Sun Ra's Arkestra.

MUSEUM OF TOLERANCE

9786 Pico Blvd. bet. Motor Ave. and Beverwil Dr., West LA, 310-553-8403; www.wiesenthal.com; Hours: Mon-Thu 10am-5pm; Fri 10am-3pm; Sun 11am-5pm

This important museum may be depressing, but in post-uprising Los Angeles, it takes an important look at race relations, bigotry, and the horrible hate crimes that they spawn. Exhibits include looks at the 1992 Los Angeles riots, hate groups, black oppression, Native American genocide, and the Holocaust. Upon admission, you are issued a passport with the name and photo of a Holocaust victim, and as you journey through the galleries you will learn about his history and find out whether he lived or died. There is even a walk-through replica of a concentration camp gas chamber, which provides a powerful and affecting experience.

SANTA MONICA MUSEUM OF ART

2525 Michigan Ave. at Cloverfield Blvd., Santa Monica, 310-586-6488; Hours: Wed-Thu 11am-6pm; Fri 11am-10pm; Sat-Sun 11am-6pm

In its new home at Bergamot Station, the Santa Monica Museum of Art is continuing its mission to present some of today's most controversial and intriguing artwork in order to reflect thoughts about modern society from fresh points of view. The museum falls somewhere between a gallery and a museum; it has no permanent collection, but instead uses its acquisition money to commission new works from emerging artists. Most of the artists represented here are newly discovered or in mid-career, and most come from Southern California. The SMMOA also likes to brag that it is the premier showcase for provocative visual arts programs. Inaugural exhibitions for its new space included "Liza Lou's Back Yard and Kitchen," made from zillions of multicolored glass beads, and "Beck and Al Hansen: Playing With Matches,"

a small show of collages by rock star Beck and his grandfather, Al, a celebrated Fluxus artist. The museum also hosts a weekly salon series on Friday nights where you can hobnob with important local artists or hear sound art by musicians from LA's celebrated experimental music scene.

museums and galleries

HOLLYWOOD MUSEUMS

There are a handful of museums celebrating Tinseltown and its checkered past. The **Hollywood Studio Museum** (2100 N. Highland Ave., Hollywood, 323-874-2276) pays tribute to the silent film era with exhibits explaining the science of old-time filmmaking. Housed in the building where Cecil B. DeMille, Samuel Goldwyn, and Jesse Lasky made Hollywood's first full-length motion picture, this was the first home of Paramount Studios. It's not just a bunch of tawdry waxen figures at the **Hollywood Wax Museum** (6767 Hollywood Blvd., Hollywood, 323-462-5991), which re-creates classic scenes from movies like *The Exorcist* and *Planet of the Apes* as well as displaying incredible waxen likenesses of all your favorite stars, from Dr. Spock to Dolly Parton. **The Hollywood Entertainment Museum** (7021 Hollywood Blvd., Hollywood, 323-960-4806) thrills with its re-creations of the beam-me-up bridge of the Star Trek Enterprise and the *Cheers* bar, which actually pulls pints on Thursday nights. The tony Los Angeles wing of New York's **Museum of Television and Radio** (65 N. Beverly Dr., Beverly Hills, 310-786-1000) has over 75,000 programs in its archives, with special exhibitions of masters of the boob tube like Andy Kaufman and Hanna-Barbera, as well the unpredictable, like a complete look at REM videos, Lenny Bruce's TV appearances, and an homage to *Monty Python's Flying Circus*.

MIRACLE MILE

This legendary strip of Wilshire Boulevard between Fairfax and La Brea was acquired in 1920 by A.W. Ross so he could develop it into a snazzy, upscale shopping district that could be navigated by automobile. The strip is the longtime home of the Los Angeles Country Museum of Art, which has spawned a half dozen special interest museums, earning the area the nickname Museum Row. Every local has gone on innumerable field trips to gawk at the bubbling tar at the **Page Museum at the La Brea Tar Pits** *(5801 Wilshire Blvd., Los Angeles, 323-934-PAGE)*, where, believe it or not, Ice Age fossils up to 40,000 years old are still being found in the heart of Los Angeles. Touch the massive leg bone of an giant ground sloth, marvel at animatronic creatures, or watch the yearly summer excavation and cleaning of bones from wolves and saber-toothed cats from the observation deck of Pit 91. The smaller-than-life world at the **Museum of Miniatures** *(5900 Wilshire Blvd., Los Angeles, 323-937-MINI)* houses the largest collection of contemporary miniatures in the world. Among the whimsical offerings are all 44 of the United States' First Ladies and a Lilliputian jazz orchestra playing the Hollywood Bowl with guest stars Ella Fitzgerald and Michael Jackson, all done in 1/12 scale. You can check out traditional folk art and crafts from around the world at the **Craft and Folk Art Museum** *(5814 Wilshire Blvd., Los Angeles, 323-937-4230)*. Besides predictable fare like quilts and masks, it's also had inventive exhibits on girls' lowrider bikes and the life of Zora Neale Hurston. The oldest museum in Los Angeles, the **Southwest Museum** *(6067 Wilshire Blvd., Los Angeles, 323-857-6000)* at LACMA West, is devoted to Native American culture. It has one of the most significant collections of Native American art in the U.S. and hosts intertribal marketplaces and textile exhibitions. The **Petersen Automotive Museum** *(6060 Wilshire Blvd., Los Angeles, 323-930-2277)* is the world's biggest museum devoted to cars and car culture and a fitting celebration of the city's love affair with the automobile. The **Los Angeles Museum of the Holocaust** *(6006 Wilshire Blvd., Los Angeles, 323-761-8170)* chronicles and preserves the history of LA's Jewish community, the second largest outside of Israel, with photos, artwork, historical displays, and, one of the more interesting collections, an assemblage of Nazi trading cards.

culture and the arts

MODERN CHIC

Mid-century furniture and design have taken Los Angeles by storm recently. But the area has long nurtured and embraced those who propelled this movement of contemporary style and clean lines. Evidence of their genius has long dotted the Los Angeles landscape and continues to be on display throughout the city — in some cases, right in our own backyard. Frank Lloyd Wright brilliantly integrated the **Ennis-Brown House** *(2655 Glendower Dr., Los Feliz, 323-668-0234)* with concrete modularity into the Hollywood hillside on which it resides. Make sure you catch a peek at the mosaic above the fireplace. One of Richard Neutra's first masterpieces, the **Lovell-Health House** *(4616 Dundee Dr., Los Feliz)* sports a steel-framed skeleton cast in stucco that's tiered into the hillside. The **Eames House** *(203 Chautauqua Blvd., Pacific Palisades, 310-459-9663)*, regarded as a standout case-study home, is composed of glass and steel and continues to be celebrated as the paragon of architectural function. Finally, no architect has had a more profound influence on Los Angeles's self-vision than Frank Gehry. **Frank Gehry's House** *(corner of Washington and 22nd Sts., Santa Monica)* was once a traditional Craftsman house and still sits on a modest corner in Santa Monica. Gehry transformed the house, however, by enveloping it in a corrugated metal and plywood shell that lends the home a startling newness.

OFFBEAT MUSEUMS

As the land of kooks, Los Angeles hosts some of the quirkiest museums in the world. These painfully wacky collections are labors of love and, as such, are sometimes located in the laborer's very own living room. So give a ring before you embark on your outing; many are open by appointment only. For starters, weird science comes alive at the **Museum of Jurassic Technology** *(9341 Venice Blvd., Culver City, 310-836-6131)*. A pseudoscientific devotion to the

culture and the arts

"advancement of knowledge and the public appreciation of the Lower Jurassic," it is, in reality, a satiric collection of relics and artifacts, emphasizing the curious and unusual. When you see the wedding cake mailbox, you'll know you've arrived at the **Mini Cake Museum** *(573 S. Boyle Ave., Los Angeles, 323-263-6195)*. The Cake Lady, Frances Kuyper, has taught cake decorating since the Korean War, and now her museum holds over 200 elaborately decorated cakes in many shapes, from the Eiffel Tower to Chihuahuas to the pièce de résistance, an airbrushed portrait of Oprah Winfrey. What started as pet names for each other ("honey bunny") turned into a enormous collection of bunny items for the proprietors of the **Bunny Museum** *(1933 Jefferson Dr., Pasadena, 626-798-8848)*, Candace Frazee and Steve Lubanski, who have crammed over 10,0000 items devoted to their floppy-eared furry friends, including stuffed bunnies, toys, decorations, utensils, and furniture into every nook and cranny in their house, with a 12-foot-high bunny in the front yard. Become a member of the International Banana Club and Ken Banninster, T.B. (top banana, don't you know), will share over 15,000 banana-related items with you from his **Banana Museum** *(2524 N. El Molino Ave., Altadena, 626-798-2272)*. Drawn from both the hard and soft collection (no dirty jokes, as Mr. Banninster insists that everything in this museum is in good taste), the highlights are the gold-sequined banana, an Italian boudoir banana, and a petrified banana. In the back room of **Frederick's of Hollywood** *(6608 Hollywood Blvd., Hollywood, 323-466-8506)* is the **International Bra Museum**, devoted to the history of restrictive undergarments, and the Celebrity Lingerie Hall of Fame. Explore the origin and development of brassieres, corsets, and stockings before gawking at the lascivious lingerie worn by the sex goddesses of history. Prime examples are Mae West's peignoir, Milton Berle's first dress, and Madonna's bustier, which was stolen (and later anonymously returned) during the LA riots. The **Holyland Exhibition** *(2215 Lake View Ave., Silver Lake, 323-664-3162)*, a self-styled archaeological museum, attempts to re-create the ancient environment of the Middle East during Jesus's time, with tour guides garbed in burnooses who serve you genuine Holyland snacks — fruit roll-ups and Kool-Aid on our visit — at the end of your tour. The women who live there today say that Bible scholar/archaeologist Antonio F. Futterer, who founded the Exhibition before leaving LA to search for the Ark of the Covenant, was the inspiration for the movie *Raiders of the Lost Ark*. Every Saturday, Forrest Ackerman, the ultimate horror movie fan and founding editor of what many credit as the world's first fanzine, *Famous Monsters*, opens up his Los Feliz home, the **Ackermansion** *(2495 Glendower Ave., Los Feliz)*, to the public. Eighteen rooms are stocked floor to ceiling with memorabilia like lifecasts of Boris Karloff and Bela Lugosi, stop-motion puppets from *King Kong*, and props, pictures, and costumes from all the finest creature features. The best part is listening to Ackerman's well rehearsed tales of hobnobbing with Tinseltown's scariest stars. The **Darby Crash Punk Rock Museum** at kitschy tchotchke store **Ka-boom** *(3816 Sunset Blvd., Silver Lake, 323-661-8697)* memorializes the Los Angeles punk scene circa 1983 with such seminal keepsakes as Iggy Pop's guitar, Debbie Harry's dress, Exene Cerkvenka's cardigan, Sex Pistols eight-tracks, and a faded yellow Devo suit.

GALLERIES AND ARTS FESTIVALS

To find out about current exhibitions at galleries around town, log on to *www.artscenecal.com*, check the listings in the *LA Weekly*, *New Times*, or *Los Angeles Times*, or check the CityTripping.com Hot Picks list. Unlike New York, there are no central art gallery neighborhoods in LA, but there are several gallery complexes.

BERGAMOT STATION

A self-styled art gallery mall, **Bergamot Station** *(2525 Michigan Ave. at Cloverfield Blvd., Santa Monica, 310-829-5854)* was opened in 1994 and now houses over 20 galleries, plus the Santa Monica Museum of Art, a café, and, most important, plenty of parking. Before public and private arts organizations transformed this desolate industrial stretch in Santa Monica to a contemporary arts campus, it was the Bergamot stop on the now dismantled Red Car line to the beach. **Track 16** *(310-264-4678)* has featured exhibitions devoted to the early years of LA punk rock and William Burroughs' paintings, as well as live performances by Karen Finley. As co-chair of the LA Biennial, longtime art player **Robert Berman** *(310-315-9507)* is one of the most influential gallery owners in town, showing both new and more established local artists. **Patricia Correia Gallery** *(310-264-1760)* features mostly abstract painting and sculpture by emerging Los Angeles and West Coast artists. **Patricia Faure Gallery** *(310-449-1479)* often shows controversial works by artists such as the Reverend Ethan Acres, a Gen-X evangelical preacher. **The Gallery of Contemporary Photography** *(310-264-8440)* showcases documentary art photography, including Max Aguilera-Hellweg's invasive-surgery photos and film director Wim Wenders' still photography. Owned by another influential bigwig on the LA art scene, The **Rosamund Felson**

culture and the arts

...allery *(310-828-8488)* represents and exhibits primarily Los Angeles artists and has brought many of them, like Meg Cranston and patron saint of pranksters Jeffrey Vallance, to worldwide attention. **Paul Fetterman Photographic Works of Art** *(310-453-6463)* shows 19th- and 20th-century photography, representing such unforgettable shutterbugs as Henri Cartier-Bresson and Weegee. **Cherry Frumkin/ Christine Duval Gallery** *(310-453-1850)* unveils contemporary painting and sculpture, including J.S.G. Boggs' fake currency, causing him quite a bit of trouble with the Feds. The **Frank Lloyd Gallery** *(310-264-3866)* focuses on modern and contemporary ceramic art, proving that there is much more to ceramics than what you made at camp. The **Shoshana Wayne Gallery** *(310-453-7535)* is run by the people who developed Bergamot Station and exhibits risky art in a variety of media, from artists like Kiki Smith and Matthew McCaslin. The **Bobbie Greenfield Gallery** *(310-264-0640)* features contemporary works on paper and diptychs and triptychs. The U.S. outpost of British gallery Flowers East, **Flowers West** *(310-586-9200)* serves as an introduction to contemporary European art. And **Sculpture to Wear** *(310-829-9960)* exhibits and sells one-of-a-kind, hand crafted wearable artwork, namely jewelry, scarves, handbags, and hats.

EASTSIDE ART CRAWL

A knock against the pretentious Westside art scene, several galleries have sprung up on the Eastside to provide a forum for under-represented artists from the struggling side of the city. Banding together with a handful of living-room galleries in the once-a-year **Eastside Art Crawl**, the following galleries form a closely knit, welcoming venue for neophyte artists. **La Luz de Jesus** *(4633 Hollywood Blvd., Los Feliz, 323-666-POOP)* is devoted to the lowbrow art world touted by magazines like *Juxtapoz*.

culture and the arts | 221

Its art openings are always a happening scene, drawing trendies from the Silver Lake, Echo Park, and Los Feliz neighborhoods, who come for the free beer (no wine or cheese here) and the zany art. Lydia Lunch and Clive Barker, as well as hipster artists like Shag and Coop, have had exhibitions here. **Plastica** *(4685 Sunset Blvd., Los Feliz, 323-644-1212)*, a retail store selling kitschy plastic products from around the world, has a gallery in back that mostly shows work from the proprietors' recent art school graduate cronies. On Echo Park Boulevard at the bottom of an overcrowded brick apartment building are three galleries that, every month, have painfully cool cooperative openings: **Ojala Fine Arts and Crafts** *(1547 Echo Park Blvd., Echo Park, 213-250-4155)*, with paintings and ceramics; **Fototeka** *(1549 Echo Park Blvd., Echo Park, 213-250-4686)*, with dazzling, cutting-edge photo exhibitions; and **Delirium Tremens** *(1553 Echo Park Ave., Echo Park, 213-861-6802)*, with bizarrely themed shows such as the recent one on sci-fi-influenced art. Nearby, on Sunset Boulevard is the **Art Park Gallery** *(1478 Sunset Blvd., Echo Park, 213-482-9469)*, an outdoor installation space.

6150 WILSHIRE

Billing itself as a vanguard gallery complex, **6150 Wilshire** *(6150 Wilshire Blvd., Los Angeles)* is home to several cutting-edge art galleries. Since it's just down the street from the Los Angeles County Museum of Art, it's worth a stop to get a taste of the flavor of the month in today's art world. **ACME Gallery** *(323-857-5942)*, run by Randy Sommer and Robert Gunderman, features boundary-shattering art from local artists. The **Dan Bernier Gallery** *(323-936-1021)* offers all manner of art, from the performance art of Tamara Fittes to the sculptural work of Martin Kersels. **Works on Paper** *(323-964-9675)* focuses on — you guessed it — paper, with intricate cutouts and collages. The **Marc Foxx Gallery** *(323-857-5571)* presents a fine selection of new work photography, projection, and sculpture. **Karyn Lovegrove Gallery** *(323-525-1755)* features photography and art from Australia in the Australian owner's cool space. A few doors down, **POST Wilshire** *(6130 Wilshire Blvd., Los Angeles, 323-622-8580)* is the Westside outlet of POST, the toast of the downtown art scene, showing the cream of the crop from the fringes with guest curators like Sue Spaid and Jeffrey Vallance.

ARTS FESTIVALS

The first Saturday of every October is the **Los Angeles County-Wide Arts Open House**, when over 100 performances, exhibitions, and other cultural events are free to the public. In May, at the **Venice Art Walk**, dozens of working artists open up their homes and studios to the public. There is also a silent art auction, food fair, and musical performances. The **LA International** is a biennial festival of artists from outside the United States, in which over 60 Los Angeles, Santa Monica, and Venice area galleries invite artists from around the world to mount special exhibitions. **The Brewery Arts Complex** *(N. Main St. at Avenue 21, Lincoln Heights)*, just east of downtown, is a 21-building arts complex where more than 100 artists live and work in studios. Twice a year, they host an Art Walk at which the public is invited to view the work of painters, sculptors, photographers, and performers in the homes and studios in which they were created.

culture and the arts | 223

index by neighborhood

santa monica/venice

The Aero 1328 Montana Ave. at 14th St., Santa Monica, 310-395-4990

Beyond Baroque Literary Arts Center 681 Venice Blvd. bet. Abbot Kinney and Lincoln Blvds., Venice, 310-822-3006

Bergamot Station 2525 Michigan Ave. at Cloverfield Blvd., Santa Monica, 310-829-5854

Eames House 203 Chautauqua Blvd. bet. Sunset Blvd. and Pacific Coast Hwy., Pacific Palisades, 310-459-9663

Frank Gehry's House corner of Washington and 22nd St., Santa Monica

Laemmle Four-Plex 1332 2nd St. bet. Arizona Ave. and Santa Monica Blvd., Santa Monica, 310-394-9741

Midnight Special 1318 3rd Street Promenade bet. Arizona Ave. and Santa Monica Blvd., Santa Monica, 310-393-2923

Santa Monica Museum of Art 2525 Michigan Ave. at Cloverfield Blvd., Santa Monica, 310-586-6488

Will Geer Theatricum Botanicum 1419 Topanga Canyon Blvd. bet. Mulholland and Pacific Coast Hwys., Topanga Canyon, 310-455-2322

brentwood/west la/westwood

Armand Hammer Museum of Art 10899 Wilshire Blvd. at Westwood Blvd., West Los Angeles, 310-443-7000

Geffen Playhouse 10886 Le Conte Ave. nr. Westwood Blvd., Westwood, 310-208-6500

Getty Center 1200 Getty Center Dr. nr. Sepulveda Blvd., Brentwood, 310-440-7300

Jazz Bakery 3233 Helms Ave. at Venice Blvd., Culver City, 310-271-9039

Museum of Jurassic Technology 9341 Venice Blvd. nr. Culver Blvd., Culver City, 310-836-6131

Museum of Tolerance 9786 Pico Blvd. bet. Motor Ave. and Beverwil Dr., West Los Angeles, 310-553-8403

Nuart 11272 Santa Monica Blvd. at Sawtelle Blvd., West LA, 310-478-6379

UCLA Film and Television Archives
James Bridges Theater, 405 Hilgard
Ave. bet. Sunset and Wilshire Blvds.,
Westwood, 310-206-FILM

beverly hills

**Academy of Motion Picture Arts
and Sciences** 8949 Wilshire Blvd.
bet. Doheny Dr. and Robertson Blvd.,
Beverly Hills, 310-247-3600

Museum of Television and Radio
465 N. Beverly Dr. at Little Santa Monica
Blvd., Beverly Hills, 310-786-1000

Writers Guild 135 S. Doheny Dr.
bet. Wilshire and Olympic Blvds.,
Beverly Hills, 323-951-4000

west hollywood

The Celebration Theater 7051B
Santa Monica Blvd. at La Brea Ave.,
West Hollywood, 323-957-1884

Comedy Store 8443 Sunset Blvd.
bet. La Cienega and Crescent
Heights Blvds., West Hollywood,
323-656-6225

Directors Guild 7920 Sunset Blvd.
bet. Crescent Heights Blvd. and
Fairfax Ave., West Hollywood,
310-289-2000

Hustler Hollywood 8920 Sunset Blvd.
bet. Doheny Dr. and San Vicente Blvd.,
West Hollywood, 310-860-9009

Improv 8162 Melrose Ave. bet. La
Cienega and Crescent Heights Blvds.,
West Hollywood, 323-651-2583

Laemmle Five 8000 Sunset Blvd. at
Crescent Heights Blvd., West Hollywood,
323-848-3500

Laugh Factory 8001 Sunset Blvd. at
Crescent Heights Blvd., West Hollywood,
323-656-1336

Stonewall Gourmet Coffee 8717
Santa Monica Blvd. bet. San Vicente
and La Cienega Blvds., West Hollywood,
310-659-8009

UnCabaret LunaPark, 665 N.
Robertson Blvd. bet. Santa Monica Blvd.
and Robertson Ave., West Hollywood,
310-652-0611

third/beverly

Acme Comedy Theater 135 N.
La Brea Ave. bet. Beverly Blvd. and 3rd
St., Los Angeles, 323-525-0202

Bang Improv Studio 457 N. Fairfax
Ave. bet, Melrose Ave. and Beverly Blvd.,
West Hollywood, 323-653-6886

Cineplex Odeon Fairfax 7907
Beverly Blvd. at Fairfax Ave.,
Los Angeles, 323-653-3117

Largo 465 N. Fairfax Ave. bet. Melrose Ave. and Beverly Blvd., Los Angeles, 323-852-1073

Masquers Cabaret 8334 3rd St. bet. La Cienega and Crescent Heights Blvds., Los Angeles, 323-653-4848

New Beverly Cinema 7165 Beverly Blvd. bet. Fairfax and La Brea Aves., Los Angeles, 323-938-4038

Silent Movie Theatre 611 N. Fairfax Ave. nr. Melrose Ave., 323-655-2520

Young Comics Exposed Farfalla, 143 N. La Brea Blvd. bet. Beverly Blvd. and 3rd St., Los Angeles, 323-954-2504

hollywood

Actors Gang 6209 and 6201 Santa Monica Blvd. bet. Vine and Gower Sts., Hollywood, 323-465-0566

American Cinematheque Egyptian Theatre, 6712 Hollywood Blvd. bet. Highland Ave. and Cahuenga Blvd., Hollywood, 323-461-2020

Attic Theater 6562 1/2 Santa Monica Blvd. bet. Highland Ave. and Cahuenga Blvd., Hollywood, 323-469-3786

Barber Shop Club 6907 Melrose Ave. bet. La Brea and Highland Aves., Hollywood, 323-939-4319

Cinegrill Hollywood Roosevelt Hotel, 7000 Hollywood Blvd. bet. La Brea and Highland Aves., Hollywood, 323-466-7000

Cinerama Dome 6360 Sunset Blvd. bet. Cahuenga Blvd. and Vine St., Hollywood, 323-466-3401

Comedy at Bat Miceli's, 1646 N. Le Palmas Ave. bet. Hollywood and Sunset Blvds., Hollywood, 323-769-5899

El Capitan 6838 Hollywood Blvd. at Highland Ave., Hollywood, 323-467-7674

Gardenia Club 7066 Santa Monica Blvd. bet. La Brea and Highland Aves., Hollywood, 323-467-7444

Groundlings, 7307 Melrose Ave. bet. Fairfax and La Brea Aves., Hollywood, 323-934-9700

HBO Workspace 733 N. Seward St. bet. Santa Monica Blvd. and Melrose Ave., Hollywood, 323-993-6099

Hollywood Bowl 2301 N. Highland Ave. bet. Mulholland Dr. and Franklin Ave., Hollywood, 323-850-2000

The Hollywood Entertainment Museum 7021 Hollywood Blvd. bet. La Brea and Highland Aves., Hollywood, 323-960-4806

Hollywood Studio Museum 2100 N. Highland Ave. bet. Mulholland Dr.

nd Franklin Ave., Hollywood, 323-874-2276

Hollywood Wax Museum
6767 Hollywood Blvd. at Highland Ave., Hollywood, 323-462-5991

Hudson Theatre 6537 Santa Monica Blvd. bet. Highland Ave. and Cahuenga Blvd., Hollywood, 323-769-5858

The Improv Olympic West Theatre 6468 Santa Monica Blvd. bet. Highland Ave. and Cahuenga Blvd., Hollywood, 323-962-7560

International Bra Museum Frederick's of Hollywood, 6608 Hollywood Blvd. bet. Highland Ave. and Cahuenga Blvd., Hollywood, 323-466-8506

Last Laughs Before the 101 Hollywood Hills Coffee Shop, 6145 Franklin Ave. bet. Vine and Gower Sts., Hollywood, 323-467-7678

Mann's Chinese Theater 6925 Hollywood Blvd. bet. La Brea and Highland Aves., Hollywood, 323-464-8111

Miceli's 1646 N. Las Palmas Ave. bet. Hollywood and Sunset Blvds., Hollywood, 323-769-5899

Outfest at the Village 1125 N. McCadden Pl. nr. Santa Monica Blvd., Hollywood, 323-960-2394

los feliz/silver lake

Ackermansion 2495 Glendower Ave. nr. Vermont Ave., Los Feliz

Art Park Gallery 1478 Sunset Blvd. bet. Echo Park and Elysian Park Aves., Echo Park, 213-482-9469

The Autry Museum of Western Heritage Griffith Park, 4700 Western Heritage Way at Zoo Dr., Los Feliz, 323-667-2000

Darby Crash Punk Rock Museum, Ka-Boom, 3816 Sunset Blvd. at Hyperion Ave., Silver Lake, 323-661-8697

Dresden Room 1760 N. Vermont Ave. bet. Franklin Ave. and Hollywood Blvd., Los Feliz, 323-665-4294

Ennis-Brown House 2655 Glendower Dr. nr. Vermont Ave., Los Feliz, 323-668-0234

Fototeka 1549 Echo Park Blvd. no. of Sunset Blvd., Echo Park, 213-250-4686

Glaxa 3707 Sunset Blvd. bet. Hyperion Ave. and Silver Lake Blvd., Silver Lake, 323-663-5295

Griffith Observatory 2800 E. Observatory Rd. north of Los Feliz Blvd., Los Feliz, 323-664-1191

Holyland Exhibition 2215 *Lake View Ave. nr. Glendale Fwy., Silver Lake,* 323-664-3162

La Luz de Jesus 4633 *Hollywood Blvd. at Vermont Ave., Los Feliz,* 323-666-POOP

Lovell-Health House 4616 *Dundee Dr. nr. Vermont Ave., Los Feliz*

Ojala Fine Arts and Crafts 1547 *Echo Park Blvd. no. of Sunset Blvd., Echo Park,* 213-250-4155

Plastica 4685 *Sunset Blvd. at Vermont Ave., Los Feliz,* 323-644-1212

Tremens 1553 *Echo Park Ave. no. of Sunset Blvd., Echo Park,* 213-861-6802

The Vista 4473 *Sunset Dr. at Hillhurst Ave., Los Feliz,* 323-660-6639

koreatown/mid-city

Bing Theater 5905 *Wilshire Blvd. bet. Fairfax and La Brea Aves., Los Angeles,* 323-857-6010

Craft and Folk Art Museum 5814 *Wilshire Blvd. bet. Fairfax and La Brea Aves., Los Angeles,* 323-937-4230

Goethe Film Institute 5750 *Wilshire Blvd. bet. Fairfax and La Brea Aves., Los Angeles,* 323-525-3388

Los Angeles Country Museum of Art 5905 *Wilshire Blvd. bet. Fairfax and La Brea Aves., Los Angeles,* 323-857-6000

Los Angeles Museum of the Holocaust 6006 *Wilshire Blvd. bet. Fairfax and La Brea Aves., Los Angeles,* 323-761-8170

Mini Cake Museum 573 *S. Boyle Ave. bet. 4th and Whittier Sts., East LA,* 323-263-6195

Museum of Miniatures 5900 *Wilshire Blvd. bet. Fairfax and La Brea Aves., Los Angeles,* 323-937-MINI

Page Museum at the La Brea Tar Pits 5801 *Wilshire Blvd. bet. Fairfax and La Brea Aves., Los Angeles,* 323-934-PAGE

Petersen Automotive Museum 6060 *Wilshire Blvd. bet. Fairfax and La Brea Aves., Los Angeles,* 323-930-2277

POST Wilshire 6130 *Wilshire Blvd. bet. Fairfax and La Brea Aves.,* 323-622-8580

6150 Wilshire 6150 *Wilshire Blvd. bet. Fairfax and La Brea Aves., Los Angeles*

Southwest Museum 6067 *Wilshire Blvd. bet. Fairfax and La Brea Aves., Los Angeles,* 323-857-6000

Downtown/chinatown

The Brewery Arts Complex
N. Main St. at Avenue 21, Lincoln Heights, 213-221-3500

Center Theater Group 135 N. Grand Ave. bet. Temple and First Sts., Downtown, 213-628-2772

The Geffen Contemporary 152 N. Central Ave. at 1st St., Little Tokyo

IMAX Theater California Science Center, 700 State Dr. bet. Vermont Ave. and Figueroa St., Downtown, 213-744-2014

Museum of Contemporary Art 250 S. Grand Ave. at 3rd St., Downtown, 213-621-2766

Orpheum 842 S. Broadway bet. 8th and 9th Sts., Downtown, 213-239-0937

Palace 630 S. Broadway bet. 6th and 7th Sts., Los Angeles, 213-239-0959

Quon Brothers Grand Star 943 Sun Mun Way bet. Hill St. and Broadway, Chinatown, 213-626-2285

---

farther afield

Actor's Forum 10655 Magnolia Blvd. bet. Vineland Ave. and Cahuenga Blvd., North Hollywood, 818-506-0600

Alex Film Society 216 N. Brand Ave. bet. California Ave. and Broadway, Glendale, 818-754-8250

American Renegade Theatre Co. 11136 Magnolia Blvd. bet. Lankershim Blvd. and Vineland Ave., North Hollywood, 818-763-4430

Azusa Foothill Drive-in 675 E. Foothill Blvd. at Alosta Ave., Azusa, 626-334-0263

Banana Museum 2524 N. El Molino Ave. at Mariposa St., Altadena, 626-798-2272

Bitter Truth Theatre 11050 Magnolia Blvd. bet. Lankershim Blvd. and Vineland Ave., North Hollywood, 818-755-7900

Bunny Museum 1933 Jefferson Dr. nr. Washington Blvd., Pasadena, 626-798-8848

Cobalt Café 22047 Sherman Way nr. Topanga Canyon Blvd., Canoga Park, 818-348-3789

Exile Books and Music 14925 Magnolia Blvd. bet. Sepulveda Blvd. and Kester Ave., Sherman Oaks, 818-986-6409

Fiesta Four Drive-in 8462 E. Whittier Blvd. nr. Paramount Blvd., Pico Rivera, 562-948-3671

Interact Theater *11855 Hart St. bet. Laurel Canyon and Lankershim Blvds., North Hollywood. 818-773-7862*

Kindness of Strangers Coffeehouse *4378 Lankershim Blvd. at Moorpark St., North Hollywood, 818-752-9566*

Laemmle Pasadena *667 E. Colorado Blvd. bet. Los Robles and Lake Aves., Pasadena, 626-844-6500*

NoHo Actors' Studio *5215 Lankershim Blvd. at Magnolia Blvd., North Hollywood, 818-990-2324*

The Old Town Music Hall *140 Richmond St. bet. Grand Ave. and El Segundo Blvd., El Segundo, 310-322-2592*

Raven Playhouse *5233 Lankershim Blvd. at Magnolia Blvd., North Hollywood, 818-509-9519*

Southbay 6 Drive-in *Main St bet. 405 and 110 Interstates, Carson, 310-532-8811*

Vineland Drive-in *443 N. Vineland Ave. bet. Valley Blvd. and Temple Ave., City of Industry, 626-961-9262*

Vitello's *4349 Tujunga Ave. bet. Moorpark St. and Venutra Blvd., Studio City, 818-769-0905*

index by type

cabaret
Cinegrill
Dresden Room
Gardenia Club
Masquers Cabaret
Miceli's
Quon Brothers Grand Star
Vitello's

cinema
Academy of Motion Picture Arts and Sciences
The Aero
Alex Film Society
American Cinematheque
The Autry Museum of Western Heritage
Azusa Foothill Drive-in
Bing Theater
Cineplex Odeon Fairfax
Cinerama Dome
Directors Guild
El Capitan
Fiesta Four Drive-in
Goethe Film Institute
IMAX Theater
Laemmle Five
Laemmle 4-Plex
Laemmle Pasadena
Los Angeles Country Museum of Art.

Mann's Chinese Theater
Midnight Special
Museum of Television and Radio
New Beverly Cinema
Nuart
Orpheum
Outfest at the Village
Palace
Silent Movie Theatre
Southbay 6 Drive-in
UCLA Film and Television Archives
Vineland Drive-in
The Vista
Writers Guild

comedy
Acme Comedy Theater
Bang Improv Studio
Comedy at Bat
Comedy Store
Groundlings
HBO Workspace
Hustler Hollywood
Improv
The Improv Olympic West Theatre
Jazz Bakery
Kindness of Strangers Coffeehouse
Largo
Last Laughs Before the 101
Laugh Factory
Masquers Cabaret
Uncabaret
Young Comics Exposed

galleries
Artwalk
Bergamot Station
Fototeka
Delirium Tremens
La Luz de Jesus
Ojala Fine Arts and Crafts
Plastica
POST Wilshire
6150 Wilshire

museums
Armand Hammer Museum of Art
The Autry Museum of Western Heritage
Banana Museum
Bunny Museum
Craft and Folk Art Museum
Darby Crash Punk Rock Museum
The Geffen Contemporary
Getty Center
The Hollywood Entertainment Museum
Hollywood Studio Museum
Hollywood Wax Museum
Holyland Exhibition
International Bra Museum
Los Angeles Country Museum of Art
Los Angeles Museum of the Holocaust
Mini Cake Museum
Museum of Contemporary Art
Museum of Jurassic Technology
Museum of Miniatures
Museum of Television and Radio

Museum of Tolerance
Page Museum at the La Brea Tar Pits
Petersen Automotive Museum
Santa Monica Museum of Art
Southwest Museum

spoken word

Barber Shop Club
Beyond Baroque Literary Arts Center
Cobalt Café
Exile Books and Music
Glaxa
Kindness of Strangers Coffeehouse
Stonewall Gourmet Coffee

stage

Actors Gang
Actor's Forum
American Renegade Theatre Co.
Attic Theater
Bitter Truth Theatre
The Celebration Theater
Center Theater Group
Geffen Playhouse
Glaxa
Hudson Theatre
Interact Theater
NoHo Actors' Studio
Raven Playhouse
Will Geer Theatricum Botanicum

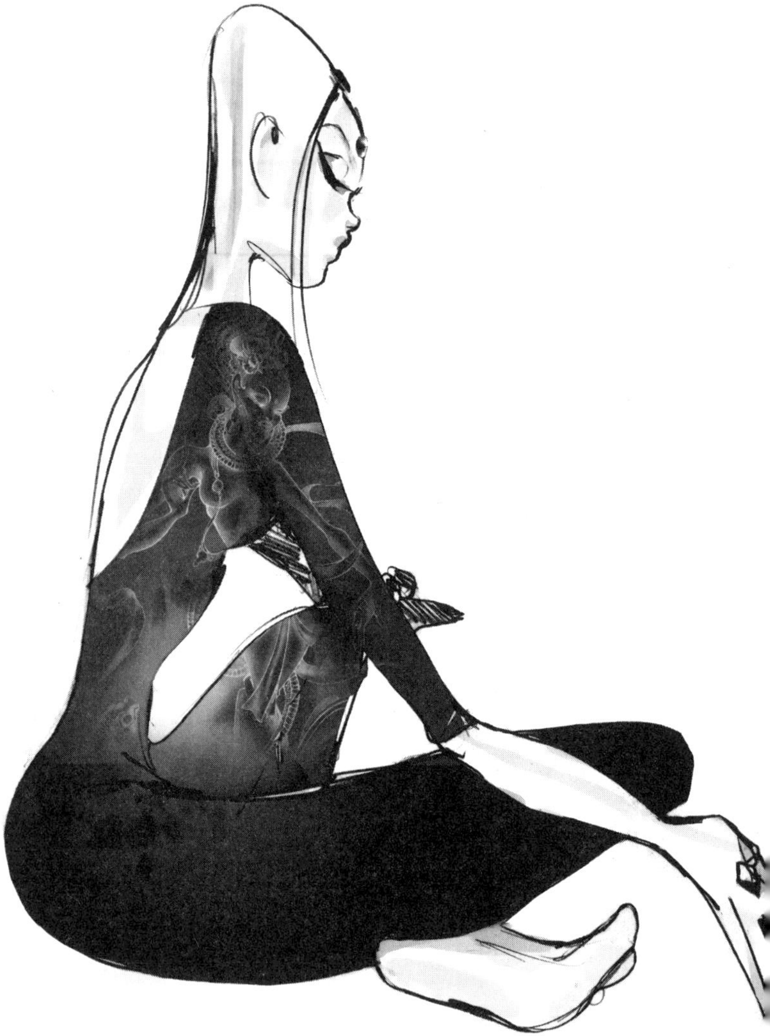

work that body

if there was ever a city prone to fitness fads, it's Los Angeles. Heat, sunshine, and a culture of body fascism make this the workout capital of the world. More than in any other city, who you are may be defined less by, well, who you are than by where and under whose tutelage you work your body. The good news is that you're bound to find something that floats your boat and tones your torso. ■ In LA, fierce debate can rage over the gym issue. Here are some of the more popular choices, along with a rock-climbing course and, for the canine-inclined, the best dog park in the city.

BARRY'S BOOT CAMP *1106 N. La Cienega Blvd. at Fountain Ave., West Hollywood, 310-360-6262; Hours: call for class schedules*

For the true masochist, Barry Jay's hard-core regimen will have you looking svelte sooner rather than later. Let's face it, your five-day-a-week workout has slipped to three days and is heading south towards two. Well, that won't fly here: Barry demands perfect attendance and punctuality. And once you're in class, there's no sleepwalking: push-ups, long jogs, and intensive body sculpting will have you begging for mercy. The popular Academy series will last four weeks and cost you $165-about $10 a pound if you're working hard, which is not a bad trade-off.

BILLY BLANKS' WORLD TRAINING CENTER *14708 Ventura Blvd. bet. Kester Ave. and Van Nuys Blvd., Sherman Oaks, 818-325-0335 Hours: call for class schedules*

Billy Blanks, the creator of Tae-Bo, is both instructor and celebrity personality. He developed Tae-Bo as a hybrid of martial arts and dance aerobics and has captured the attention of the conditioning world. A Saturday morning at this expansive studio in the Valley resembles a Saturday night on the Sunset Strip. Lines queue out the door in anticipation for classes; participants cheer over the thumping music as the session draws to a close. The workout itself is graceful, challenging, and, to those who've committed themselves to the regimen, addictive. Best of all, you won't have to worry about scheduling; the studio offers classes almost hourly during the morning and evenings.

CRUNCH *8000 Sunset Blvd. at Crescent Heights Blvd., West Hollywood, 323-654-4550; Hours: Mon-Thu 5am-11pm; Fri 5am-9pm; Sat 7am-8pm; Sun 8am-8pm*

No national fitness club has placed more emphasis on image management and niche marketing than Crunch. The niche, you ask? Any urbanite under 45 with a desire for a bird's-eye view of what's going on. In addition to the scenester element, Crunch offers everything from power yoga to Internet terminals on its stationary bikes. There's even a class called "Brand New Butt." And Crunch's management always does a nice job of making what could be an insufferably snotty place very user-friendly. Sleek design and superior locker and shower facilities lend this gym an air of cleanliness that you'll grow to appreciate. One problem: The subterranean garage at Sunset Plaza (home to the Laemmle 5 Theaters) can be a real bitch during the evening rush.

GOLD'S GYM HOLLYWOOD

1016 Cole Ave. bet. Santa Monica Blvd. and Romaine St., Hollywood, 323-462-7012; Hours: Mon-Fri 5am-12am; Sat-Sun 7am-9pm

Without question, Gold's Hollywood has the highest porn star quotient of any gym in the nation. Just don't stare or you'll incriminate yourself. Once you've perused

work that body | 237

the clientele, the facility is pretty straightforward and functional. A large, open space of free weights and weight machines dominates the ground floor; upstairs, you'll discover the two dance and workout studios of the Madonna Grimes Dance Studio, which offers everything from Latin to hip-hop dance classes (be advised, the participants include dozens of professionals; watch first, then enroll). If all this isn't enough for you, Gold's also has a juice bar.

SPORTSCLUB LA *1835 S. Sepulveda Blvd. bet. Santa Monica and Olympic Blvds., West LA, 310-473-1447; Hours: Mon-Fri 5am-11pm; Sat-Sun 7am-8pm*

A visit to Sportsclub LA isn't a workout, it's a day's outing. The Olympic-sized pool, track, full-court basketball, and every conceivable class and activity you can imagine just begins to scratch the surface. Start your morning with 25 laps, then down some coffee at the bar. After that, visit one of the half dozen weight rooms for a few sets. If you're really lucky, you may hook onto a game of horse with a Laker or two on the courts. Lunch at the in-house restaurant is healthy and savory (particularly the veggie burger). Spend the next hour digesting and tanning on the outdoor patio, just in time for your stretch class, and then a couple of miles on the track. And don't forgot to bring your checkbook; both the annual cost and initiation fees are far above anything you'd pay at other gyms.

ROCKREATION *11866 La Grange Ave. bet. Bundy Dr. and Barrington Ave., West LA, 310-207-7199; Hours: Mon, Wed, Fri 12pm-11pm; Tue, Thu 6am-11pm; Sat-Sun 10am-6pm*

If you're bored with the same old gym regimen and have an urge to defy gravity, you should head over to Rockreation and sign up for

"Fight Gravity One," their rock-climbing intro course. In a couple of hours, you'll learn all the basics — tying the knots, using the belay, and general strategy on the wall. The four-story walls have hundreds of climbs of varying levels; just follow the color-coded footholds. You can rent all the gear you'll need, including shoes. Because you have to climb in pairs, Rockreation is more fun with a friend.

SILVER LAKE DOG PARK

2000 Silver Lake Blvd. bet. Glendale and Sunset Blvds., Silver Lake

People look cuter when tending to their dogs. Luckily for you, on the south side of Silver Lake Reservoir lies a civic treasure and a bare necessity for any dog owner — or anyone who wants to meet a dog owner.

The Silver Lake Dog Park is a great place to toss the Frisbee around with your pup, and it isn't too shabby for meeting potential dates, either. Just make sure to bring your scooper and a supply of plastic bags.

A DAY AT THE BEACH

With dozens of miles of coastline within an hour's drive, the question in LA isn't "should we go to the beach?" but "where?" Starting north of the city, **Zuma Beach** offers everything you could want in a beach escape. The views on the Pacific Coast Highway from Santa Monica are so breathtaking, you may have trouble keeping your eyes on the road. A southern-exposed beach (most conducive to killer surf breaks), Zuma's silky sand and cobalt blue water make it easy to forget the teeming masses just ten miles south. A bit up the road is **El Matador Beach**, a beautiful, rocky cove that unveils gorgeous summer sunsets. Be sure to pack light, though; the descent from the parking lot to the beach is steep and rugged. El Matador's privacy has attracted its share of nudists, who congregate near the eroded sand pillars lining the shore. If big crowds and hyperactive children don't bother you, **Santa Monica Beach** is the most convenient option in town, sitting right at the end of the 10. Be forewarned that the bay has seen cleaner days, although a concerted preservation effort is underway. More attractive for its assortment of characters than for the gritty sand, **Venice Beach** is still something to see, especially on a Sunday, when the freaks come out in force. If you're more interested in looking at smooth torsos and bare midriffs, then **Manhattan Beach** and **Hermosa Beach** both come highly recommended. On weekends, the sand will be packed with volleyball players, surfers, and local families. And, unlike Malibu, you're only steps away from a quaint local string of shops, restaurants, and bars.

BOWLING

That's right, bowling is cool again. Lanes can be hard to come by at **Bay Shore Bowl** *(234 Pico Blvd., Santa Monica, 310-399-7731)*, particularly on Tuesday nights when they turn off the lights and crank up the music. Even better, it's all-you-can-bowl for $11. **Hollywood**

work that body

Star Lanes *(5227 Santa Monica Blvd., Hollywood, 323-665-4111)* probably hasn't updated its astral decor since 1954, which is why the Coen brothers made it the centerpiece of *The Big Lebowski*. Insomniacs can stumble in for a few frames anytime: the lanes operate 24-7. The real fun can be found on Saturday nights at Bowl-a-rama at **All Star Lanes** *(4459 Eagle Rock Blvd, Eagle Rock, 323-254-2576)*, when it's Greaser Night in an all-out tribute to the heyday of bowling, the 1950s.

CATCH SOME WAVES

If you're planning to adopt surfing as a recreational cornerstone in your life, get ready to exercise great patience. Once you get the hang of it, however, few sports are more exhilarating, not to mention cheap — except for the occasional trip to the emergency room. As a beginner, find a beach with an open break, such as **El Porto** on Manhattan Beach or **Zuma Beach** at Malibu during the summer months.

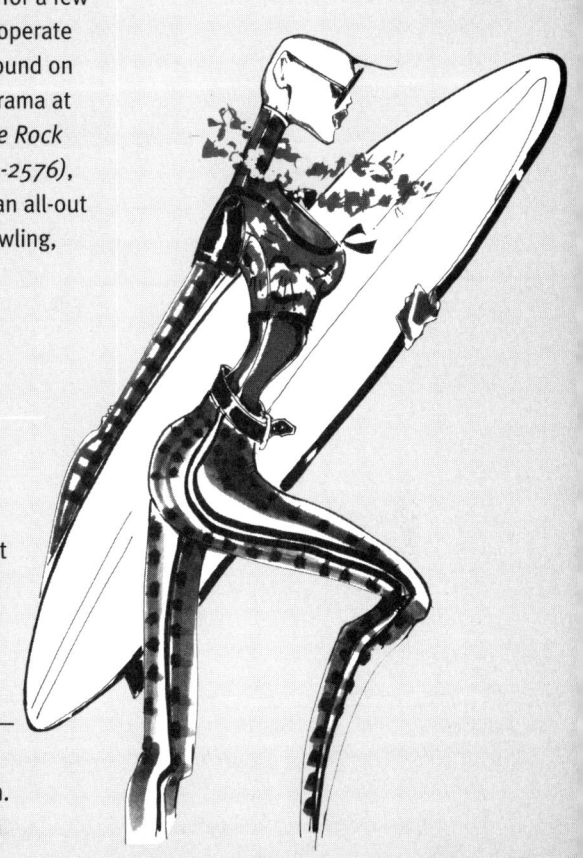

A southwestern-facing beach is your best bet as an intermediate, particularly **Sunset Beach** *(Sunset Blvd. at Pacific Coast Hwy.)*. Once you've gotten the hang of it, challenge yourself at Orange County's **Huntington Beach** *(Main St. at Pacific Coast Hwy.)*, where the waves can get pretty feisty. The water begins to cool during the fall months and won't warm again until early summer; during that period, you'll need a wet suit. And if you're used to more southern climes, you might very well need one year-round.

GEAR UP

For many, the true fun in taking up an outdoor sport is buying all the gear — never mind that much of it won't emerge from the hallway closet. Los Angeles, surrounded by mountains and ocean on all sides and populated by feverish consumers, makes for the perfect retail market for all things outdoorsy. As every instructor will tell you, mastery of any sport begins with the appropriate footwear. At **Surefoot** *(1426 Montana Ave., Santa Monica, 310-393-3331)*, the first thing you do is step on the foot scanner which takes 538 measurements in seconds. In 30 minutes you'll have a pair of custom orthotics to slip into your ski boots, in-line skates, cross-trainers, cycling shoes, or even golf cleats. Cyclists on the Westside swear by **Helen's Cycles** *(2501 Broadway, Santa Monica, 310-829-1836; 1071 Gayley Ave., Westwood, 310-208-8988)* and their dutiful and efficient maintenance staff. Their wide selection of cool jerseys and bike-wear will ensure that you're not a fashion victim on wheels. For wilderness stuff, **Adventure 16** *(11161 Pico Blvd., West LA, 310-473-4574)* is a mecca. They even have a wedding registry for the rugged couple who'd rather spend their honeymoon climbing the north face of El Capitan than the stairs to their bungalow in Bali. You can test-ride almost any bike in the shop at **I. Martin Imports** *(8330 Beverly Blvd., Los Angeles, 323-653-6900)*, which may outfit more AIDS Riders than any other sport shop in Southern California. **Val Surf** *(4810 Whitsett Ave., North Hollywood, 818-769-6977)* can stake its claim as the best extreme sport shop in America. They focus primarily on three sports: surfing (including bodyboarding), skateboarding, and snowboarding. Even if you're just working the X-aesthetic, stop in for some glasses or skate shoes. For a smaller surf shop closer to the beach, **ZJ's Boarding House** *(2619 Main St., Santa Monica, 310-392-5646)* fits the bill for the essentials, and the staff won't sneer if you're a neophyte.

GOLF FOR HIPSTERS

Hipster golf fiends are coming out of the closet in hordes to declare their allegiance to the maddeningly addictive sport that has roared back with a vengeance in the past decade. This is Southern California, after all, where there is no such thing as a space shortage. Refugees from Fox, Sony, and the nearby agencies are known to sneak away at lunch to focus their aggression at the **Rancho Park Golf Course** *(10460 Pico Blvd., West LA, 310-838-7373)*. Over the hill, the **Studio City Golf Course** *(4141 Whitsett Ave., Studio City, 818-761-3250)* has a nice par-three course and a driving range, just a nine-iron's shank away from Disney, Warner's, and Universal, where you're likely to spot television talent chasing their Titleists around the green. Noplace beats the **Los Feliz Par 3** *(3702 Los Feliz Blvd., Los Feliz, 323-663-7758)* for its laid-back attitude — that's where Jon Favreau and his slacker friends hit eight on a hole in *Swingers*. If you're a serious golfer, though, the real plan is to get yourself invited to one of the elite private courses in the area for 18 holes at Bel Air, Hillcrest (next door to Rancho Park), Sherwood, or Lakeside.

IN-LINE SKATING

Grab your skates and head immediately down to Venice's **Ocean Front Walk** for the quintessential Los Angeles experience. The traffic can be fierce, particularly on the weekends, when you'll have to dodge

work that body

indignant cyclists, joggers, and strollers who are oblivious to everyone. But the paved path extends for miles and miles, past Topanga Beach and beyond. On the other side of town, **Griffith Park** has miles of paved roads, both flat and inclined, for cyclists and in-liners alike, with far less traffic — not to mention potential for collision.

JOGGING

There are few things more satisfying than running into a casual acquaintance while pounding the pavement on your daily jog. After all, your panting and soaked shirt demonstrate a willfulness and discipline that's always attractive. Your sweat is doubly sexy if you're climbing the **Santa Monica Stairs**, à la *Rocky*. The steps run from sea level near the Santa Monica Pier up the cliff near Santa Monica's shopping district. One of the prettier streets on the Westside is **San Vicente Boulevard** from Santa Monica to Brentwood. Few traffic lights will hinder you, and you won't have to look at the commercial blight that lines most major thoroughfares in LA. A run in and around **Hollywood Reservoir and Lake Hollywood Boulevard** is also one of the most picturesque jogs in the city. You can park in the gravel area just beyond the gate to the reservoir.

PILATES

Pilates may be displacing yoga as the next fitness craze to enthrall Westsiders. Although not a traditional cardiovascular workout, Pilates challenges your body in more ways you thought possible, employing the overriding principle that the power center of the body is the abdomen, from which you harness the strength to perform the balletic stretch movements that'll have you schvitzing. Pilates veterans regard **PAPT** and **The Pilates Studio** *(8704 Santa Monica Blvd., West Hollywood, 310-659-1077)* as the true Pilates headquarters in Southern California, and the only studio that offers certification for instructors. There are mat classes (similar to yoga on the surface) and

Pilates training using spring resistance machines. **The Pilates Gym** at Rapid Rehab International *(13050 San Vicente Blvd., Brentwood, 310-312-0022)* also offers several classes in conjunction with its sports therapy center.

SKATEBOARD CITY

Though Saturday morning TV shows might have convinced you otherwise, youth culture in LA is really more about the street than the beach. And though on every corner you'll likely to find skaters making do with what space they have, everyone generally regards the **Graffiti Pit** as skate central. It's an abandoned outdoor theater on Venice Beach with layers of graffiti laminating the walls, concrete tables, handrails, and strange monoliths that balance on some of the benches. There's also the **Sand Gap**, where Ocean Park meets the beach in Santa Monica; skaters there like to dare themselves with the big holes in the pavement. For most skaters, however, almost any local school ground will do, whether it's the corner of **Hoover Street and Exposition Boulevard** on the USC Campus, the bleacher seats at **UCLA's Stadium**

work that body | 245

Tennis Court *(325 Westwood Plaza, Westwood)*, **Los Feliz Elementary** *(1740 N. New Hampshire Ave., Los Feliz)*, or **Fairfax High** *(7850 Melrose Ave., Hollywood)*. Near Fairfax High, the Fairfax-Melrose neighborhood is establishing itself as the skate-or-die mecca of the city. The best part about all these places that the likelihood of getting busted is low or nonexistent. Be sure to check out the well-written 'boarder magazine *Big Brother* for all local events.

SPINNING

A daily bike ride after work is a tough proposition in Los Angeles, and quite possibly suicidal. Spinning has surfaced as the next best thing. LA-based Johnny G. created spinning in 1986 and continues to operate his studio, **Johnny G.'s World Headquarters** *(8729 Washington Blvd., Culver City, 310-559-4949)*. **Todd Tramp** *(624 N. La Cienega Blvd., West Hollywood, 310-657-4140)* has an extensive schedule of spinning classes and some great instructors, particularly in the early morning. Nowadays, most large gyms will also have fairly decent spinning programs. One of the better ones is at **Gold's Gym Hollywood** *(1016 Cole Ave., Hollywood, 323-462-7012)*, where Michelle Segal, one of the better instructors, will run you ragged, steaming up the mirrors and glass walls until you're begging for mercy. **Crunch** *(8000 Sunset Blvd., West Hollywood, 323-654-4550)* has an equally extensive range of classes and, unlike Gold's, offers spinning free to its members.

TAKE A HIKE

Few cities have the advantage of a mountain range within city limits. In the Santa Monica Range, a hike up **Runyon Canyon** *(Fuller Ave., north of Franklin Ave., Hollywood)* offers a fantastic view of downtown and gorgeous sunsets to the west. Dog owners will appreciate the off-the-leash hiking trails. **Temescal Canyon** *(off Sunset Blvd., Pacific Palisades)* is a perfect Sunday morning hike. Follow the signs to the waterfall, then continue up for

work that body

beautiful views of the Malibu shoreline. For an easy walk above Los Feliz and some dramatic views, start at the Observatory in Griffith Park and follow the trail from the north end of the parking lot to **Mount Hollywood** and a panoramic view of the Basin. Over in Pasadena, the **Arroyo Seco Canyon** offers some of the best hikes in town. (Parking in Pasadena can be found on Windsor Avenue just south of Ventura Street.) If you're feeling more adventurous and want to get farther out of town, pick up the **Mount Wilson Trail** off the Angeles Crest Highway.

YOGA

Although it's been around for centuries, yoga has hit full stride in recent years as the rage on the fitness circuit. It may not look like much work, but yoga converts will tell you that you'll work up quite a sweat in the right class. Come early to **Yoga Works** (*1426 Montana Ave., Santa Monica; 2215 Main St., Santa Monica, 310-393-5150*) or risk fighting over mat space with the likes of Meg Ryan. About once a month, they offer intro classes to provide you with the basics of posture and breathing. At **Maha Yoga** (*13050 San Vicente Blvd., Brentwood, 310-899-0047*), crowds flock to Steve Ross's hip-hop yoga class, a perfect alternative if you find most yoga to be too New-Agey. Those in the know insist that there isn't a better yoga instructor in the nation than Bryan Kest, who teaches about a dozen classes a week of **Santa Monica Power Yoga** (*522 Santa Monica Blvd., Santa Monica, 310-281-1170*). On the other side of town, the **Center for Yoga** (*230 S. Larchmont Blvd., Larchmont, 323-464-1276*) has a loyal Hancock Park celebrity following.

work that body

index by neighborhood

santa monica/venice

Bay Shore Bowl 234 Pico Blvd. at 3rd St., Santa Monica, 310-399-7731

Helen's Cycles 2501 Broadway bet. 25th and 26th Sts., Santa Monica, 310-829-1836

Santa Monica Power Yoga 522 Santa Monica Blvd. bet. 5th and 6th Sts., Santa Monica, 310-281-1170

Santa Monica Beach end of the 10 Freeway, Santa Monica

Surefoot 1426 Montana Ave. bet. 14th and 15th Sts., Santa Monica, 310-393-3331

Temescal Canyon off Sunset Blvd., Pacific Palisades

Venice Beach off Ocean Front Walk bet. Rose Ave. and Washington Blvd.

Yoga Works 1426 Montana Ave. bet. 14th and 15th Sts., Santa Monica & 2215 Main St. bet. Pico and Ocean Park Blvds., Santa Monica, 310-393-5150

ZJ's Boarding House 2619 Main St. at Ocean Park Blvd., Santa Monica, 310-392-5646

brentwood/west la/ westwood

Adventure 16 11161 Pico Blvd. bet. Sawtelle and Sepulveda Blvds., West LA, 310-473-4574

Helen's Cycles 1071 Gayley Ave. bet. Weyburn and Kinross Aves., Westwood, 310-208-8988

Johnny G.'s World Headquarters 8729 Washington Blvd. bet. National and La Cienega Blvds., Culver City, 310-559-4949

Maha Yoga 13050 San Vicente Blvd. at 26th St., Brentwood, 310-899-0047

Rapid Rehab International 13050 San Vicente Blvd. at 26th St., Brentwood, 310-312-0022

Rancho Park Golf Course 10460 Pico Blvd. at Beverly Glen Blvd., West LA, 310-838-7373

Rockreation 11866 La Grange Ave. bet. Bundy Dr. and Barrington Ave., West LA, 310-207-7199

Sportsclub LA 1835 S. Sepulveda Blvd. bet. Santa Monica and Olympic Blvds., West LA, 310-473-1447

work that body

west hollywood

Barry's Boot Camp 1106 N. La Cienega at Fountain Ave., West Hollywood, 310-360-6262

Crunch 8000 Sunset Blvd. at Crescent Heights Blvd., West Hollywood, 323-654-4550

The Pilates Studio 8704 Santa Monica Blvd. bet. San Vicente and La Cienega Blvds., West Hollywood, 310-659-1077

Todd Tramp 624 N. La Cienega Blvd. at Melrose Ave., West Hollywood, 310-657-4140

third/beverly

I. Martin Imports 8330 Beverly Blvd. at Flores St., Los Angeles, 323-653-6900

hollywood/larchmont

Center for Yoga 230 S. Larchmont Blvd. bet. Beverly Blvd. and 3rd St., Larchmont, 323-464-1276

Gold's Gym Hollywood 1016 Cole Ave. bet. Santa Monica Blvd. and Romaine St., Hollywood, 323-462-7012

Hollywood Star Lanes 5227 Santa Monica Blvd. bet. Western and Normandie Aves., Hollywood, 323-665-4111

Runyon Canyon Fuller Ave., nr. Franklin Ave., Hollywood

los feliz/silver lake

Griffith Park Los Feliz Blvd. at Riverside Dr., Los Feliz

Los Feliz Par 3 3702 Los Feliz Blvd. bet. Griffith Park and Riverside Drs., Los Feliz, 323-663-7758

Mount Hollywood Griffith Observatory, Los Feliz, follow trail from north end of parking lot

Silver Lake Dog Park 2000 Silver Lake Blvd. bet. Glendale and Sunset Blvds., Silver Lake

farther afield

All Star Lanes 4459 Eagle Rock Blvd. nr. York Blvd., Eagle Rock, 323-254-2576

Arroyo Seco Canyon Windsor Ave. south of Ventura St., Pasadena

Billy Blanks' World Training Center 14708 Ventura Blvd. bet. Kester Ave. and Van Nuys Blvd., Sherman Oaks, 818-325-0335

work that body

El Matador Beach *Pacific Coast Hwy., six miles north of Malibu*

Hermosa Beach *Hermosa Beach Strand nr. Pier Ave., Hermosa Beach*

Manhattan Beach *Manhattan Beach Strand nr. Manhattan Beach Blvd., Manhattan Beach*

Mount Wilson *Trail off the Angeles Crest Hwy., Arcadia*

Studio City Golf Course *4141 Whitsett Ave. bet. Moorpark St. and Ventura Blvd., Studio City, 818-761-3250*

Val Surf *4810 Whitsett Ave. at Riverside Dr., North Hollywood, 818-769-6977*

Zuma Beach *Pacific Coast Hwy., four miles north of Malibu*

index by type

beaches
El Matador Beach
Hermosa Beach
Manhattan Beach
Santa Monica Beach
Venice Beach
Zuma Beach

bowling
All Star Lanes
Bay Shore Bowl
Hollywood Star Lanes

gear
Adventure 16
Helen's Cycles
I. Martin Imports
Surefoot
Val Surf

golf
Los Feliz Par 3
Rancho Park Golf Course
Studio City Golf Course

gyms
Crunch
Gold's Gym Hollywood
Sportsclub LA
Todd Tramp

hikes
Arroyo Seco Canyon
Mount Hollywood
Mount Wilson
Runyon Canyon
Temescal Canyon

work that body

in-line skating
Griffith Park
Ocean Front Walk

jogging
Hollywood Reservoir and Lake
Hollywood Boulevard
San Vicente Boulevard
Santa Monica Stairs

parks
Griffith Park
Silver Lake Dog Park

skateboarding
Fairfax High
Graffiti Pit
Los Feliz Elementary
Sand Gap
UCLA's Stadium Tennis Court Bleachers
USC Campus

spinning
Crunch
Gold's Gym Hollywood
Johnny G.'s World Headquarters
Sportsclub LA
Todd Tramp

surfing
El Porto
Huntington Beach
Sunset Beach
Zuma Beach

yoga and pilates
Center for Yoga
Crunch
Maha Yoga
Rapid Rehab International
The Pilates Studio
Santa Monica Power Yoga
Sportsclub LA
Yoga Works

work that body | 251

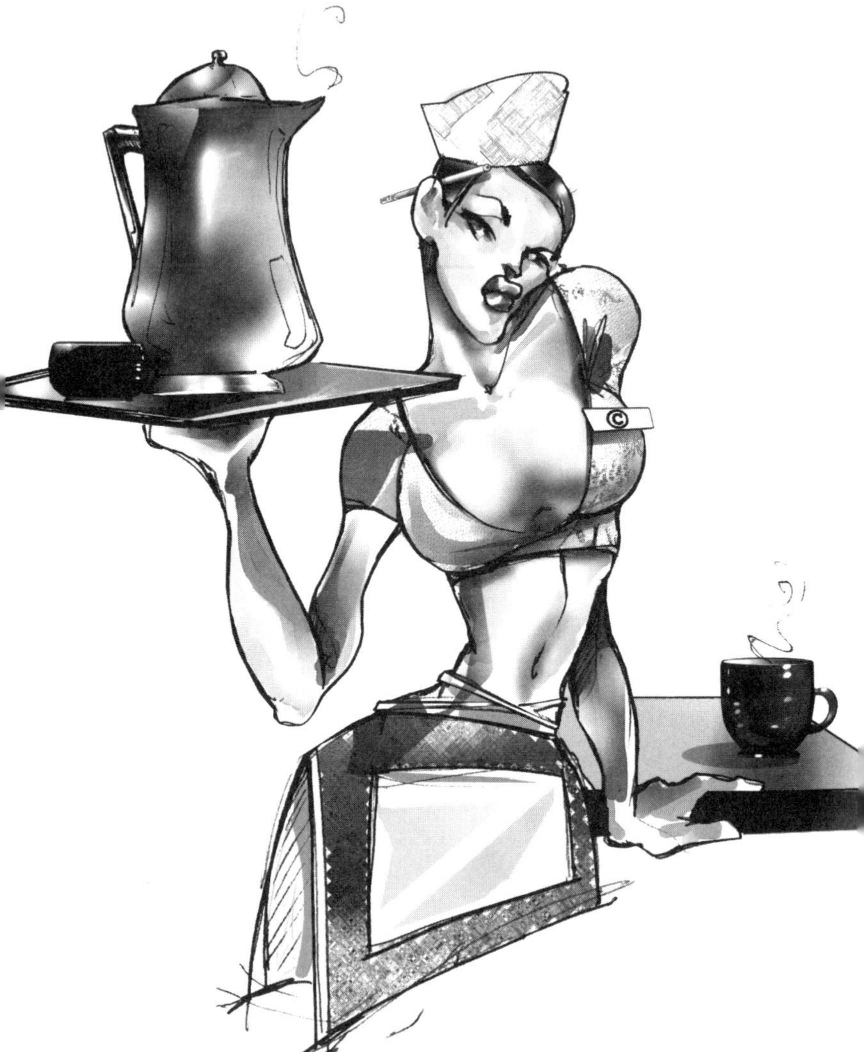

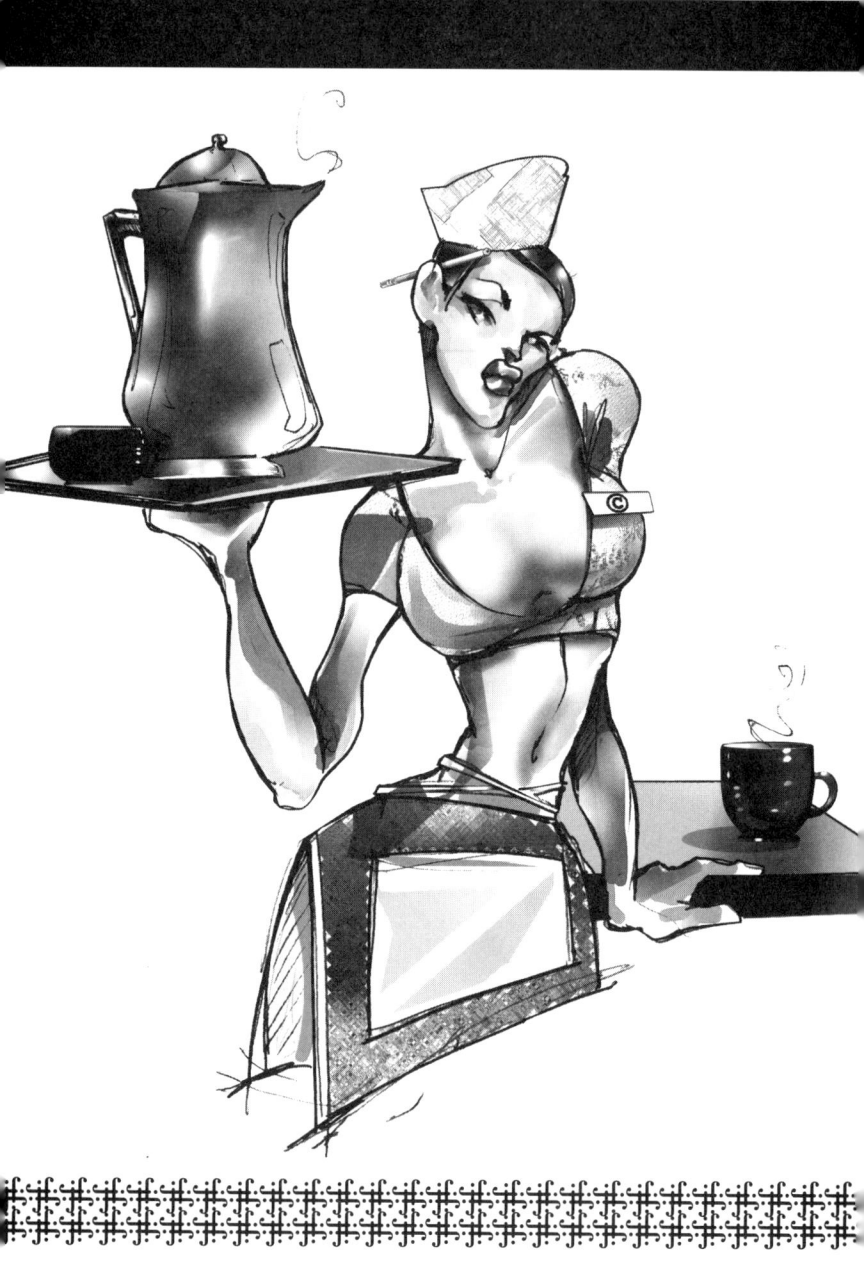

coffee

coffee in los angeles has elevated itself not only as the beverage of choice, but also as the catalyst in a public space movement. Cafés and coffee bars, once strictly the domain of students, bohos, and other urbane types, can now be found at virtually every major intersection, not merely the city's arts districts. Today you're just as likely to see a 52-year-old empty nester on her way to yoga as you are a 26-year-old poet at your local coffee joint. Everyone has an excuse and a yearning for a visit; whatever your reason for a $4 latte, you have nearly unlimited choices.

THE ABBEY *692 N. Robertson Blvd. bet. Santa Monica Blvd. and Melrose Ave., West Hollywood, 310-289-8410; Hours: daily 7am-3am*

Situated on the doorstep of West Hollywood's gay mecca, this coffee-and-drinks hangout is the jewel of WeHo's materialistic and misspent energy. Showing up here for the first time may be daunting (upon entering the handsome open-air courtyard, about 50 pairs of eyes look you up and down like a lollipop), but it's a trial by fire that every young gay guy in LA must endure. When you emerge from the flames and begin to hear the bad diva music, you will either embrace the scene, reject it, or simply make your peace with it. Most choose the latter, because there's nothing like having a Corona or a cappuccino beneath the moon. On weekend nights, the Abbey checks ID, and the place begins to look more like a bar.

ANASTASIA'S ASYLUM *1028 Wilshire Blvd. bet. 10th and 11th Sts., Santa Monica, 310-394-7113; Hours: Mon-Thu 6:30am-1am; Fri 6:30am-2am; Sat 8am-2am; Sun 8am-1am*

Getting a crowd of people into this narrow coffee house is like trying to stuff clowns into a car. The tight quarters don't obscure the fact that the folks at the Asylum have a good thing going. Several nights a week, acoustic musicians serenade the crowd below from the loft overlooking the primary seating area. If your stomach growls, Anastasia's also offers vegetarian items.

BACK DOOR BAKERY & CAFÉ *1710 Silver Lake Blvd. at Effie St., Silver Lake, 323-662-7927; Hours: Tue-Sun 7am-7pm*

A hole in the wall along a quaint stretch of Silver Lake Boulevard, the Back Door Bakery and its resident whiz, baker Deborah Gross, make Sunday mornings worth getting up for. Grab your paper and get your ass down to Back Door for their famous cinnamon sticky bun. If that's not enough for you, the Apple Uglies Muffin, the homemade Ding Dong, and the Lemon Sex (a pedestrian variation would be a "lemon bar") will boost your sugar count. For a more traditional breakfast, order the fruit pancake.

BOURGEOIS PIG *5931 Franklin Ave. bet. Gower St. and Western Ave., Hollywood, 323-962-6366; Hours: daily 9am-2am*
This block of Franklin may be the cutest stretch of street anywhere in town. The dark and moody Bourgeois Pig, however, stands in stark defiance of this mood; this is yet another joint where California's nonsmoking law is in a state of noncompliance. No one seems to mind, though, from the goth counter staff to the scruffy velveteers (those who hold court on the plush furniture). Besides, with a pool table in the back and the most comfortable couches in the 323 area code up front, who can complain?

CACAO *11609 Santa Monica Blvd. bet. Barrington Ave. and Sawtelle Blvd., West LA, 310-473-7283; Hours: Mon-Fri 4:30pm-2am; Sat-Sun 12pm-2am*
Most of the time, this is where the tough people on the Westside hang out. You'll see the kaleidoscope of hair colors, wallet chains, heavy piercings, black accoutrements, and a general mood of disgruntlement, all of it spilling onto the sidewalk, since the Cacao is pretty small. Inside, it's three parts '50s tiki room and one part space-age pad, in addition to some colorful local art on the walls.

CAFÉ TROPICAL *2900 Sunset Blvd. at Silver Lake Blvd., Silver Lake, 323-661-8391; Hours: Mon-Sat 6am-10pm; Sun 7am-10pm*
For sheer coffee consumption, nothing beats Café Tropical. This little bit of South Beach in Silver Lake sits adjacent to

coffee

long-standing dive Silver Lake Lounge and offers Cuban pastries that'll make you proud to be an Eastsider: a guava and cheese pie or a honey horn with your café con leche will provide you just the right combination of sugar and caffeine. Conversation, both in the sparse café and at the sidewalk tables, is heavily punctuated with Spanish.

and a procession of regulars. You needn't hover over chatty customers while waiting for a table, because the Coffee Table has tons of seats in two large rooms and a patio, so there's always somewhere to park yourself. You'll find a good selection of magazines for sale behind the coffee bar. The kitchen closes at 9:30pm.

THE COFFEE TABLE *2930 Rowena Ave. bet. Hyperion Ave. and Glendale Blvd., Silver Lake, 323-644-8111; Hours: Sun-Thu 7am-11pm; Fri-Sat 7am-12am*
Functional and sleek rather than cozy and cramped, this Silver Lake hangout is a user-friendly café with a cute staff

HOME *1760 Hillhurst Ave. bet. Franklin Ave. and Hollywood Blvd., Los Feliz, 323-669-0211; Hours: winter 8am-10pm; summer 8am-11pm*
As the name suggests, Home is a rec room turned café where a quick sandwich can easily be extended into a long evening gossiping on the comfy couches. After placing your order, your first instinct may be to slip off your shoes and recline à la King Farouk; feel free to do so. The food at Home mimics its persona, with offerings like a turkey and cranberry sauce sandwich just like the day after Thanksgiving. A cool jukebox and a friendly atmosphere on the garden patio make it feel just like…you get the picture.

URTH CAFÉ *8565 Melrose Ave. bet. San Vicente and La Cienega Blvds., West Hollywood, 310-659-0628; Hours: Mon-Thu 6:30am-11pm; Fri 6:30am-12am; Sat-Sun 7am-12am*
The unpretentious young industry set comes here when it doesn't want to deal with cleavage and Cosmos. Just pull on a sweatshirt (something moderately fashionable, natch) after your workout and come by for a Honey Vanilla Latte. Urth also has remarkably tasty food by any standard (try the Italian bean soup), particularly for a coffee bar. Free tables during the evening hours are at a premium, particularly on the smoker-friendly outside deck and sidewalk, so get ready to maneuver and pounce.

WEDNESDAY'S HOUSE *2409 Main St. bet. Pico and Ocean Park Blvds., Santa Monica, 310-452-4486; Hours: Mon-Sat 8am-12am; Sun 12pm-12am*
The ceiling is decorated with cutouts of David Cassidy, Leif Garrett, and the like and the vintage clothing is all for sale. The joint's Wednesday open-mic night, which draws in daffy musicians and poets, is a throwback to a long-lost bohemia. Stop in regularly and before you know it, the friendly workers will know your name too.

CHAIN GANG

The Coffee Bean & Tea Leaf *(8591 Sunset Blvd., West Hollywood, 310-659-1890; 135 N. Larchmont Blvd., Larchmont, 323-469-4984; 950 Westwood Blvd., Westwood, 310-208-8018)* is a fast-growing LA chain, largely due to the overwhelming demand for their Ice Blended, the Bean's take on a Frappuccino. Another in a series of local chains, **Buzz Café** *(8200 Santa Monica Blvd., West Hollywood, 323-650-7742)* has been adopted by West Hollywood's gay community. As is so often true, coffee and biscotti take a backseat to the game of eye pinball going on inside the café and on the sidewalk. **Starbucks** *(7624 Melrose Ave., Hollywood, 323-852-9690; 701 Montana Ave., Santa Monica, 310-394-8020; call for other locations)* has brought espresso preparation to a Fordian level, brewing thousands of concoctions a day. The Melrose location attracts its share of scenester urchins and out-of-work actors; residents of idyllic Santa Monica can walk to the location on Montana and cozy up with their papers.

LATE NIGHT

If you enjoy caffeinating yourself until all hours of the night, you'll want to check out of a few of LA's all-night coffee offerings. **Van Gogh's Ear** *(796 Main St., Venice 310-314-0022)* has an open-air deck upstairs and pornographic stills on the walls, and it serves some pretty decent food. This color-saturated Westside staple is mostly popular, however, for its 24-hour access, offering young'uns a clean, well-lighted place to wait for the sunrise, and a spread that's surprisingly hearty. As the name suggests, **Insomnia** *(7286 Beverly Blvd., Los Angeles, 323-931-4943)* also stays open comparatively late, perfect for a late-night sobriety session after an evening of boozing at the café's nearby alcoholic counterparts. During the day, a frothy latte from Insomnia serves as a respite from shopping at the showroom floors up and down Beverly.

SCREENWRITER'S BLUES

The life of the budding screenwriter can be very isolating, all cooped up in a studio apartment, tapping away at the keyboard, etching lives and dialogue onto a blank screen. Enter the laptop computer and the café, a marriage of function and space. The Thinkpad quotient is high at **Stir Crazy** *(6917 Melrose Ave., Hollywood, 323-934-4656)* on Melrose, a bare-bones coffee joint with plenty of tabletop room. Move farther west to **Who's on Third** *(8369 3rd St., Los Angeles, 323-651-2928)* for more active street life (more distractions, more eye candy). On the Westside, the creative juices flow at **Novel Café** *(212 Pier Ave., Santa Monica, 310-396-8566)* in Santa Monica. It doesn't hurt to be surrounded by a few hundred books and dozens of inviting reading chairs at this hangout, which doubles as a secondhand bookstore. More important, Novel Café stays open 24-7 — and it sure beats Denny's. Farther down the way in Venice, the spartan **Abbot's Habit** *(1401 Abbot Kinney Way, Venice, 310-399-1171)* generally stays quiet throughout the day and serves smooth coffee from the Gourmet Coffee Warehouse around the corner.

Finally, if you need to procrastinate by checking your e-mail, **Cyber Java** *(7080 Hollywood Blvd., Hollywood, 323-466-5600)* prides itself on being the leading wired coffee joint in Southern California, with terminals available for surfing the Internet, processing words, and spilling your coffee.

TO A TEA

Let's face it, coffee can get old. More evolved taste buds have graduated to **Zen Zoo Tea** *(13050 San Vicente Blvd., Brentwood, 310-576-0585)* and its ZenFusion, an iced tea drink (either black or green) prepared "martini style" with various flavored syrups and soy milk. Zen Zoo also offers several dozen varieties of teas and some dim sum items from their minimalist Asian bar. It might register fairly high on the New-Age index, but as long as **Elixir** *(8612 Melrose Ave., West Hollywood, 310-657-9300)* keeps serving up those yummy concoctions at its Gan Bei tonic bar, we won't complain. Elixir also sells teas by the tin and some cute gift items that complement the store's apothecary mission.

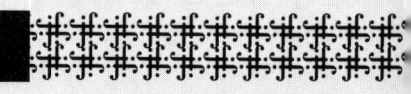

index by neighborhood

santa monica/venice

Abbot's Habit 1401 Abbot Kinney Way at California Ave., Venice, 310-399-1171

Anastasia's Asylum 1028 Wilshire Blvd. bet. 10th and 11th Sts., Santa Monica, 310-394-7113

Novel Café 212 Pier Ave. bet. Main and 2nd Sts., Santa Monica, 310-396-8566

Starbucks 701 Montana Ave. at 7th St., Santa Monica, 310-394-8020

Van Gogh's Ear 796 Main St. bet. Rose and Brooks Aves., Venice, 310-314-0022

Wednesday's House 2409 Main St. bet. Pico and Ocean Park Blvds., Santa Monica, 310-452-4486

brentwood/westwood/west la

Cacao 11609 Santa Monica Blvd. at Federal Ave., West LA, 310-473-7283

The Coffee Bean & Tea Leaf 950 Westwood Blvd. bet. Le Conte Ave. and Wilshire Blvd., Westwood, 310-208-8018

Zen Zoo Tea 13050 San Vicente Blvd. at 26th Street, Brentwood, 310-576-0585

west hollywood

The Abbey 692 N. Robertson Blvd. bet. Santa Monica Blvd. and Melrose Ave., West Hollywood, 310-289-8410

Buzz Café 8200 Santa Monica Blvd. bet. La Cienega Blvd. and Fairfax Ave., West Hollywood, 323-650-7742

The Coffee Bean & Tea Leaf 8591 Sunset Blvd. bet. Doheny Dr. and La Cienega Blvd., West Hollywood, 310-659-1890

Elixir 8612 Melrose Ave. bet. San Vicente and La Cienega Blvds., West Hollywood, 310-657-9300

Urth Café 8565 Melrose Ave. bet. San Vicente and La Cienega Blvds., West Hollywood, 310-659-0628

third/beverly

Insomnia 7286 Beverly Blvd. bet. Fairfax and La Brea Aves., Los Angeles, 323-931-4943

Who's on Third 8369 Third St. bet. La Cienega and Crescent Heights Blvds., Los Angeles, 323-651-2928

hollywood

Bourgeois Pig *5931 Franklin Ave. bet. Gower St. and Western Ave., Hollywood, 323-962-6366*

Cyber Java *7080 Hollywood Blvd. at La Brea Ave., Hollywood, 323-466-5600*

Starbucks *7624 Melrose Ave. bet. Fairfax and La Brea Aves., Hollywood, 323-852-9690*

Stir Crazy *6917 Melrose Ave. bet. La Brea and Highland Aves., Hollywood, 323-934-4656*

hancock park/larchmont

The Coffee Bean & Tea Leaf *135 N. Larchmont Blvd. bet. Beverly Blvd. and 3rd St., Larchmont, 323-469-4984*

los feliz/silver lake

Back Door Bakery & Café *1710 Silver Lake Blvd. at Effie St., Silver Lake, 323-662-7927*

Café Tropical *2900 Sunset Blvd. at Silver Lake Blvd., Silver Lake, 323-661-8391*

The Coffee Table *2930 Rowena Ave. bet. Hyperion Ave. and Glendale Blvd., Silver Lake, 323-644-8111*

Home *1760 Hillhurst Ave. bet. Franklin Ave. and Sunset Blvd., Los Feliz, 323-669-0211*

Checking In

sleeping around

if you've got friends in town or are visiting yourself, you may need a place to stay. With more than 93,000 hotel rooms to choose from in this town, you're destined to find something to your liking. With the boutique hotel craze hitting its stride and notable architects and designers turning their attention to hotels more than ever, the Los Angeles hotel scene is certain to see even more growth and remodeling in the coming years. ■ A couple of pointers before you roll up to valet parking: Always book ahead, and don't be afraid to demand the best room in the house. Reception desks here are accustomed to prima donnas and are trained to absorb attitude. Ask about views, check in early, and beware of parking charges (some hotels charge up to $24 per day per car). Prices listed are the basic room rate; all are subject to 14 percent tax unless otherwise noted.

expensive

ARGYLE *8358 Sunset Blvd. bet. La Cienega and Crescent Heights Blvds., West Hollywood, 323-654-7100; $260*

Once home to Marilyn, Clark, Errol, and other Hollywood stars and now a cozy place to shuffle back to after a night on the town, the Argyle has managed to keep its art deco interior looking polished and tasteful amid the sterile architecture popping up around it. You may remember the adjacent Fenix — the cozy piano bar with a stunning patio — from *The Player*. Because of its prime real estate on the Strip, the Argyle fetches $260 for a room, unless you'd like the penthouse apartment with wraparound balcony for $1,200.

CHATEAU MARMONT

8221 Sunset Blvd. bet. La Cienega and Crescent Heights Blvds., West Hollywood, 323-656-1010/800-CHATEAU; $210

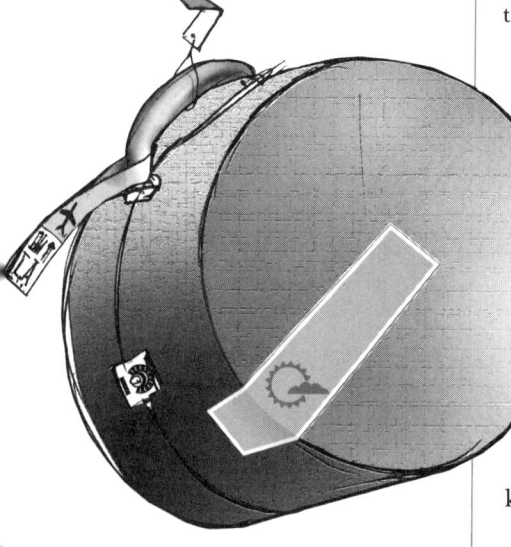

The Chateau Marmont is like the naughty old auntie to the nearby Standard — she's very well kept, but has stories that would make your jaw drop. If she weren't so discreet, she'd tell you that Howard Hughes used to keep his harem here, John Belushi died here, Tim Burton lived here for an entire year, Sharon Tate hung out in the penthouse, and on and on. The hotel has since become home to an illustrious crowd of celluloid heroes and real live human beings. Owner Andre Balazs has rounded up the best staff of any hotel in Los Angeles, unfailingly friendly and helpful without being obsequious. While you may not get the exhaustive amenities you might at one of the Goliath luxury hotels, you are in for a real taste of Hollywood living at the Chateau. At $350, the funky poolside cottages are worth the cash if you have it.

MONDRIAN *8440 Sunset Blvd. at La Cienega Blvd., West Hollywood, 323-650-8999/800-525-8029; $260*
The Mondrian is not the kind of place where you'd want to be caught in the hallway looking for ice in your flannels. One goes to the Mondrian, after all, to be seen. Why else would you put up with rooms that look like a high school infirmary? Star hotelier Ian Schrager has the art of sterile modernity down pat with sharp clean lines, stunning sight-lines, and minimal use of color. Be sure to get a room with pool or city exposure. The pool is heated and boasts the latest in hotel technology: underwater music. A suite will set you back $450 and includes a kitchenette. The best part about staying at the Mondrian? You won't have any problems getting into the hotel's famed Sky Bar.

THE STANDARD *8300 Sunset Blvd. bet. La Cienega and Crescent Heights Blvds., West Hollywood, 323-650-9090; $95*
The Standard is currently the hottest game in town, thanks to owner Andre Balazs' magic touch. More so than his timeless Chateau Marmont, the

Standard's atmosphere is charged with electricity. Once the home of the Golden Crest Retirement Home (yes, the irony kills us, too), the building has since been purged of anything remotely geriatric. Bright blue poolside AstroTurf, exotic cacti arrangements, and young bodies lying nearly naked behind glass are all part of the Standard's fare. The lobby is alive with activity: a DJ spins at the reception desk, slender and stylish folks cross-pollinate in the "conversation pits," drinks are downed in a faux Joshua Tree setting, and the restaurant serves 'round the clock. With a basic room running an amazingly low $95 and suites under $200, you won't get more for your dollar at any hotel in Los Angeles, let alone on the hopping Sunset Strip. The rooms can be a bit starchy, but most have balconies overlooking the pool (be sure to ask — the higher the better!), and all are well appointed with groovy toys, T-1 lines, inflatable sofas, bean bags, and Warhol-print curtains. One caveat: The Standard often hosts swank parties till midnight and you may have to prove that you're worthy of reentry, so bring your key and know the password!

W HOTEL *930 Hilgard Ave. bet. Sunset and Wilshire Blvds., Westwood, 310-208-8765; $259*
With boutique hotels more popular than ever, Starwood Hotels and Resorts — the folks that own Westin and Sheraton — developed the W as an alternative to their more traditional business hotels. Brand new and situated in Westwood (a neighborhood long in need of overnight options), this branch of the W works with the clean lines, lush woods, and fluffy white linens that have become synonymous with smart urban minimalism. The casual bar area, with silky ottomans for seating, works as an extension of the sexy foyer. Rooms, sparingly decorated in

the spirit of Philippe Starck, are equipped for the digital age with high-speed ethernet connections and CD players. Unlike most of the notable boutique hotels that line the busy Sunset Strip, the W is in cloistered and residential Westwood, only a short walk away from the collegiate village, but in a more placid setting that underscores its decor.

expensive

DOWNTOWN, UPMARKET

The **New Otani** *(120 S. Los Angeles St., Downtown, 213-629-1200/800-421-8795)* in Downtown's Little Tokyo is a standard upscale business hotel with one special exception — the "Japanese Experience" package ($599, parking and taxes included), which includes one night in a suite with tatami mats, futons, a balcony view of the half-acre Japanese garden, a complimentary sushi dinner, and a shiatsu session at the Sanwa spa. This treatment is especially pleasant in late October, during the orchid show. For more of a European boutique feel, check into the art deco **Wyndham Checkers** *(535 S. Grand Ave., Downtown, 213-624-0000)* across the street. Be sure to visit the rooftop lap pool.

LIVING IT UP

For those on an expense account looking for the quintessential Beverly Hills experience, we nominate four hotels that cater to your most extravagant — even venal — desires. When Eddie Murphy showed up with only his gray laundry bag at the front desk of the **Beverly Hills Hotel** *(9641 Sunset Blvd., Beverly Hills, 310-276-2251/800-283-8885)* in *Beverly Hills Cop*, the staff gave him the high hat. Rooms range from $310 for a single to $4,700 for the Presidential Bungalow, which comes with a 24-hour butler and a private pool. Perfectly landscaped gardens surround surreal carpeted sidewalks that lead to the private bungalows. The plush, luxury-ocean-liner interiors are wired with high-tech temperature controls and sound and video systems. Tucked away in a wooded corner of Stone Canyon, the **Hotel Bel Air** *(701 Stone Canyon Blvd., Bel Air, 310-472-1211/800-648-4097)* once belonged to an oil baron who made the grounds his primary residence and developed the area as the most exclusive neighborhood in the United States. Almost 80 years later, the hotel — which offers rooms ranging from $325 to $2,500 for the most desirable cabana-reigns as the standard of luxury in Los Angeles. Back down in the flats of Beverly Hills, the **Regent Beverly Wilshire** *(9500 Wilshire Blvd., Beverly Hills, 310-275-5200)* thrives on its celebrated name and unrivaled location. Inside, the European-style hotel exudes warmth, and the staff bends over backward to please. Rooms start at $265. President Clinton stayed at the **Regal Biltmore** *(506 S. Grand Ave., Downtown, 213-624-1011)* until he began bedding down with the Katzenbergs and Spielbergs when in town. The Presidential Suite is the biggest hotel room in the city, with two floors, five bedrooms, and three bathrooms. Built in 1923, this landmark hotel now houses mostly conventioneers and the odd philandering politician.

STAYING BY THE SEA

Situated right on the beach, **Shutters on the Beach** *(One Pico Blvd., Santa Monica, 310-458-0030/800-334-9000)*, has old-school charm, lent to it by tasteful art, vaulted ceilings, and weathered tile. A non-ocean view room starts at $335, though the price jumps to $550 for a mere glimpse of the sea. Each room is equipped with a Jacuzzi, so you can sit in a warm bubble bath and look at the chilly ocean. **Casa del Mar** *(1910 Ocean Front Walk, Santa Monica, 310-581-5533)* is a restored Italian renaissance revival hotel located next door to Shutters, with which it shares owners, ocean views, and uncannily, the same Italian sheets and room layout. Non-ocean view rooms start at $335; ocean view rooms are $575.

sleeping around

moderately priced

AVALON *9400 Olympic Blvd. at Beverly Dr., Beverly Hills, 310-277-5221/800-535-4715; $175*
A refurbished Holiday Inn south of Beverly Hills' shopping district, the Avalon Hotel offers real value and a decidedly *Jetsons* feel. Guest rooms, which curve around the pool area, are splashed with color and functional furnishings, giving them an Ikea-meets-Almodovar aura. Although Olympic Boulevard doesn't glint with the lights and buzz of the Strip (only ten minutes away), at least you won't be sitting in traffic on a Friday night.

BEVERLY PLAZA HOTEL *8384 3rd St. bet. La Cienega and Crescent Heights Blvds., Los Angeles, 323-658-6600; $139*
Nestled in the heart of Third Street's funky boutique district, the Beverly Plaza Hotel gives guests an off-the-beaten-path neighborhood quaintness with all the amenities of a high-end hotel, including tapas favorite Cava downstairs. Guest rooms are enormous, decorated in tasteful neutrals and custom furnishings. Visitors rave about the agreeable staff and the thoughtful extras, such as free newspapers and bath goodies. In close proximity to local coffee shops and cute design stores, the Beverly Plaza remains a favorite of visiting parents. Just as rents along Third Street have continued to rise, rates at the Beverly Plaza have increased as well, yet are still reasonable at $139-$189 per night.

HOLLYWOOD ROOSEVELT HOTEL *7000 Hollywood Blvd. bet. La Brea and Highland Ave., Hollywood, 323-466-7000/800-950-7667, www.hollywoodroosevelt.com; $159*
A taste of old Hollywood right on the Boulevard (the first Academy Awards were held here), the Roosevelt is the only hotel that houses a museum on its premises. A historical exhibit on the second floor mezza-

nine tracks the history of the Boulevard of Dreams, complete with great old photos and memorabilia. You'll be keeping company with a middle-American crowd — nothing too glamorous — but the rooms are reasonable and retain some of their charming 1920s accoutrements, like built-in vanities. Bungalows overlooking the pool are also available. Rates range from $159 to $299, depending on the tourist season.

LE PARC *733 West Knoll Dr. bet. Holloway Dr. and Santa Monica Blvd, West Hollywood, 310-855-8888/800-5-SUITES, www.leparcsuites.com; $199*
Centrally located and easy to access, Le Parc offers anonymity and low-key, high-quality service for travelers weary of lobby melodrama. You won't have to battle traffic on Sunset, endure staff attitude, or remember the name of that little-known actor. While the suites need a little refurbishing, they are spacious and well laid out and have become popular with music and film industry types in the market for laid-back comfort. Perks include private balconies, a lighted tennis court, a basketball hoop, a rooftop heated pool with cabanas, and fireplaces in every room. Rates include free parking, a rarity and luxury in West Hollywood.

sleeping around

moderately priced

FARTHER AFIELD

Meetings in the Valley? **Sportsman's Lodge** *(12825 Ventura Blvd., Studio City, 818-769-4700)* is the place to stay. A country-style hotel with an Olympic-sized pool, the Lodge brings charm to the "other side of the hill." The furnishings are cozy antique pine, and the grounds include eight wooded acres. Rates start at $118 for a single and $300 for a two-room suite. Although the decor at the **Malibu Beach Inn** *(22878 Pacific Coast Hwy., Malibu, 310-456-6444)* imparts the teals and mauves of the mid-1980s, this beachfront hideaway makes for the perfect romantic weekend. Rates fluctuate between $169 and $325, based upon proximity to the beach and amenities such as fireplace and Jacuzzi. Way down the coast on Dana Point and considerably higher in price, the **Ritz Carlton Hotel Laguna Niguel** *(1 Ritz Carlton Dr., Dana Point, 949-240-2000)* is perched atop a bluff overlooking the Pacific. In addition to sitting on the most romantic stretch of coastline in Southern California, the Ritz offers every activity imaginable, from a golf course to bicycle trails.

cheap

BANANA BUNGALOW

2775 Cahuenga Blvd. nr. Mulholland Dr., Hollywood, 323-851-1129/ 800-4-HOSTEL; $55

Nestled in the Santa Monica Mountains and seemingly staffed by a crop of guests who never left, the Banana Bungalow has the atmosphere of a mutinous camp of pirates. Look closely and you're sure to find clues to the hostel's prankish patrons: an indoor waterfall spurts soapy bubbles; a sunburned Brit snores in the bar; various multilingual yelps of play and pleasure echo from the dorm rooms. While it's a treasure for international travelers on a tight budget, its coed rooms are closed to Americans unless you have a ticket to cross the border. The dorms, which sleep 6-10 people, range between $15-$18 per person. Singles and doubles are available to anyone for $55 for two people, plus $10 per additional person. Other perks include Internet access, sanctioned parties three times a week, a video room with free movie nights, shuttles to the beach, laundry, luggage storage, a communal kitchen, complimentary (but questionable) coffee and toast, and free airport pickup.

BEST WESTERN HOLLYWOOD HILLS HOTEL

6141 Franklin Ave. bet. Vine and Gower Sts., Hollywood, 323-464-5181/800-528-1234, www.bestwestern.com/hollywoodhillshotel; $129

This well placed hotel at the foot of Beachwood Canyon offers many positives: free parking, an outdoor pool, and low room rates. You're within walking distance of great restaurants, close to the funky corridor of Los Feliz, and convenient to both Studio City and the 101. The Hollywood Hills Coffee Shop, the unique lobby restaurant featured in *Swingers*, beats any breakfast in LA and is worth a visit even if you're not staying here.

sleeping around

cheap

BUDGET BONANZA

Like many travelers, you may have Ian Schrager taste on a Motel 6 budget. Luckily, Los Angeles has a host of options in great locations that offer reasonable comfort. At the **Magic Hotel** *(7025 Franklin Ave., Hollywood, 323-851-0800)*, the suites are spacious apartments with living rooms, bedrooms, and dining rooms and are a favorite for bands on tour. Rates vary from $60 to $129 in this great location at the base of the Hollywood Hills. The **Beverly Laurel Hotel** *(8018 Beverly Blvd., Los Angeles, 323-651-2441)* is a classic postwar motor lodge situated in the middle of Beverly Boulevard's swanky design shops and excellent restaurants. Ask for the $79 kitchenette suite, only $10 more than the regular rooms. The decor is retro with a few classic pieces thrown in, and with the Swingers Diner right downstairs, you won't go to bed hungry. We can't resist telling you about the chintzy and cheap **Farmer's Daughter Motel** *(115 S. Fairfax Ave., Los Angeles, 323-937-3930/800-334-1658)*. It's across the street from the Farmer's Market, where you'll find fresh food and great coffee. Rooms range from $58 for a queen-size bed to $85 for a suite. The **Cadillac Hotel** *(8 Dudley Ave., Venice, 310-399-8876)* is a restored 1905 art deco landmark in the thick of Venice and a magnet for European travelers on a shoestring budget. For $69 (suites are $120), you get the same stunning ocean views that would set you back $550 at Shutters down the road. Amenities include a rooftop AstroTurf sundeck, free parking, a pool table, a sauna, a gym, and a real piece of the Berlin Wall on display. Make sure you get a room that's high and away from the noise; we recommend the Charlie Chaplin Room, where it is whispered that the silent one spent his holidays.

index by neighborhood

santa monica/venice/malibu

The Cadillac Hotel 8 Dudley Ave. at Ocean Front Walk, Venice, 310-399-8876

Casa del Mar 1910 Ocean Front Walk at Pico Blvd., Santa Monica, 310-581-5533

Malibu Beach Inn 22878 Pacific Coast Hwy. nr. Malibu Pier, Malibu, 310-456-6444

Shutters on the Beach One Pico Blvd. at Ocean Ave., Santa Monica, 310-458-0030/800-334-9000

brentwood/westwood/west la

W Hotel 930 Hilgard Ave. bet. Sunset and Wilshire Blvds., Westwood, 310-208-8765

beverly hills

Avalon 9400 Olympic Blvd. at Beverly Dr., Beverly Hills 310-277-5221/800-535-4715

Beverly Hills Hotel 9641 Sunset Blvd. at Beverly Dr., Beverly Hills 310-276-2251/800-283-8885

Hotel Bel Air 701 Stone Canyon Blvd. nr. Sunset Blvd., Bel Air, 310-472-1211/800-648-4097

Regent Beverly Wilshire 9500 Wilshire Blvd. nr. Rodeo Dr., Beverly Hills, 310-275-5200

west hollywood

Argyle 8358 Sunset Blvd. bet. La Cienega and Crescent Heights Blvds., West Hollywood, 323-654-7100

Chateau Marmont 8221 Sunset Blvd. bet. La Cienega and Crescent Heights Blvds., West Hollywood, 323-656-1010/800-CHATEAU

Le Parc 733 West Knoll Dr. bet. Holloway Dr. and Santa Monica Blvd., West Hollywood, 310-855-8888/800-5 SUITES

Mondrian 8440 Sunset Blvd. at La Cienega Blvd., West Hollywood, 323-650-8999/800-525-8029

The Standard 8300 Sunset Blvd. bet. La Cienega and Crescent Heights Blvds., West Hollywood, 323-650-9090

sleeping around

third/beverly

The Beverly Laurel Hotel *8018 Beverly Blvd. bet. Crescent Heights Blvd. and Fairfax Ave., Los Angeles, 323-651-2441*

Beverly Plaza Hotel *8384 3rd St. bet. La Cienega and Crescent Heights Blvds., Los Angeles, 323-658-6600*

Farmer's Daughter Motel *115 S. Fairfax Ave. bet. Beverly Blvd. and 3rd St., Los Angeles, 323-937-3930/ 800-334-1658*

hollywood

Banana Bungalow *2775 Cahuenga Blvd. nr. Mulholland Dr., Hollywood, 323-851-1129/800-4-HOSTEL*

Best Western Hollywood Hills Hotel *6141 Franklin Ave. bet. Vine and Gower Sts., Hollywood, 323-464-5181/800-528-1234*

The Hollywood Roosevelt Hotel *7000 Hollywood Blvd. bet. La Brea and Highland Aves., Hollywood, 323-466-7000/800-950-7667*

Magic Hotel *7025 Franklin Ave. bet. La Brea and Highland Aves., Hollywood, 323-851-0800*

downtown

New Otani, *120 S. Los Angeles St. bet. 1st and 2nd Sts., Los Angeles, 213-629-1200/800-421-8795*

Regal Biltmore *506 S. Grand Ave. bet. 5th and 6th Sts., Los Angeles, 213-624-1011*

Wyndham Checkers *535 S. Grand Ave. bet. 5th and 6th Sts., Los Angeles, 213-624-0000*

farther afield

Sportsman's Lodge *12825 Ventura Blvd. at Coldwater Canyon Ave., Studio City, 818-769-4700*

index by price

under $100

Banana Bungalow
Best Western Hollywood Hills Hotel
The Beverly Laurel Hotel
The Cadillac Hotel
Farmer's Daughter Motel
Magic Hotel
The Standard

$100-$250

Avalon
Beverly Plaza Hotel
Chateau Marmont
The Hollywood Roosevelt Hotel
Le Parc
Malibu Beach Inn
New Otani
Sportsman's Lodge
The Standard
Wyndham Checkers

$250 and over

Argyle
Beverly Hills Hotel
Casa del Mar
Hotel Bel Air
Mondrian
Regal Biltmore
Regent Beverly Wilshire
Shutters On The Beach
W Hotel

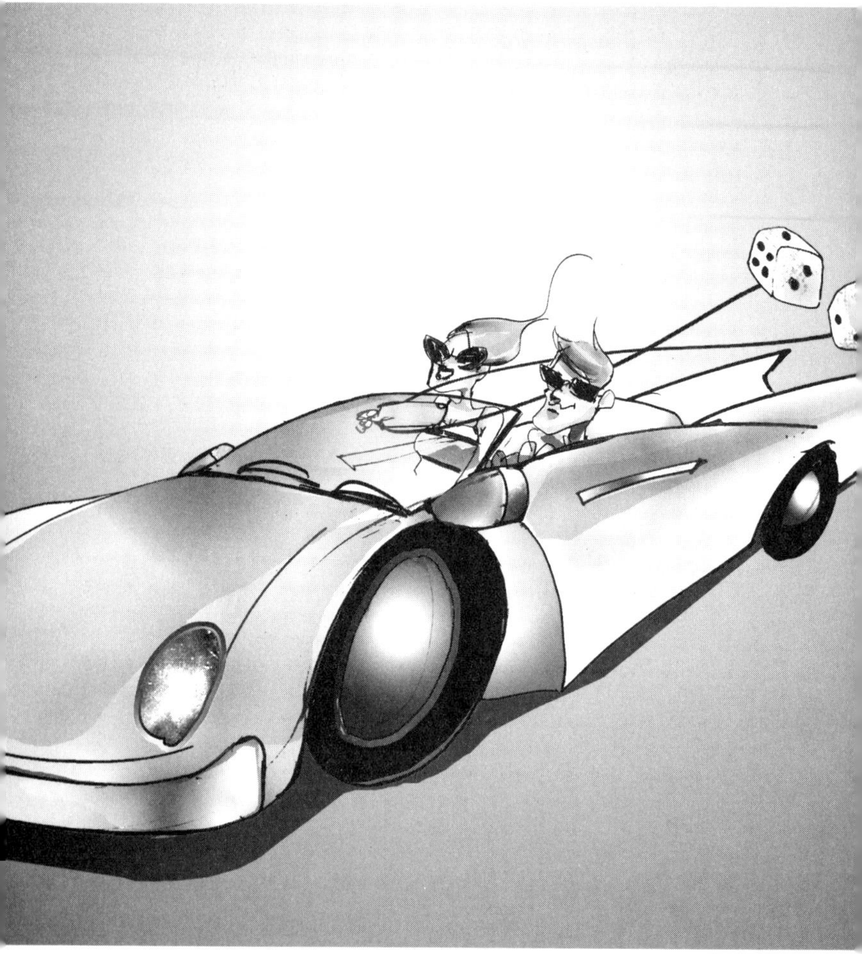

las vegas

Until quite recently, Las Vegas was largely the domain of conventioneers and a small constituency of repeat tourists, those who thrived on gambling, big portions of food at cheap prices regardless of quality, and forlorn past-their-prime entertainers like Dionne Warwick. To many Americans, especially those with taste, Las Vegas was a veritable punch line. However, with the economic recovery of the early '90s, the stars began to realign for Las Vegas. ■ First, developers such as Steve Wynn realized that there was a tremendous upside to expanding Vegas's base. Why couldn't Las Vegas be a sought-after destination among big-city professionals, yuppies, families, and those seeking a little hedonism with a touch of class? With that mission in mind, Wynn proceeded to build an upmarket Vegas, a place where you could you could wake up, go to the gym, get a professional massage, and have an egg-white omelette before hitting the tables. Soon, notable national chefs like the populist Wolfgang Puck and Le Cirque's Sirio Maccioni began to set up annexes in Vegas. And, ten years ago, who would have thought that Prada, Armani, Gucci, and Tiffany would be competing for prime retail space in the Strip's designer malls?

Second, kitsch and retrology became the rage among hipsters all over the country, particularly in Los Angeles — which has never really suspended its love affair with Hollywood's Golden Age. All of the sudden, aesthetic liabilities became assets in Las Vegas. Kids began to realize that Vegas was a living, breathing thrift store and vintage shop where you could float an outfit or ensemble without a trace of eye rolling. Adults finally had something besides craps, cheap booze, and hookers to waste their money on.

Despite its face-lift, Vegas's new digs belie its greatest attraction — as human microscope. People watching remains the most interesting game in town. Whether you're lurking behind a $1,000-per-hand blackjack table or studying the chain-smoking truckers' wives on the slots downtown, there's no better place to spy on humanity.

This list of the city's unique offerings is far from complete but should be enough to entertain you and your buddies for a three-day weekend. With this desert oasis of sin only a 45-minute flight away, it may be just the thing to recharge your batteries.

tips to get you started

If you're looking to budget yourself but still want to stay in the hotel of your choice, strongly consider hitting Vegas during the middle of the week. Designer hotels such as the Hard Rock Hotel & Casino and Mandalay Bay drop their nightly rates steeply during the week, unless there is a big convention in town. You may not see the scene in its full glory, but the neon is just as bright.

Don't be bashful about asking for handouts, particularly if you're spending substantial time at the tables. Remember, the hotels and casinos want you to be happy and accommodated — even as they rob you of your hard-earned cash. And you don't have to be a high roller to score a comp. If you've played at the same blackjack table for a couple of hours and have been pleasant and courteous, feel free to ask the pit boss if he'll treat you to lunch or a line pass.

to sleep and wager

Nightly rates at the following hotels, and around Las Vegas in general, vary wildly. During holiday weekends and busy conventions, you can expect to pay anywhere from $200 to $350 per night for a standard room. Conversely, during the dog days of summer, the Hard Rock Hotel & Casino will occasionally offer rooms for free midweek in conjunction with a special promotion, and Mandalay Bay's rate will hover below $100 per night. Do note that some hotels, including the Hard Rock, will not allow you to book a Saturday night without also staying the preceding Friday night. You should research each hotel's rates and policies carefully before making a reservation. Quite often, the difference between one weekend and the next may be several hundred dollars. Of course, if you qualify as a high roller, then it's an entirely different story. Discounts and in some cases comps will be afforded to those playing high stakes. If you fall into this category, ask for a casino host when making your reservation.

The rates listed below are an approximation for a standard room on an average Friday or Saturday night. Again, mid-week rates are significantly lower.

BELLAGIO
3600 Las Vegas Blvd. S. at Flamingo Rd., Las Vegas, 888-987-6667; $398

In a town where hype qualifies as a civic duty, few events were more anticipated than the opening of the Bellagio in 1998. The project was the realization of Steve Wynn's high-end strategy — a Vegas for the gentry class. By all accounts, he has fulfilled this goal. The Bellagio recently expanded its Impressionist art gallery, and its two daily performances of Cirque du Soleil's *O* have nary an empty seat. Throngs of people stroll through the marble lobby to stare at the glass sculpture overhead and then drift over to the botanical gardens. In what's becoming commonplace for the newer, upscale hotels, the Bellagio also boasts its share of designer boutiques. The hotel's self-created majesty can be overwhelming for a entire weekend - it's easy to get lost on a simple walk from the tables to the sports book — but for luxury, it's the best game in town.

DESERT INN
3145 Las Vegas Blvd. S. at Desert Inn Rd., Las Vegas, 800-634-6906; $180

Made famous by the Rat Pack in the '50s and '60s, the

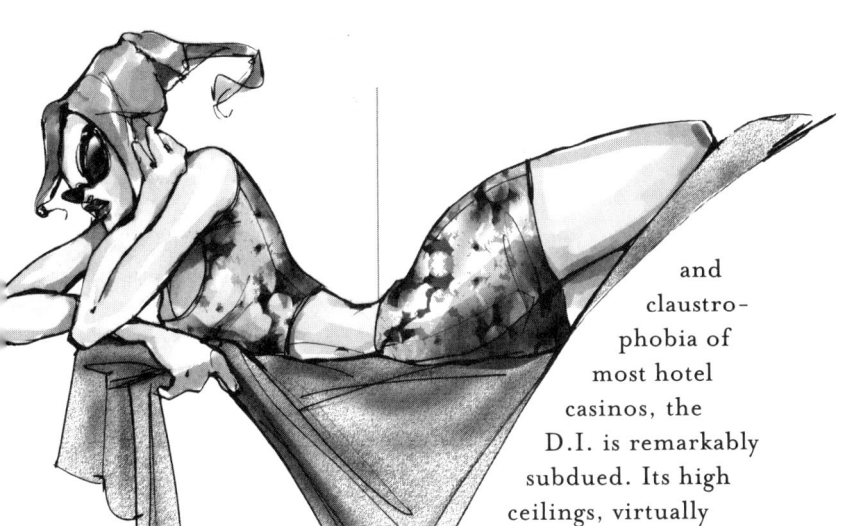

Desert Inn is a throwback to the old Vegas, the purist's Vegas — the place that existed before family-friendliness and multiple towers became prerequisites for excellence. The D.I. was a place where the guys went to gamble, drink, and play 36 holes over the weekend. For those who prefer gambling over spectacle, golfing over arcades, and scotch over a frozen buttery nipple, the D.I. is the place. In contrast to the incessant ringing, bleeping, and claustrophobia of most hotel casinos, the D.I. is remarkably subdued. Its high ceilings, virtually inaudible music, and quiet surroundings make for a mellow experience. You'll find few kids running around the pool area or the golf course (the only one on the Strip). In a town famous for 10-minute weddings, the D.I. is a great change of pace, particularly for a romantic weekend.

HARD ROCK HOTEL & CASINO *4455 Paradise Rd. at Harmon Ave., Las Vegas, 800-473-7625; $179*
If you're looking for a home base, this is it. Peter Morton

las vegas | 285

has created an environment that caters to the style-obsessed whose median birth date is around 1973. In contrast to the frilly rooms on the Strip, Morton hired the progressive design firm of Tsao and McKown to create the Hard Rock's sleek, clean rooms. The multitiered pool and lagoon snakes around the backside of the hotel and allows for wading from the sandy shore (like a real beach) before falling off to a concrete-bottomed clear pool. The Hard Rock is most distinctive, however, because of its clientele — mostly young, well-heeled urbanites from across the nation who put up with the sometimes attitude-laden hotel staff. Most of the gaming is low-impact, and the $5 tables tend to fill up early on the weekends.

MANDALAY BAY 3950

Las Vegas Blvd. S. at Hacienda Ave., Las Vegas, 877-632-7000; $209
Mandalay Bay belongs to the "size counts" school of Las Vegas hotels: the idea that where you stay should be more than just a hotel and casino, but a megaresort. In that spirit, you could spend an entire weekend at Mandalay Bay never eating in the same restaurant, never drinking at the same bar, never playing at the same table (much less in the same pit), hitting the House of Blues one night and seeing a fight the next. What separates Mandalay Bay from many of the other superhotels is a commitment to innovative design in its entertainment emporium. You'll have so much fun in RumJungle, for example, basking in the Jeffrey Beers-designed, glowing lunar wonderland that drinking becomes almost superfluous. Mandalay also snagged Adam Tihany of Le Cirque 2000 to lend his eye toward Trattoria del Lupo and Aureole, where a real-life angel descends from the ceiling to pluck your wine selection from a towering glass structure.

MIRAGE *3400 Las Vegas Blvd. S. Spring Mountain Rd., Las Vegas, 00-374-9000; $259*

It's hard to believe that we can now regard the Mirage as a middle-aged cousin to its fantastical neighbors. When it first opened over a decade ago, the Mirage revolutionized the Strip with its otherworldliness — spectacles that walked the tightrope between the sublime and the ridiculous but were always worth a look. Out front, a man-made volcano erupts every 15 minutes and tourists will line the adjacent walkway five and six deep merely to snap a photo of the event. Everybody's favorite German tanning victims, Siegfried & Roy, present a multimillion-dollar act at the Mirage with their white tigers and magic. Sharks swim behind glass, menacing drunk visitors. And the walk from the lobby to the main casino mimics a tropical rain forest. The Mirage remains a damned good place to set up shop for the weekend, and many high rollers have remained loyal to the hotel. The buffet rivals any in town, and the hotel, despite having over 3,000 rooms, is amazingly compact and manageable for its size. And the standard hotel rooms still offer a lot for your money, including good-sized bathrooms.

---

eating out in vegas

Key (cost per person)
$ — $15 and under
$$$ — 16-$25
$$$ — $26 and over

AUREOLE *Mandalay Bay, 3950 Las Vegas Blvd. S. at Hacienda Ave., Las Vegas, 702-632-7401 $$$*
The menu here mirrors Charles Palmer's midtown Manhattan restaurant of the same name — contemporary American without the needless complications of fennel, reductions, and the like. If nothing else, make sure that you order a bottle of wine. Your server-angel, like something out of a

circus act, will be lifted four stories by harness to retrieve your selection from the Adam Tihany-designed standing glass wine "cellar."

BINION'S RANCH STEAKHOUSE *Binion's Horseshoe, 128 Fremont St. bet. 1st St. and Casino Center Blvd., Downtown Las Vegas, 702-382-1600 $$$*
In steak house terms, we're talking about the real thing here — potbellied, mustached waiters in starched white shirts, cigar smoke, wood paneling, portions that could feed a family of four for a week (the 20-ounce porterhouse steak may be the best value in town). Sure, you could go to Morton's or Smith & Wollensky, but with a panoramic view of Vegas and prime seats in a worn leather booth, what more could you possibly want?

CHINA GRILL *Mandalay Bay, 3950 Las Vegas Blvd. S. at Hacienda Ave., Las Vegas, 702-632-7404 $$*
At China Grill (a descendant of the restaurant in Manhattan), you'll ask yourself, "What's more seductive? The lamb ribs or Jeffrey Beers's industrially groovy space?" Although you're eating on a veritable movie set, China Grill is, at heart, a family-style Chinese joint — the kind of place where you order five entrees for six people and pluck one delicacy after another off each other's plates. While you wait, watch the waiters cross the working drawbridge over the restaurant's circular moat to serve you.

MR. LUCKY'S *Hard Rock Hotel & Casino, 4455 Paradise Rd. at Harmon Ave., Las Vegas, 800-473-7625 $*
Open all day, every day, Mr. Lucky's menu is similar to Sean McPherson's Swingers on Beverly Boulevard in Los Angeles. We're talking about non-greasy diner fare: burgers (beef, turkey, veggie), salads, bagels and lox, and turkey and avocado sandwiches. In contrast to its neighbors at the

NOBU *Hard Rock Hotel & Casino, 4455 Paradise Rd. at Harmon Ave., Las Vegas, 800-473-7625 $$$*
A meal at Nobu transcends anything you may encounter at your local sushi bar — it's like *Babette's Feast* in a kimono. Be sure to try out chef Nobu Matshuhisa's multicourse *omakase* menu: A prix fixe fare of $65, $85, or $105 entitles you to a procession of culinary masterpieces. Even if you're normally a control freak at the table, trust Nobu — you can't possibly go wrong.

PINK TACO *Hard Rock Hotel & Casino, 4455 Paradise Rd. at Harmon Ave., Las Vegas, 800-473-7625 $*
Conveniently located a chip's throw from the Hard Rock Casino, Pink Taco evokes a college-spring-break Mexican cantina — the sort of place where you'd throw back four margaritas without the slightest bit of guilt. The best thing about Pink Taco is that the food's good, cheap, and relatively healthy and light.

RUMJUNGLE *3950 Las Vegas Blvd. S. at Hacienda Ave., Las Vegas, 702-632-7408 $$*
In addition to being one of the cooler spaces in Vegas, RumJungle serves up Brazilian barbecue — grilled meats, poultry, and fish — and some tiki island appetizers that will go perfectly with your rum IV.

eating out in vegas

GORGING YOURSELF

If you fail to indulge in at least one buffet during your visit to Las Vegas, well, you're just not true Glitter Gulch material. For value, variety, and indigestion, nothing can compete with an all-you-can-eat Dionysian feast, Vegas style. That said, you should be selective in choosing your buffet. Some of these spreads resemble your high school cafeteria, but the good ones are worth waiting in line for. When it opened in 1989, the **Mirage Buffet** *(Mirage, 3400 Las Vegas Blvd. S., 702-791-7111)* upped the ante on buffet quality and variety, from Chinese specialties to a frozen yogurt station. More recently, the Rio has cornered the market on buffets. Their **Carnival World** *(Rio, 3700 W. Flamingo Rd., 702-252-7777)* is so extensive that you can burn off half of what you eat walking from one end of the line to the other. The atmosphere may feel like the food court at the mall, but you won't leave hungry — provided that you don't chew off your limbs during the interminable wait. For an equally long wait but a more specialized spread, the **Village Seafood Buffet** *(Rio, 3700 W. Flamingo Rd., 702-252-7777)* at the Rio has it going on, with hot and chilled king crab legs, mounds of fresh peel-and-eat shrimp, and Chinese seafood specialities. Finally, the Gospel Brunch at the **House of Blues** *(Mandalay Bay, 3950 Las Vegas Blvd. S., 702-632-7600)*, may be well worth the steep $34 price (including tax & tip), provided that you're up on Sunday morning. Unlike the usual amusement park maze at most buffets, the House of Blues hosts two seatings on Sundays at 10am and 1pm. Once inside, you can help yourself to grits and peach cobbler while you tap your silverware to rousing gospel tunes.

LA ANNEXES

Over the course of your visit, you're bound to hear locals bemoaning the Los Angelization of Las Vegas. True, it seems like every industry brat on the Westside invades Vegas on any given weekend, bringing with it the style and attitude that governs LA. But that's just the way Vegas tycoons like it; they salivate over free-spending Angelenos, many of whom have made the "weekend in Vegas" a monthly fixture. There's more to the Los Angeles fascination in Vegas than the bottom line, though. Vegas entrepreneurs recognize that when it comes to developing a nightlife, they could do a lot worse than replicating a Los Angeles sensibility. On the club tip, Peter Morton brought in Sean McPherson of LA's El Carmen, Good Luck Bar, Bar Marmont, and Jones Hollywood to design and develop **Baby's** *(Hard Rock Hotel, 4455 Paradise Rd., 800-473-7625)*, the Hard Rock's feverish nightspot. Can't get anything earlier than a 10pm reservation for Spago Beverly Hills? Nail one down in prime hours at the **Spago** *(Caesar's Palace, 3570 Las Vegas Blvd. S., 702-369-6300)* in Caesar's Palace. The Venetian has hopped on the bandwagon too, with an annex of Brentwood's highly regarded **Valentino** *(Venetian, 3355 Las Vegas Blvd. S., 702-414-1000)*. And everyone's favorite culinary duo, Susan Milliken and Susan Feniger (better known as television's *Too Hot Tamales*) opened Hollywood fave **Border Grill** *(Mandalay Bay, 3950 Las Vegas Blvd. S., 702-632-7403)*.

nightlife in vegas

Not the gambling type? Don't sweat it. There's plenty to keep you busy while your traveling companion pisses away his paycheck. Nightlife, which formerly consisted of an Eddie Rabbit performance followed by a treacherous evening of rolling dice, has been elevated to top priority for Vegas hotel brass.

BABY'S *Hard Rock Hotel & Casino, 4455 Paradise Rd. at Harmon Ave., Las Vegas, 800-473-7625*
This Sean McPherson brainchild is the only game in town for a New York-Los Angeles-style dance club (MGM's dreadfully derivative 54 notwithstanding). Dark but lush in its pre-*Saturday Night Fever* '70s cheesiness, the basement bar and adjacent disco floor have a decidedly underground, rave-ish feel, but the glowing blue aquarium is unmistakably Vegas showmanship. The sounds are '80s and '90s hits — from Depeche Mode to Dee-Lite — with nothing too obscure or trancy.

GIPSY *4605 Paradise Rd. bet. Harmon and Tropicana Aves., Las Vegas, 702-731-5171*
A block south of the Hard Rock sits Vegas's primary gay dance club. For the city mouse, there's nothing here you can't find at your haunts in LA. But the crowd is a nice combination of local kids and tourists who find themselves a bit more loose and less self-conscious than at home. For celebs like Janet Jackson, this is the only credible place outside the gawking hotel scene to boogie without being bothered.

HARD ROCK CASINO BAR *Hard Rock Hotel & Casino, 4455 Paradise Rd. at Harmon Ave., Las Vegas, 800-473-7625*
At the center of the Hard Rock's circular main floor, you'll find the busiest meat market in town. Surrounded by tables at all sides, the casino bar serves as the hub for Camelot of the Beautiful People. Those who prefer to hang on to their cash but want the action and frenzy

of a dynamic casino will enjoy checking out the faces and bodies here while sipping Cosmos.

HOUSE OF BLUES *Mandalay Bay, 3950 Las Vegas Blvd. S. at Hacienda Ave., Las Vegas, 702-632-7600*
The Foundation Room has become the most sought-after admission in town on weekend nights. If you're staying at Mandalay Bay, make sure to secure some passes upon check-in. Atop the towering hotel, the outdoor patio may have the best view this side of the Stratosphere. The decor inside is strangely hipster-Eastern, with bronzed Buddhas that belie the joint's constant revelry.

RED DRAGON LOUNGE *Mandalay Bay, 3950 Las Vegas Blvd. S. at Hacienda Ave., Las Vegas, 702-632-7404*
Nothing in Vegas rivals the sound and lavish style of Wednesday nights at China Grill, when Red Dragon Lounge takes over at 1am. DJ Michael Fuller spins roaring house music against the sleek, contemporary backdrop. And hey, everybody looks great dancing on a granite floor.

RED SQUARE *Mandalay Bay, 3950 Las Vegas Blvd. S. at Hacienda Ave., Las Vegas, 702-632-7407*
An airy, velvety space, Red Square greets you with a huge Marxist wall mural that looks like the cover of a Billy Bragg album. Wear your mittens if you choose to sit at the frozen bar, where a selection of over 100 vodkas are dispensed to the proletariat. Your best bet is the vodka tasting menu at one of the cushy booths.

quickies

best place to score a lapdance

CLUB PARADISE, *4416 Paradise Rd. at Harmon Ave., Las Vegas, 702-734-7990*
In town for a bachelor party? Stumble across Paradise Road from the Hard Rock to this upscale gentlemen's club. You'll have to wrangle your way down to the intimate seating area, but for $20 a song you'll have a good seat for inspecting the merchandise.

best place to play eighteen

DESERT INN, *3145 Las Vegas Blvd. S. at Desert Inn Rd., Las Vegas, 702-733-4444*
The Desert Inn has the only golf course on the strip. It'll cost you, though — approximately $150 a round.

best place to learn craps

BINION'S HORSESHOE CASINO, *128 Fremont St. bet. 1st St. and Casino Center Blvd., Downtown Las Vegas, 702-382-1600*
If you're a craps novice, don't try to squirm your way into a busy $10 table on a Saturday night. Instead, hit the $1 minimum bet tables during the afternoon at Binion's to pick up the nuances of the game and to practice your strategy. The tables will be a lot less crowded, and the seasoned dealers will offer sound advice and explanations.

best place to blow your winnings

FORUM SHOPS AT CAESAR'S, *3570 Las Vegas Blvd. S. at Flamingo Rd., Las Vegas, 702-731-7110*

VIA BELLAGIO, *3600 Las Vegas Blvd. S. at Flamingo Rd., Las Vegas, 888-987-6667*

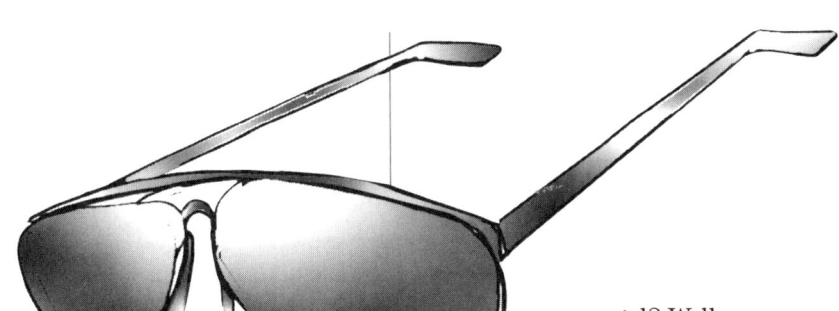

Start your afternoon on the west side of the Strip inside the cool confines of the Forum Shops, then continue on to Via Bellagio. All the usual suspects are represented, including Prada, Hugo Boss, Gucci, Armani, and Moschino, as well as more casual wear, with Abercrombie, Armani Exchange, and Gap.

best place to outfit yourself vegas-style

THE ATTIC, *1018 S. Main St. nr. Charleston Blvd., Las Vegas, 702-388-4088*
Remember that Visa commercial? Well, here it is: the only vintage clothing store in America that charges a cover (one dollar). Sequins and polyester are the orders of the day; they mix well with the zebra shag carpeting. Set aside a couple of hours and go nuts.

index by type of venue

hotels/casinos

Bellagio 3600 Las Vegas Blvd. S. at Flamingo Rd., Las Vegas, 888-987-6667

Binion's Horseshoe Casino 128 Fremont St. bet. 1st St. and Casino Center Blvd., Downtown Las Vegas, 702-382-1600

Desert Inn 3145 Las Vegas Blvd. S. at Desert Inn Rd., Las Vegas 800-634-6906

Hard Rock Hotel & Casino 4455 Paradise Rd. at Harmon Ave., Las Vegas, 800-473-7625

Mandalay Bay 3950 Las Vegas Blvd. S. at Hacienda Ave., Las Vegas, 877-632-7000

Mirage 3400 Las Vegas Blvd. S. at Spring Mountain Rd., Las Vegas, 800-374-9000

restaurants

Aureole Mandalay Bay, 3950 Las Vegas Blvd. S. at Hacienda Ave., Las Vegas, 702-632-7401

Binion's Ranch Steakhouse Binion's Horseshoe, 128 Fremont St. bet. 1st St. and Casino Center Blvd., Downtown Las Vegas, 702-382-1600

Border Grill Mandalay Bay, 3950 Las Vegas Blvd. S. at Hacienda Ave., Las Vegas, 702-632-7403

Carnival World Rio, 3700 W. Flamingo Rd. at Valley View Blvd., Las Vegas, 702-252-7777

China Grill Mandalay Bay, 3950 Las Vegas Blvd. S. at Hacienda Ave., Las Vegas, 702-632-7404

House of Blues Mandalay Bay, 3950 Las Vegas Blvd. S. at Hacienda Ave., Las Vegas, 702-632-7600

Mirage Buffet Mirage, 3400 Las Vegas Blvd. S. at Spring Mountain Rd., Las Vegas, 702-791-7111

Mr. Lucky's, Hard Rock Hotel & Casino, 4455 Paradise Rd. at Harmon Ave., Las Vegas, 800-473-7625

Nobu Hard Rock Hotel & Casino, 4455 Paradise Rd. at Harmon Ave., Las Vegas, 800-473-7625

Pink Taco Hard Rock Hotel & Casino, 4455 Paradise Rd. at Harmon Ave., Las Vegas, 800-473-7625

RumJungle 3950 Las Vegas Blvd. S. at Hacienda Ave., Las Vegas, 702-632-7408

Spago Caesar's Palace, 3570 Las Vegas Blvd. S. at Flamingo Rd., 702-369-6300

Valentino Venetian, 3355 Las Vegas Blvd. S. at Sands Ave., Las Vegas, 702-414-1000

Village Seafood Buffet Rio, 3700 W. Flamingo Rd. at Valley View Blvd., Las Vegas, 702-252-7777

nightlife

Baby's Hard Rock Hotel & Casino, 4455 Paradise Rd. at Harmon Ave., Las Vegas, 800-473-7625

Club Paradise 4416 Paradise Rd. at Harmon Ave., Las Vegas, 702-734-7990

Gipsy 4605 Paradise Rd. bet. Harmon and Tropicana Aves., Las Vegas, 702-731-5171

Hard Rock Casino Bar Hard Rock Hotel & Casino, 4455 Paradise Rd. at Harmon Ave., Las Vegas, 800-473-7625

House of Blues Mandalay Bay, 3950 Las Vegas Blvd. S. at Hacienda Ave., Las Vegas, 702-632-7600

Red Dragon Lounge Mandalay Bay, 3950 Las Vegas Blvd. S. at Hacienda Ave., Las Vegas, 702-632-7404

Red Square Mandalay Bay, 3950 Las Vegas Blvd. S. at Hacienda Ave., Las Vegas, 702-632-7407

shopping

The Attic 1018 S. Main St. nr. Charleston Blvd., Las Vegas, 702-388-4088

Forum Shops at Caesar's 3570 Las Vegas Blvd. S. at Flamingo Rd., Las Vegas, 702-731-7110

Via Bellagio 3600 Las Vegas Blvd. S. at Flamingo Rd., Las Vegas, 888-987-6667

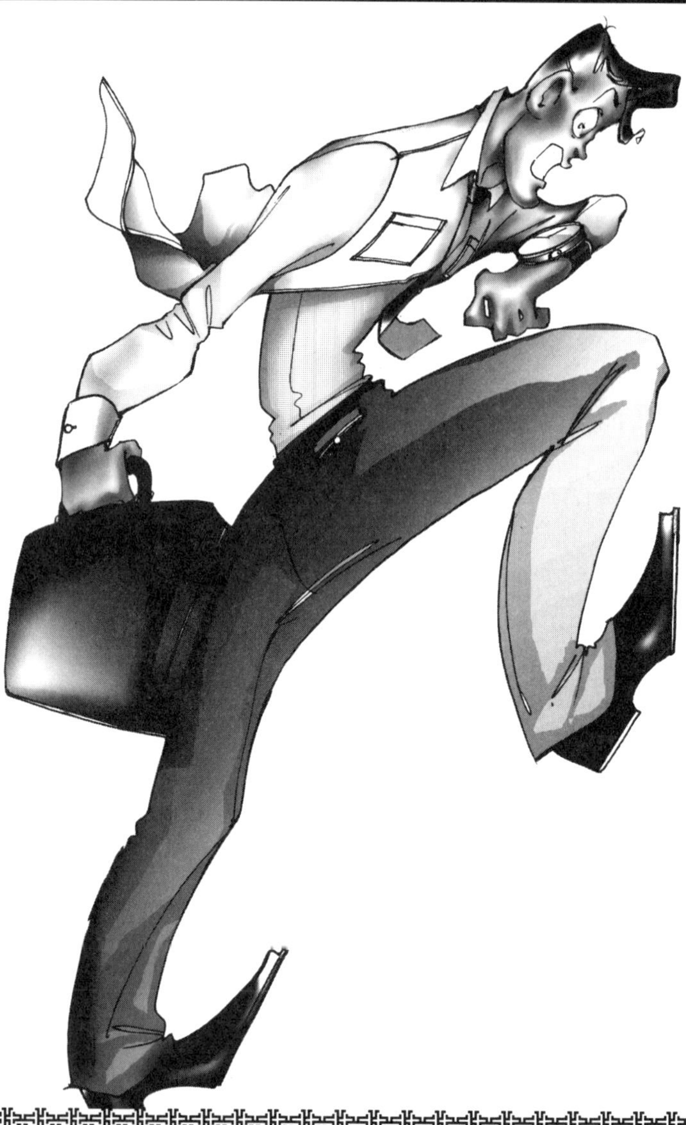

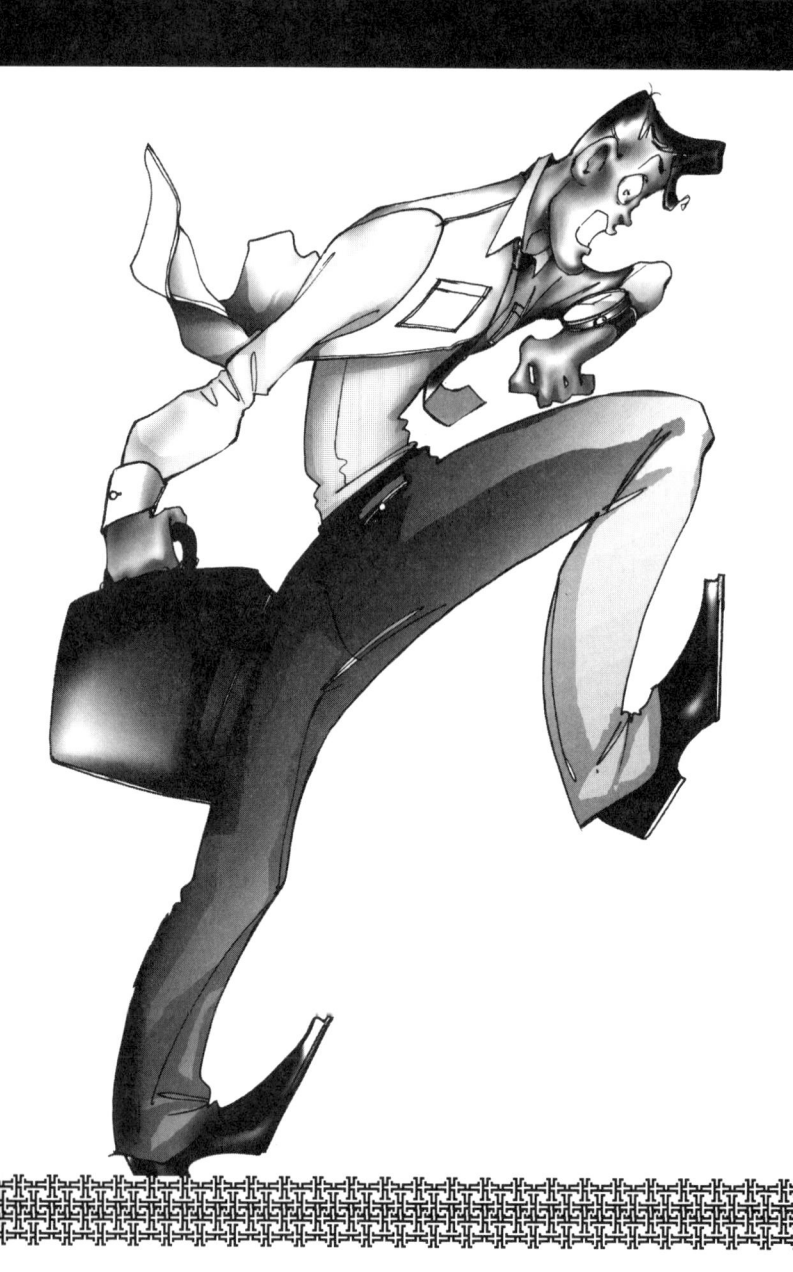

getting around

to fully understand the Los Angeles experience, you must engage in the drive. Only in LA can the road to marriage start with a wink at a red light and end at a drive-in church. The city is slowly expanding its paltry, badly managed public transportation system — the latest addition being a Downtown to Hollywood subway — but locals know better than to depend on the inconvenient schedules and roundabout routes of city buses. Besides, identity and social status is forged by the car you drive. Struggling hipsters drive vintage Dodge Darts, gangsters drive lowriders with souped-up sound systems, wanna-be starlets drive cherry-red convertibles, white-trash greasers put the pedal to the metal in customized hot rods, goths drive hearses, and suburban moms take over the freeways in their urban assault vehicles. To navigate the urban sprawl that is Los Angeles, you *need* your own ride. In LA, if you have no wheels, you have no life — and you can forget about getting a date. Don't listen to out-of-town naysayers: The traffic's not that bad, and parking is rarely a problem.

So make your first stop in LA at the car rental agency, splurge on a convertible or an exotic sports car, and blend in with the natives. And don't forget to wear your seat belt, or you'll be faced with a stiff fine from the LAPD.

To rent a car, you'll need your own plastic (credit card) and a driver's license. If you rent by the week, you'll save a bundle. If money is no object, rent a luxury car like a Lamborghini, Ferrari, Jaguar, or a restored classic car with free cellular phone, natch, at **Beverly Hills Rent-A-Car** (*9220 S. Sepulveda Blvd., Beverly Hills, 310-337-1400/800-479-5996*). Many of the major chain rental companies at LAX have a pool of luxury-mobiles to choose from, as well. If you're on a budget, hightail it over to **Ugly Duckling** (*5555 Van Nuys Blvd., Van Nuys, 818-563-9303/800-THE-DUCK*), **Rent-A-Wreck** (*12333 W. Pico Blvd., West LA, 310-478-0677*), or **Avon** (*7080 Santa Monica Blvd., Hollywood, 323-850-0826*) for low rates on anything from a Yugo to a convertible to a four-wheel SUV. If you don't have a credit card, you can sign over your life at **Cash Car Rental** (*1600 N. La Brea, Hollywood, 323-464-4147*) and you'll roll out of their driveway in no time.

If you're planning on spending more than a couple of days in smog city, invest in a *Thomas Guide to Los Angeles*, available at bookstores and gas stations. This phone book-sized tome has maps to every nook and cranny in the city and is appropriately venerated by the automobile-dependent hordes.

A good introduction to Los Angeles is to drive the length of Sunset Boulevard. Start at Union Station, where East LA's main drag, Cesar Chavez Boulevard, gets renamed Sunset just after it passes Olvera Street, the city's first-ever street. Drive past the cholos in Echo Park, the hipsters and working-class immigrants of Silver Lake and East Hollywood, the gutter punks and Japanese and midwestern tourists in Hollywood, and the gay boys and heavy-metal posers of the Sunset Strip. Continue snaking on the manicured boulevard through Beverly Hills, Bel-Air, Brentwood (just a few blocks from O.J.'s former digs), and Pacific Palisades, until you spill out onto the Pacific Coast Highway alongside the ocean, just a couple of miles from Malibu. You'll feel the satisfaction of having done LA like a native — from the driver's seat.

index

Avon *7080 Santa Monica Blvd. at La Brea Ave., Hollywood, 323-850-0826*

Beverly Hills Rent-A-Car *9220 S. Sepulveda Blvd. bet. Century Blvd. and Westchester Pkwy., Beverly Hills, 310-337-1400/800-479-5996*

Cash Car Rental *1600 N. La Brea Ave. bet. Hollywood and Sunset Blvds., Hollywood, 323-464-4147*

Rent-A-Wreck *12333 W. Pico Blvd. at Centinela Blvd., West LA, 310-478-0676*

Ugly Duckling *5555 Van Nuys Blvd. at Burbank Blvd., Van Nuys, 818-563-9303/800-THE-DUCK*

index of venues

A

A Different Light 167, 207
A Votre Santé 62
A-1 Record Finders 170
Aardvark's 142
The Abbey 24, 254
Abbot's Habit 259
Academy of Motion Picture Arts and Sciences 196
Ackermansion 219
Acme Comedy Theater 205
Actor's Forum 206
Actors Gang 208
Adventure 16 242
The Aero 198
AFI International Film Festival 192
Ago 47
Akbar 99
Al Gelato 161
Al's Bar 103
Alex Film Society 195
The Alley 140
All Star Lanes 241
American Cinematheque 190
American Rag 116
American Renegade Theatre Co. 205
Anastasia 147
Anastasia's Asylum 254
Andrew Dibben 134
Angel City Books 168
Angelus Awards Student Film Festival 193
Anime Expo 193
Anna Sui 132
Anti-Mall 137
Antica Pizzeria 47
Apothia 147
Apple Pan 52
Argyle 266
Armand Hammer Museum of Art 209
Armani 138
Aron's Records 170
Arroyo Seco Canyon 247
Art Park Gallery 222
Asia de Cuba 90
Asian Pacific Film & Video Festival 193
Astro Burger 53
Astro Family Restaurant 54
Atlas Bar & Grill 59
The Attic (Las Vegas) 295
Attic Theater 207
Aureole (Las Vegas) 287
The Autry Museum of Western Heritage 194
Avalon 272
Avon Car Rental 300
Azusa Foothill Drive-in 192

B

Baby Jane of Hollywood 130
Baby's (Las Vegas) 291, 292
Back Door Bakery & Café 156
Back Lot 156
Bahooka's Ribs and Grog 61
Banana Bungalow 275
Banana Museum 218
Bang Improv Studio 205
Bar Marmont 83
Barber Shop Club 149, 206
Barfly 90
Barnes & Noble 167
Barneys New York 24, 139
Barry's Boot Camp 236
Bay Shore Bowl 240
Bellagio (Las Vegas) 284
Beige 27
Belvedere 57
Bergamot Station 220
Best Western Hollywood Hills Hotel 275

302 | index

Beverly Center	25, 136
Beverly Hills	24
Beverly Hills Beauty Center	147
Beverly Hills Farmers Market	161
Beverly Hills Hotel	270
Beverly Laurel Hotel	276
Beverly Plaza Hotel	272
Beyond Baroque Literary Arts Center	206
Beverly Hills Rent-A-Car	300
Bigfoot Lodge	84
Bijan	138
Billy Blanks World Training Center	236
Bing Theater	194
Binion's Horseshoe Casino (Las Vegas)	294
Binion's Ranch Steakhouse (Las Vegas)	206
Bitter Truth Theatre	206
Black Wave Tattoo	145
Blue	101
Blueberry	46
Blueprint	150
Boardner's	101
Bob's Big Boy	49
The Body Shop	104
Book Soup	164, 207

Border Grill	54
Border Grill (Las Vegas)	291
Borders	168
Bourgeois Pig	255
Brentwood	23
Brentwood Bread Company	162
Brewery Arts Complex	29, 223
Bristol Farms	162
Britannia Inn	93
Bunny Museum	218
Burke Williams	149
Buzz Café	258

C

Ca' del Sole	58
Cacao	255
The Cadillac Hotel	276
Café Stella	28, 33
Café Tropical	255
Caffé Luna	55
Caioti Pizza Café	47
California Mart	140
California Pizza Kitchen	47
Camden Lock	131
Canal Club	33
Canter's	26, 55, 161
Carnival World (Las Vegas)	290

Cartier	138
Casa Bianca	47
Casa del Mar	271
Cash Car Rental	300
Cassell's	52
Cat 'N' Fiddle	93
Cat Club	84
Catalina Bar & Grill	27, 59
Cava	54
Celebration Theater	208
Center for Yoga	247
Center Theater Group	200
Century City Shopping Center	136
Chameli	63
Chanel	138
Chateau Marmont	266
Cheetah's	104
Cherry	100
Chestnuts and Papaya	156
Chicken Little	159
China Grill (Las Vegas)	288
Chinese Theater	197
Christian Dior	138
Cinefile	171
Cinegrill	202
Cinema Glamour Shop	130

Cineplex Odeon Fairfax	198	
Cinerama Dome	197	
Circus	99	
Citadel	141	
Ciudad	29,53	
Clark Nova	149	
Clearman's North Woods Inn	61	
Clifton's	62	
Club 7969	98,99,105	
Club Lingerie	97	
Club Paradise (Las Vegas)	294	
CM Bookshop	168	
Coach and Horses	89	
Cobalt Café	207	
Coconut Club	58	
Coconut Teaszer	104	
The Coffee Bean & Tea Leaf	258	
The Coffee Table	256	
Cole's P.E. Buffet	56	
Comedy at Bat	204	
Comedy Store	203	
The Conga Room	101	
Contempo Nails	147	
Continental	48	
The Cook's Library	167	
The Cooper Building	140	
Craft and Folk Art Museum	216	
Crate & Barrel	154	
Crazy Girls	104	
Crunch	236,246	
Curve	117	
Cuvee	162	
Cyber Java	260	
Cynthia Rowley	25,133	

D

D&G	132
Daddy's	85
Daisy Arts	157
Damon's	61
Dances With Films	193
Darby Crash Punk Rock Museum	219
Daryl K.	137
Decades, Inc.	117
Delirium Tremens	222
The Derby	94
Desert Inn (Las Vegas)	284,294
Destroy All Music	170
Directors Guild	196
DKNY	133
Doctober	193
Domingo's	162
Dominick's	34
Donut Hole	49
Doug Weston's Troubadour	102
Downtown	28
Dragonfly	27,97
Dragstrip 66	98
Dream Dresser	134
Dresden Room	28,85,202
Du Vin	163
Dublin's Irish Whiskey Pub	93
Dutton's Brentwood Bookstore	166,207

E

Eames House	217
Eat Well	45
Eduardo Lucero	134
8B	142
El Capitan	199
El Cholo	55
El Cid	59
El Coyote	35
El Floridita	101
El Matador Beach	240
El Rey Theatre	100,102
Elat Market	162,163
Electric Lotus	54
Elixir	260
Empire Snowboards	155
Emporio Armani	133
Empress Pavilion	51

icounter	86	Frederic Fekkai	149	Goldfingers	97
inis-Brown House	217	Frederick's of Hollywood	134, 218	Golyester	142
picurus	163			The Good Luck Bar	28, 92
ewhon	162	Friends of the Orpheum	196	Good Old Times	143
piritu de Vida	156			Gotta Have It	143
ile Books and Music	207	The Frolic Room	89	Grand Central Market	163
		Further	156	Griffith Observatory	210
		Futurama	155	Griffith Park	244
				The Grill	58
he Factory/ Ultra Suede	97, 99	**G**		Groundlings	204
		Gabah	103	Gucci	138
airfax Avenue	25	Gallo's Grill	50	Guelaguetza	50
is Do-Do	97, 100	Gap	135		
rfalla	204	The Garage	103		
rmer's Daughter Motel	276	Gardenia Club	202	**H**	
		Gardens	57	H.K. Korean Supermarket	162
nix	90	Gardens of Taxco	56		
esta Four Drive-in	192	Geffen Contemporary	211	Hal's Bar & Grill	37
gtree's Café	63	Geffen Playhouse	201	Hampton's Hollywood Café	52
refly	159	Gelson's	162		
rehouse	46	Genghis Cohen	93	Hancock Park	26
icker	196	Getty Center	209	Hard Rock Casino Bar (Las Vegas)	285, 292
int's	59	Ginza Sushiko	xxx		
rmosa Café	87	Gipsy (Las Vegas)	292	Hard Rock Hotel & Casino (Las Vegas)	285
rum Shops at Caesar's (Las Vegas)	294	Gladstone's 4 Fish Malibu	36		
				HBO Workspace	205
ototeka	222	Glaxa	206, 208	Helen's Cycles	242
ank Gehry's House	217	Goethe Film Institute	195	Hermosa Beach	240
ed 62	35	Gold's Gym Hollywood	237, 246	HMS Bounty	91
ed Segal	25, 119, 132			Hollywood	27
				Hollywood Bowl	201

Hollywood Black Film Festival	193	Hollywood
Hollywood Discovery Awards	193	
Hollywood Entertainment Museum	215	**I**
Hollywood Farmers Market	161	I. Martin Imports 242
Hollywood Film Festival	193	Ikea 154
Hollywood Hills Coffee Shop	45, 204	Il-Literature & Pulp 166
Hollywood Palladium	102	Ilan Dei Studios 150
Hollywood Roosevelt Hotel	272	Illume 157
Hollywood Star Lanes	240	IMAX Theater 199
Hollywood Studio Museum	215	Improv 203
Hollywood Tropicana	105	The Improv Olympic West Theatre 205
Hollywood Wax Museum	215	Independent Film Festival 193
Holyland Exhibition	219	In House 151
Home	45, 257	In-N-Out Burger 53
Hotel Bel Air	270	Inn of the Seventh Ray 63
House of Blues	102	Insomnia 258
House of Blues (Las Vegas)	290, 293	Interact Theater 208
House of Freaks	145	International Bra Museum 218
Hudson Theatre	207	It's a Wrap 130
Hugo's	45	Itacho 51
Huntington Beach	242	
Hustler	134, 204	**J**
		Jack Sprat's Grille 63
		Jack's Sugar Shack 103
		James' Beach 38
		Janice McCarty 119
		Jason Vass Gallery 156

Jazz Bakery	20
Jerry's Video Room	17
Jet Rag	14
Jim Bridges Boutique	13
Joe Peep's	4
John O'Groats	4
Johnnie's Pastrami	1
Johnny B. Wood	15
Johnny G.'s World Headquarters	24
Jones Hollywood	9
Julian's	14
Jumbo's Clown Room	10

K

Ka-Boom	28, 159, 21
Kane	26, 9
Kate Spade	13
Kenneth Cole	13
Key Club	9
Key Sunday Cinema Club	19
Kindness of Strangers Coffeehouse	204, 20
King Taco No. 2	4
King's Head	9
King's Road Café	4
Kokomo Café	26, 4
Kozmo.com	17

rispy Kreme	49	Lisa Kline	120	(Las Vegas)	
ruang Tedd	51	Liza Bruce	132	Manhattan Beach	29, 240
		Loehmann's	140	Mann's Chinese Theater	197
a Boca del Conga Room	59	Lola's	92	Manuel's El Tepeyac	50
		Los Angeles Conservancy	196, 199	Maple Drive	58
a Brea Bakery	161	Los Angeles County Museum of Art	211	Marla's Jazz Supper Club	48
a Conversation	161				
a Luz de Jesus	221	Los Angeles Independent Film Festival	193	Marouch	51
a Serenata de Garibaldi	56			The Martini Lounge	26, 92
		Los Angeles Short Film Festival	192	Masquers Cabaret	202
aemmle Five	197			Matsuhisa	60
aemmle Four-Plex	197	Los Feliz	27	Maxfield	121
aemmle Pasadena	197	Los Feliz Par 3	243	The Mayan	101
anger's Deli	49	Louis Vuitton	138	McCabe's	103
anny Nails	147	Lovell-Health House	217	McCormick & Schmick's	53
archmont	26	Lowenbrau Keller	61		
archmont Beauty Center	147	Lucky Brand Dungarees	141	Mel's Drive-In	55
				Melrose	25
argo	103, 203	Lucques	39	Mexico City	56
arry Edmunds Cinema & Theater Bookshop	166	Lucy's El Adobe Café	56	Miceli's	57, 202, 204
		LunaPark	97, 203	Michelle's XXX Topless Review	99
		Lura Starr	120		
ast Laughs Before the 101	204	Lydia's TV Fashions	135	Midnight Special	164, 196
				Milky Way	48
augh Factory	203	**M**		Millie's Diner	28, 40
ava Lounge	91	Magic Hotel	276	Mini Cake Museum	218
e Parc	273	Maha Yoga	247	Mirage (Las Vegas)	287
es Deux Café	38	Makeup!	100	Mirage Buffet (Las Vegas)	290
ily et Cie	143	Malibu Beach Inn	274		
iquid Kitty	91	Mandalay Bay	286	Mishima	51

Miu Miu	132	
Modernica	155	
Molly Malone's Irish Pub	93	
Mondrian	267	
Morton's	58	
Mount Hollywood	247	
Mount Wilson	247	
Mr. Lucky's (Las Vegas)	288	
Mulberry Street Pizza	47	
Museum of Contemporary Art	195, 211	
Museum of Jurassic Technology	217	
Museum of the Holocaust	216	
Museum of Miniatures	216	
Museum of Television and Radio	215	
Museum of Tolerance	213	
Musso and Frank Grill	56, 91	
My Secret Garden	163	

N

Nate 'n' Al's	57
Neiman Marcus	24, 139
Neptune's Net	51
New Beverly Cinema	198
New Otani	270
Newsroom Café	25, 63
Nicole Miller	133
No Problem	137
Nobu (Las Vegas)	289
NoHo Actors' Studio	206
North	87
Not So Far East	155
Novel Café	259
Nuart	24, 197
Nyala	51
NYSE	121

O

O'Brien's	93
Off the Wall	159
Ojala Fine Arts and Crafts	222
The Old Town Music Hall	198
Oliver Peoples	122
Omelette Parlor	46
Opium Den	97
Original Pantry Café	56
Orpheum	199
Osteria Romana Orsini	58
Outfest at the Village	192, 195
Ozzie & Moosy	157
Ozzie Dots	143

P

Pacé	4.
Pacific Dining Car	5.
Page Museum at the La Brea Tar Pits	21(
Palace	102, 19!
The Palm	5(
The Palms	9!
Pan African Art & Film Festival	194
Papa Cristos	5(
Paper Bag Princess	14!
Petersen Automotive Museum	21(
Phillipe the Original	4.
Pie 'n' Burger	5!
Pier One Imports	154
Pigments	14!
Pilates Gym	24!
The Pilates Studio	244
Pink Dot	17
Pink Taco (Las Vegas)	28!
Pink's	5!
Planet Funk	12!
Plastica	22!
Playmates	134
The Playroom	27, 94, 10(
Pleasure Chest	13!
Polka Dots and Moonbeams	12!

308 index

lo Lounge	57
)ST Wilshire	223
stobello	151
ttery Barn	154
ada	133,138
adeeps	63
ime Cuts	170
imi	58
ivé Salon	148
oduct	123
ll My Daisy	144
rple Circle	149

uality Food & Beverage	46
uon Brothers Grand Star	29,202

-23	29,60
ge	24,99
alph Lauren	138
ancho Park Golf Course	243
pid Rehab International	245
ven Playhouse	206
-Mix	124
al Food Daily	63

Red	42
Red Balls	131
Red Dragon Lounge (Las Vegas)	293
Red Lion Tavern	91
Red Square (Las Vegas)	293
Redemption	131
Reel Clothes	130
Regal Biltmore	271
Regent Beverly Wilshire	271
Reign	48
Rent-A-Wreck	300
Resfest Digital Film Festival	193
Retail Slut	131
Revolver	24,99
Richard Tyler	134
Rita Flora	163
Ritz Carlton Laguna Miguel	274
Rix	90
Rizzoli	168
Robertson Blvd.	24
Rockaway Records	170
Rocket Video	171
Rockreation	238
Rodney's English Disco	100
Ron Herman Sportswear	23
Roscoe's House of Chicken 'n' Waffles	55
Rose Bowl Flea Market	152
Rose Café	46
Roxy	102
Rubin's Red Hot	49
Rudolpho's	98,101
Rudy's Barbershop	149
RumJungle (Las Vegas)	289
Runyon Canyon	246

S

Saks	24,140
Samuel French Theater & Film Bookshop	166
Sanamluang	50
Santa Monica	22
Santa Monica Beach	240
Santa Monica Farmers Market	161
Santa Monica Film Festival	193
Santa Monica Museum of Art	213
Santa Monica Place	136
Santa Monica Power Yoga	247
Serious	131
Shabby Chic	22,152
Shelter	152

index | 309

Shibucho	55	Starbucks	258	Todd Tramp	24
Short Film Festival	192	Stevie Joe's Lounge and Supper Club	59	Tommy Tang's	9
Shutters on the Beach	22, 271			Tommy's	5
		Stir Crazy	259	Tower Records	16
Silent Movie Theatre	199	Stonewall Gourmet Coffee	206	Tracey Ross	12
Silver Lake	28			Trader Joe's	16
Silver Lake Dog Park	239	Studio City Golf Course	243	Trader Vic's	9
Sinister Store	131			Traveler's Bookcase	16
6150 Wilshire	222	Stüssy	141		
Sky Bar	88	Suburban	141		
Skylight Books	166, 207	Suehiro	54	**U**	
Slave	131	Sugar	22, 103	U	14
Slow	125	Sunset Beach	242	UCLA Film and Television Archives	19
The Smog Cutter	89	Sunset Room	58, 90		
Soap Plant/Wacko	159	Surefoot	242	Ugly Duckling	30
Sonrisa	153	Sushi Nozawa	60	UnCabaret	x
Soolip	157	Sushi on Tap	60	Uncle Jer's	15
Soot Bull Jeep	51	Sushi Roku	60	Union	14
South Bay Beach Towns	29	Swingers	43	Urban Outfitters	22, 126, 1
South Coast Plaza	136	Syren	135		
Southbay 6 Drive-in	192			Urth Café	25
Southwest Museum	216				
Spaceland	28, 95, 104, 196	**T**			
Spago	46	Target	154	**V**	
Spago (Las Vegas)	291	Taylor's Prime Steaks	43	Val Surf	24
Spago Beverly Hills	58	Temescal Canyon	246	Valentino	13
Sportsclub LA	238	Tempest	101	Valentino (Las Vegas)	2
Sportsman's Lodge	274	Tiffany	138	Valerie	14
Squaresville	144	Tiki Ti	91	Van Gogh's Ear	25
The Standard	90, 267	Time After Time	130	Vegas	x

nice	22	Whisky a Go-Go	102	
nice Beach	240	Who's on Third	45, 259	
rsailles	51	Wild Oats	162	
a Bellagio (Las Vegas)	294	Will Geer Theatricum Botanicum	208	
brator	99	Wolfgang Puck Café	46	
diots	171	The Woods	163	
llage Coffee Shop	45	Workmens	137	
llage Seafood Buffet (Las Vegas)	290	World Café	54	
n Baker	127	Writers Guild	196	
neland Drive-in	192	The Writers' Store	167	
per Room	95	Wyndham Checkers	270	
rgin Megastore	169			
he Vista	198			
tello's	202			
to's	47			
roman's	165, 207			
ynyl	98			

X

X-Large/X-Girl	128

Y

Y Que Trading Post	159
Yoga Works	247
Young Comics Exposed	204

J

J Hotel	268
&V Dailey Rare Books	168
ally's	163
asteland	128
ednesday's House	257
est Hollywood	24
estside Pavilion	136
estwood/Westside	23

Z

Zankou Chicken	50
Zen Grill	44
Zen Zoo Tea	260
Zipper	158
ZJ's Boarding House	243
Zuma Beach	240, 241

who we are

Tom Dolby *(Executive Editor)* is the CEO of CityTripping Productions, Editor of CityTripping.com, and Director of New York Operations. A graduate of Yale University, Tom has worked at *The Village Voice* and *Details* magazine; his writing has appeared in *The Village Voice* and *Time Out New York*, among others. He is the author of *CityTripping New York* (City & Company, 1998). A writer, journalist, and entrepreneur, Tom spends his days and nights in search of new trends for CityTripping to cover.

Tina Hay *(Executive Editor)* is the President of CityTripping Productions and Director of Los Angeles Operations. Prior to that, she was a development executive with Scott Rudin Productions at Paramount Pictures. A long-time resident of Los Angeles, Tina has worked at the Cannes Film Festival, Miramax Films, and TriStar Pictures. She is a graduate of UCLA's Communications Program. From the editing room to the board room, Tina is a force to be reckoned with.

Kevin Arnovitz *(Managing Editor)* is a writer and editor for CityTripping.com. A former political consultant turned development brat, Kevin has lived, dined, raged, and pouted in New York, Atlanta, Seattle, Washington, D.C., and, presently, Los Angeles. In addition to working with CityTripping, he is currently pursuing a career in writing for television. Kevin is a graduate of Columbia University.

m Williams (*Managing Editor*) is a writer and editor for tyTripping.com. Born and raised in Manhattan, he was dragged kicking and screaming to LA by his parents right before he turned 18. After ur years at Yale, he decided to stop whining and love Los Angeles. He ow lives within golfing distance of the Santa Monica beach and divides s time between fetching decaf espressos for a top Hollywood producer d exploring his new hometown for CityTripping.

lia Calle (*Illustrator*) is an illustrator for CityTripping.com. Her work s appeared in *Paper*, *Bust*, and *ESPN* magazine, as well as in presentans for MTV Networks, Jean-Paul Gaultier Jeans, Calvin Klein, and lo Ralph Lauren. She graduated from the Parsons School of Design th a BFA in Fashion Design. More of her work can be viewed at vw.celiacalle.com.

n Stein (*Foreword*) is a well-known Hollywood figure and pop culture on who frequently writes for publications about life in Los Angeles. e is the Emmy award-winning host of Comedy Central's *Win Ben ein's Money*.

ennis Hensley (*Introduction*) is the author of the *Los Angeles Times* bestling novel *Misadventures in the (213)*, recently optioned by Imagine TV. s a journalist, his articles have appeared in *Movieline*, *Us*, *Cosmopolitan*, *Guide*, *Detour*, *The Advocate*, and *Maxim*. He recently released his singing d songwriting debut, *The Water's Fine*. He can be stalked on-line at vw.dennishensley.com.

who we are

YOU'VE GOT THE BOOK. NOW SEE THE SHOW.

Lights... Camera... Action!
Check out CityTripping in full-motion, TV-quality video powered by LOADtv and get the 411 on everything that matters in Los Angeles and New York.

CityTripping and LOADtv offer the latest insider tips on where to drink, dine, and shop in America's two greatest cities.

So get over to CityTrippingTV.com to watch the CityTripping shows and stop acting like such a tourist.

LOADtv
www.loadtv.com

CITYTRIPPING

Cosmetics committed to the power of color.

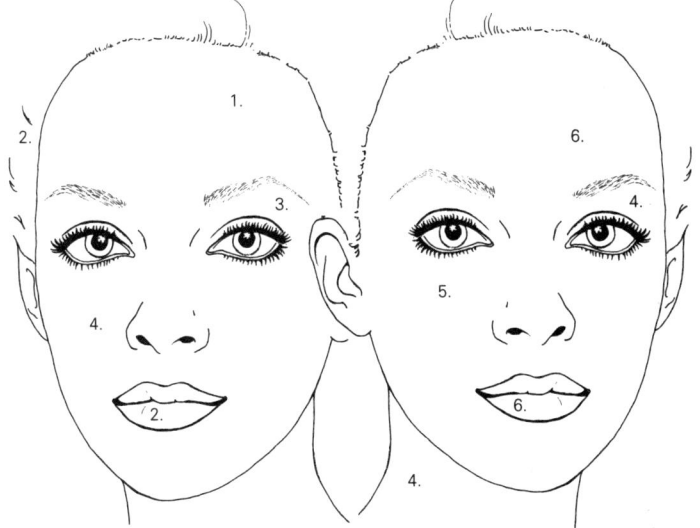

1. blue 2. red 3. green 4. yellow 5. orange 6. violet

Aromatherapy. Colortherapy. Positive Thought. TONY&TINA
tonytina.com

NEWSROOM CAFE

SANTA MONICA
6TH & WILSHIRE BLVD.
310.319.9100

WEST HOLLYWOOD
120 N. ROBERTSON BLVD.
310.652.4444

The healthy way to light up your day!

Wake up to Bliss!

Experience a GUAYAKÍ Chai Latté™ and discover a delicious healthful alternative to coffee.

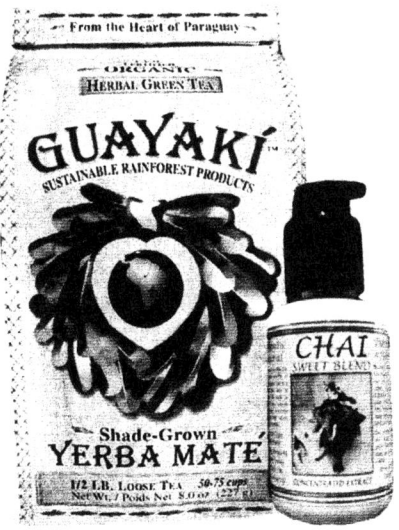

Fall into your **natural rhythm** of **life** and **embrace** all bouts of **inspiration**.

Available in most natural food stores.
WWW.GUAYAKI.COM
(888) GUAYAKI (482-9254)

GUAYAKÍ YERBA MATÉ provides a natural energy lift and a mental clarity unparalled by any other herb. Sweeten it with honey and milk and add a blast of *Primal Essence Chai* to instantly enliven your GUAYAKÍ latté with exotic spicy flavor. A few sips and you'll understand why we say, "Step on the Feel-Good Express!" All aboard!

· **GUAYAKÍ YERBA MATÉ** & *Primal Essence Chai* ·

Electric Lotus

Village Cuisine from India
Music and Food

4656 Franklin Avenue
Los Angeles, CA 90027
323-953-0040

428 South San Vicente
Los Angeles, CA 90048
310-659-3903

FEELING WIPED OUT?

Get back on your feet Hawaiian style.

Ola Loa's Tropical Power Powder gives you instant and long lasting energy, all naturally, with our complete formula of vitamins, minerals, amino acids, herbs, Coenzyme Q10 and Hawaiian ingredients like bromelain and pineapple. None of which get stuck in your throat. Developed by Richard Kunin M.D., this Tropical Power Powder is the most extensive vitamin available and it even tastes good. To find out more about Ola Loa or to place an order, contact us at 1-888-2OLALOA or www.olaloa.com or DrinkYourVitamins.com.